WITHDRAWN

The Jews of
North Africa
during the
Second World War

The Jews of North Africa during the Second World War

MICHEL ABITBOL

Translated by Catherine Tihanyi Zentelis

 WAYNE STATE UNIVERSITY PRESS   DETROIT   1989

Les Juifs d'Afrique du Nord sous Vichy copyright © 1983 by
G.-P. Maisonneuve et Larose, Paris, France. English translation
copyright © 1989 by Wayne State University Press,
Detroit, Michigan 48202. All rights are reserved.
No part of this book may be reproduced without formal permission.
93 92 91 90 89   5 4 3 2 1

Library of Congress Cataloging-in-Publication Data

Abitbol, Michel.
   [Juifs d'Afrique du Nord sous Vichy. English]
   The Jews of North Africa during the Second World War / Michel
Abitbol ; translated by Catherine Tihanyi Zentelis.
   p. cm.
   Translation of: Les Juifs d'Afrique du Nord sous Vichy.
   Bibliography: p.
   Includes index.
   ISBN 0-8143-1824-X (alk. paper)
   1. Jews—Africa, North—Persecutions. 2. World War, 1939-1945—
Jews—Africa, North. 3. Africa, North— Ethnic relations.
I. Title.
DS135.A25A2513 1989   88-23247
961'.004924—dc19   CIP

Grateful acknowledgment is made to the Institute for Contemporary
Jewry, Hebrew University, for financial assistance in the publication of
this volume.

Contents

Introduction 7

PART ONE While Awaiting Vichy: North Africa on the Eve of World War II

1 A Colonial Phenomenon: Algerian Anti-Semitism 19

    Men and an Idea 22

    The Administration and Anti-Semitic Agitation 26

    Moslem Population and the Jewish Problem 29

    Algerian Jewry in the Face of Anti-Semitism 31

2 Moroccan and Tunisian Jews in the Face of the French Extreme Right and German and Italian Agitation 35

    The Extreme Right 35

    Maghrebian Nationalism and German and Italian Propaganda 36

    Jewish Response 39

3 Toward Pétain's "National Revolution" 41

PART TWO North Africa on Vichy Time

4 The Maghreb after the Armistice: Attempts at Resistance and Militant Pétainism 47

5 Vichy and the Jews of North Africa 56

    Ideological Background 56

    Anti-Jewish Legislation and Its Application in North Africa 59

    The abrogation of the Crémieux decree 59

    The "Statut des Juifs" 62

CONTENTS

The Aryanization of education and of the Youth Service Corps 68
The Aryanization of property 71
North African Public Opinion and the Jewish Statute 74
The Internal Life of North African Jewish Communities under Vichy 83
Jewish Refugees and Internees in North Africa 90
Help for the emigrants 93
Relief for the refugees 94
The trans-Saharan rail and the work camps of North Africa 96

PART THREE A Difficult Liberation

6 Operation Torch and Its Consequences 105
The Allied Landing and the North African Resistance 106
Vichyst Africa under American Protection 110
7 The Germans in Tunisia (November 1942 to May 1943) 116
Jews and Germans in Tunis: First Contacts 119
The Testing of the Community's Organization 125
Camp Life 130
Tunisian Public Opinion and the Fate of the Jews 136
8 The Jews of North Africa from Darlan to Giraud 141
The Jews of Algeria and Morocco after the Allied Landing 141
The Problem of the Political Prisoners and of the Refugees 147
9 Toward the Abolition of Racial Laws 152
The Effect of Allied Public Opinion and of American Jewish Organizations 152
The Struggle for the Reestablishment of the Crémieux Decree 159
Conclusion 166
Abbreviations 171
Notes 172
Bibliography 199
Index 206

Introduction

On the eve of World War II there were 400,000 Jews in French North Africa. They were spread out over more than 400 settled districts but comprised only 3 percent of a total population of 14 million of which 1,200,000 were Europeans.

The Maghrebian Jews still often lived in areas where almost all of the inhabitants were Moslem. At the same time, they were more and more irresistibly attracted to cities and neighborhoods with high ratios of European population. Thus Algiers, Oran, Bône,[1] Sidi-bel-Abbès, Casablanca, and Tunis alone sheltered about a third of the Jewish population of Algeria, Morocco, and Tunisia, while a sizable segment lived in the traditional cities of Constantine, Tlemcen, Rabat, Fez, Meknes, Marrakech, Sousse, Gabès, and Nabeul, which, even though not predominantly French, nonetheless felt the sway of a strong French presence. The remaining Jews were spread out in smaller urban centers and in the villages of the Atlas and of the edge of the Sahara.

The socioeconomic makeup of North African Jewish communities had changed drastically since the arrival of the French. Traditionally, Jews had been attracted to trade and crafts. As tradesmen, they had been the middlemen between local producers and the outside world, but that role had been chipped away by the arrival of businessmen, settlers, and metropolitan and European bankers. As craftsmen, their small technical and financial means had not provided them with enough protection in the face of the flooding of Maghrebian markets with imports.

Except a few wealthy families whose assets had, at any rate, been greatly affected by the drop in value of movable and landed property during the depression, almost all the Jewish population was made up of individuals of modest means. According to statistics, peddlers, craftsmen, clerks, and blue-collar workers made up 60 percent of the working masses. They lived from hand to mouth and many were gradually joining the ranks of the unemployed and the beggars, who, for instance in Casablanca, made up about one-fourth of the Jewish population in 1936. The rise of a middle class was more pronounced in Algeria and Tunisia than in Morocco, and it had come out of the first generations of graduates from secondary and postsecondary schools. This group did not significantly modify the nature of North African communities but it nonetheless was an indicator of the apparition of new criteria of social mobility: modern learning, and more specifically French learning, came to be viewed by all as an absolutely new and total mean of social success.

French education was lay and widespread in Algeria but it was offered only parsimoniously in the two neighboring countries. This was particularly so in Morocco where despite its best efforts the Alliance Israélite Universelle could not enroll more than fifteen thousand children in schools. This closely matched the number of children enrolled in Tunisia despite the fact that the Jewish population there was two-thirds smaller than in Morocco.

In this domain as in others, the developmental gaps between the three communities were a function, on the one hand, of the length of French presence and on the other, of the nature of colonial policies toward the Jewish populations of the three countries.

Colonial policy was assimilationist in Algeria, reformist in Tunisia, but pretty much conservative in Morocco. Consequently, French citizenship had been granted to the Jews of Algeria (except those of the southern territories) according to the terms of the Crémieux decree of 1870. The decree was applied in Algeria after the abolition of the juridical autonomy theoretically enjoyed by Jewish minorities in Islamic lands, after the setting up of consistories[2] along the metropolitan model. Thus the decree completed the total emancipation of Algerian Jews who, from *dhimmi*[3] more often tolerated than protected, were moved up to a rank equal to that of the masters of the country, which was no small privilege, given the colonial situation. This upgrading was poorly accepted by the greater part of the European population of Algeria, which, setting aside their various political leanings, was to unite in an unusually virulent anti-Semitism. This drive had no real connection to the Kabyle revolt of 1871 the causes of which had been falsely attributed to the Crémieux decree, nor was it even connected to the Dreyfus affair. Conservatives, Radicals, Anarchists, and Freemasons sacrificed their differences to this movement, which brought to the French Parliament several fanatically anti-Jewish representatives among which were Edouard Drumont and Emile Morinaud, elected respectively at Algiers and Constantine in 1898.

The Algerian troubles, added to the fact of the peculiar nature of the protectorate system in Tunisia and Morocco, which at least formally set limits to colonial prerogatives, led to the failure of any attempt at extending the granting of French citizenship to the Jews of Tunisia and Morocco:

> Résident-Général[4] Millet noted in 1899 that it is not at the time when Algeria suffers from the consequences that political parties have succeeded in making out of the Crémieux decree that it is feasible to consider creating in Tunisia the slightest privilege that would set the Jewish population the least bit above Moslem natives. Any reform that would lead the regency's Jews toward assimilation with French citizens would create in Tunisia an anti-Semite problem all the more serious in that we have here sixty thousand Jews and barely sixteen thousand French. (A.E.P., vol. 131, Jan. 14, 1899)

The French authorities mostly ignored as well demands for the modernization of Jewish community structures and for a long time opposed all projects propounded on this matter by the Central Consistory of France:

> The résident-général's office and the government of the protectorate have always sought to maintain the complete independence of the Jewish community in Tunisia. The Algerian events have more than clearly shown the political drawbacks of consistorial organization and centralization of the Jewish forces. Any reform that would put the religious leadership of their communities in the hands of the wealthy, influential, and active individuals would create in Tunisia a power that we would soon be forced to take into account. It may be true that the present organization of the rabbinate is outdated but it nevertheless strongly guarantees us security and stability. (A.E.P., vol. 131, March 4, 1899)

However, from 1910 on, under the threat of Italian territorial covetousness, the authorities of the Tunisian protectorate were forced to mollify their position. They made the selective and individual naturalization of the young Jewish elite easier[5] and created as well new structures for the Jewish community, thereby allowing a broader representation of the population.

In Morocco, the French administration took shelter behind the clauses of the Madrid Convention (1880), which established the principle of perpetual allegiance to the sultan. Thus demands for French naturalization were systematically denied, even those by individuals who could claim ". . . a higher than average level of education, who traveling frequently in France had undertaken studies there" and were aspiring ". . . to a political status consonant with their culture and the orientation of their sympathies" (C.D.J.C., 82-5: 22).

Moroccan Jews were juridically and politically assimilated to the Moslem native population. Their community organizations were headed by quasi-unremovable notables appointed by the administration. Lacking in significant freedom of action and in specific powers, the committees in charge of the communities were nothing more than benevolent associations whose meager resources had to be devoted to helping the indigent, thus freeing municipal authorities from a burdensome responsibility. These committees had not been conceived as organs that could represent their brethren to the public authorities and even less guide them on the difficult path of westernization and modernization. Consequently, they could not win over the support of the younger generation that looked elsewhere for frameworks of action more in keeping with its aspirations and ambitions.

This disaffection was not limited to the young Jewish generation of Morocco; it was a general phenomenon in varying degrees in Tunisia and Algeria where the intellectual elite, when it did not seek anchor in the movement of ideas and the political currents of the time, preferred to choose modes of action peripheral to that of the community organizations, which were passively absorbed in problems of cult and charity.

Thus in Algiers, as early as 1917, a group of young intellectuals created a Comité Juif Algérien d'Etudes Sociales (Algerian Jewish committee for social studies), which, headed by Dr. Henri Aboulker, took upon itself the task of ". . . seeing that the free exercise of the rights of Jewish citizens would be neither violated nor ignored."

In Tunis, the most brilliant among these young people chose to exercise their talents in political journalism. They wrote in the great dailies of the regency such as *Tunisie Française, Tunis Socialiste,* and the *Petit Matin* as well as in the specifically Jewish press such as *La Justice*, which represented the "assimilationist" stance, its competitor *L'Egalité*, which propounded the defense of the traditionalists and the conservatives, or in *Réveil Juif*, a Zionist weekly with revisionist tendencies. A Tunisian Zionist Federation operated freely since the end of World War I. It had been organized by Alfred Valensi, who combined a dozen Zionist associations and support groups that had spread out across the country at the turn of the century.[6]

The young Jewish elite generations of the three Maghrebian countries

Introduction

enjoyed comfortable economic circumstances: They often came from families who had climbed the social ladder during the last years of the precolonial era, or for Algeria, during the first years of the colonial era. They had many traits in common, one of the most important being their attachment to France and their belief in the "eternity" of French presence in North Africa.

This faith was shared by all concerned, even by militant Zionists for whom "the Jewish ideal" was at best only supplementary and complementary to "the French ideal": "To remain Jewish is the best bet that you will become excellent French citizens," propounded *Avenir Illustré*, the organ of Moroccan Zionists, in its editorial of January 9, 1930, reprinted in its entirety on the eve of the armistice of 1940: "We offer the rebirth of Zion as example to our brothers in Morocco and we say to them: What our fellow Jews have accomplished alone in their ancient fatherland after so many years of oppression can't you, in the shelter of the maternal arms of Great France, achieve here?" (*L'Avenir Illustré*, Jan. 9, 1930, and April 16, 1940).

The "France" that so electrified everyone's mind was "this great republic whose civilizing mission has been idealized in history books and which has brought liberty to the world, a liberty symbolized by those famous names so dear to the Jewish people: Father Grégoire, Adolphe Crémieux, Emile Zola . . ." (Cohen-Hadria 1980:5). It was also and firstly "official France," the France of the "outside," and it was this France, and not the "African," or "pied-noir,"[7] France that was the "only France."[8]

The aim of this work is to study the situation of the Jews of Africa when the Jewish people experienced one of the bloodiest tradegies of its history. Far removed from Hitler's Europe and the Nazi death camps, the clock of Maghrebian Judaism was set to Vichy time and, except for the six months of German presence in Tunisia, it experienced no direct contact with Hitlerian Germany. And yet, the North African Jews were not to be spared by the French regime that came out of the armistice. Even while the Germans abstained from making any demands in this regard, Pétain and his administration proceeded to strip Algerian Jews of their citizenship and extended to the three Maghrebian countries most of the racial laws enacted in France non-occupied territory ("Free Zone"). North African Jews had to live at the heart-wrenching pace of the deliveries of the *Journal Officiel*, which, every time, brought the text of a new law or a new decree of enforcement concerning them. Thousands of children were chased away from their schools, hundreds of civil servants were

INTRODUCTION

fired, dozens of landowners were deprived of their property, and convoys of refugees, of former enlisted volunteers, and of political prisoners were thrown into the work camps of the Saharan oven.

In this study, we hope to go beyond an analysis of the specifically North African data, which we will try to place in as large a context as possible, and aim to contribute to the history of the "fringes" of the Holocaust universe, fringes that understandably have been neglected by World War II scholars.

Undoubtedly, the situation of the Jews of North Africa between 1940 and 1943 was in no way comparable to the infernal lot of European Jewry during the same period. All things considered, this period presented less danger for them than some other critical phases of their long history in the Maghreb. Without going back to the Almohads, we can say, without exaggeration, that the three bloody days of Constantine (August 3–5, 1934) resulted in as many dead and wounded Jews as the three years of Vichy regime and German occupation.

Nonetheless, never had persecution in North Africa been prepared with so great an effort of ideological mobilization, nor with so much juridical "care." Taking inspiration from anti-Semitic "models" totally alien to the Maghreb, Vichy made use of the vocabulary and of the methods that, on the other side of the Rhine, were to stake out the path to the Final Solution. Furthermore, and regardless of opinions on the degree of responsibility of "foreign influence" on the behavior of the Vichy regime, it is undeniable that the anti-Jewish policy of the French government aimed as well at satisfying interests and wishes of long standing of a segment of the local population. Otherwise, it would be difficult to comprehend why the first measure adopted by Vichy in North Africa was the repeal of the Crémieux decree, which, since 1971, had become the battle cry of all the anti-Semitic factions in Algeria. In fact, as much in the North African periphery as in the European centers of the Holocaust universe, public opinion played a significant role in the evolution of the fate of the Jews. This holds equally for the Vichy period as for when Tunisian Jews came to be under the Nazi heel.

The promulgation in North Africa of the anti-Jewish legislation in the fall of 1940 was hardly a bolt from the blue. It had been prepared for by a lengthy period of anti-Semitic agitation that had overtaken in varying degrees the three Maghrebian territories. Consequently, we have felt it necessary to study the relations of the Jews with their European and Moslem neighbors during the last prewar years.

The Archives de France d'Outre-Mer (archives of overseas France) at Aix-en-Provence have yielded the most varied and detailed documents for researching this period. The collection we consulted is made up of reports generated at every administrative level, and in particular by the police department. It includes some now unique newspaper clippings, posters, and "official" syntheses dealing with the state of mind of the North African people on the eve of the war and after the armistice. The quality of this documentation is uneven in that unverified rumors are given the same prominence as solidly confirmed information. But despite its evident weaknesses, the collection provides first-class material enabling the researcher to get a feel for the heavily threatening atmosphere permeating North African Jewish communities.

Official reports contain little information on the attitude of North African Jews in the face of anti-Semitic agitation. They must thus be complemented with Jewish sources and first of all with the Jewish press. Jewish newspapers, so prolific between the two world wars, became silent after the armistice except for the Tunisian *Petit Matin* and the Algerian *Bulletin de la Fédération des Sociétés Juives d'Algérie*. Despite its subheading "Tunisian Jewish Daily," the *Petit Matin* is a mediocre source on matters relating to the history of the Tunisian Jewish community under Vichy because, outside a few occasional articles devoted to Jewish community life, it differed very little from the other newspapers of the regency. The title "Jewish Daily" would have at any rate been more suitable for the Algerian *Bulletin*. Thanks to it, the result of French governmental policies in the most metropolitan of the French North African colonies can be apprehended in the most subtle nuances of the responses and wrenching heartbreaks of the Jewish milieu. On the other hand, the general North African press is disappointing as a source of information. Conformist and, moreover, censored, it serves at best to uncover official declarations and legal texts of the period, which because of postwar vagaries are not always available.

The English-language press is of much better quality. It is an indispensable tool for the study of the period spanning "Operation Torch" of November 1942 to the reestablishment of the Crémieux decree in the fall of 1943. It abounds in information and in in-depth articles of all kinds pertaining to the general situation in North Africa as well as to its Jewish population. It also contains the record of drives by Jewish organizations in the United States and in Great Britain for the suppression of the racial laws maintained for several long months after the Allied landing of November 8. American papers were particularly interested in the fate of European Jewish refugees who had sought asylum or a transit point in Morocco or Algeria. An important segment of these ended in Saharan work camps where they had been preceded by hundreds of former Jewish

INTRODUCTION

volunteer enlisted men of the French army. These internees became the concern of various aid committees organized for them by the Jewish communities of both countries. Probably the most active of these committees was the one organized in Casablanca by Hélène Cazès-Benathar, who a few years ago gave her personal archives to the Central Archives for the History of the Jewish People in Jerusalem. These personal archives form a substantial store of documents including, among other things, the letters exchanged by Mrs. Benathar with the French authorities and with the American Jewish organizations American Jewish Joint Distributor Committee (JOINT) and United Hebrew Sheltering and Immigrant Aid Society (HIAS), as well as the complete lists of in-transit or interned individuals. This collection, after a systematic reading, should prove to be invaluable in uncovering the history of the rescue of Jewish refugees during World War II.

The archives of the Centre de Documentation Juive Contemporaine (Paris), particularly those from the Commissariat-General for the Jewish Question (which, at any rate, did not fundamentally differentiate between metropolitan Jews and those of the colonies) have provided us with the most invaluable source of information on the situation of North African Jews during the Vichy regime. These archives deal as much with Moslem and European responses to anti-Jewish legislation as with the various internal debates within ministries and the civil services; they were made much use of by M. Ansky and J. Sabille in their excellent works on the Jews of Algeria and Tunisia. Besides the documents "bequested" by the Commissariat-General for the Jewish Question, the archives of the Centre also contain collections of unpublished official reports, official documents, and in-depth reports drafted by various Jewish organizations. The latter were following the example of the World Jewish Congress and the American Jewish Committee, which took an active part in the protection of North African Jews after November 8, 1942.

Some of these documents can be found in several other libraries, notably at the Central Zionist Archives and the Yad Vashem Museum in Jerusalem. In the latter repository we were able to consult documents from the Nuremberg trials and from official German archives, which, even though they shed little light on the Nazi perspective on the Maghreb Jews, nonetheless contain useful information on Berlin's contacts with various North African and Arab nationalist movements, on the difficulties encountered by German and Italian armistice commissions at Casablanca and Algiers, on the relations cultivated by German "diplomats" with certain North African French personalities, and on the Germans' plans in Tunisia and the vexations caused by their Italian allies.

Introduction

Few North African Jews wrote memoirs. Besides the Algerian resistants who have left us detailed accounts of their clandestine activities before the Allied landing, few important Jewish witnesses have written accounts. Maurice Eisenbeth for Algeria and Robert Borgel and Paul Ghez for Tunisia are practically the only ones who took the trouble of having their journals published after the war.

This lack has in part been made up by the Oral Division of the Institute of Contemporary Jewry of the Hebrew University of Jerusalem, which for the last twenty years has collected eyewitness accounts of the life of the Jewish communities of North Africa during the war. We have made extensive use of the collection of accounts of the situation of Tunisian Jews during the German occupation.

This work could not have been done without the generous help I have received in France and in Israel. I would like to express my heartfelt thanks to the Center for the Integration of the Patrimony of Oriental Jewry of the Israeli Ministry of Education and to the Faculty of Humanities of the Hebrew University of Jerusalem, which have sponsored my research. I am also grateful to the directorial staff of the Archives de France d'Outre-Mer at Aix-en-Provence and to the staff of the Centre de Documentation Juive Contemporaine at Paris, who have offered me a most cordial welcome and have often allowed me to consult documents that were difficult to access or not yet catalogued.

The warm interest for my research shown by the personnel in charge of the Yad Vashem Museum has been a great encouragement to me. Finally, I owe the opportunity to pursue this topic to my colleagues, friends, and students at the Institute of Contemporary Jewry. To all, I express my deepest gratitude.

PART ONE

While Awaiting Vichy:
North Africa on the
Eve of World War II

1

A Colonial Phenomenon: Algerian Anti-Semitism

Anti-Semitism appears to have practically been one of the basic elements of the *pied-noir* mind-set. It was, to an extent, the only current of ideas, the only mass ideology ever to be popular with Algerian Europeans. Many "explanations" for this phenomenon have been offered: the Crémieux decree and the Kabyle revolt of 1871, the religious clericalism of the refugees from Alsace-Lorraine as well as that of the *pied-noirs* of Italian and Spanish origins, the "anti-clerical" republicanism of the Radicals and the Socialists, the Dreyfus affair and Edouard Drumont's political activity in Algiers, economic troubles spanning the phylloxera epidemics of the end of the nineteenth century and the depression of the 1930s, Léon Blum, the Popular Front and the project Blum-Violette, and so on.

These "causes," set in a timeline, span all the political and social history of Algeria and, in parts, that of France during the Third Republic. Rather than providing explanations for the essential bases of Algerian anti-Semitism, they illustrate the perennial nature of this movement, which was rooted in the social and cultural structures of colonial Algeria.[1]

Anti-Semitism in Europe in the second half of the nineteenth century banished Jews from national societies. Similarly, Algerian anti-Semitism centered on the absolute negation of the "Frenchness" of Jews and of their rights to assume the title of French citizen, in the name of the Crémieux decree. It also centered on the refusal to let them participate in French political life and on the rejection of their modes of behavior, their manners, their accented speech of "French Arabs." In short, anti-Semites constantly objected to the insertion of Algerian Jews into the dominant colonial ethnic group that perceived in the insularization of its own cultural traits — principally of its Latin origins and Catholic religion — not only the main basis but the guarantee itself of the social order established in 1830, after the French conquest of Algeria.

In this light, one can better comprehend why, in Algeria, the adherents of every political persuasion that accepted the legitimacy of the colonial order used and abused anti-Semitic slogans. One can better comprehend, as well, why the close of every electoral term became an anti-Jewish crisis, the scope and intensity of these crises being determined more by the importance of the electoral stake than by current anti-Semitic phantasms ranging from accusations of ritual murders to that of the "conspiracy of the elders of Zion." Above all, it becomes clear why this movement remained a "white domain," affecting the Moslem native masses very little. "Arab anti-Semitism," called into being by the wishful thinking of Max Regis, Emile Morinaud, Paul Bidaine, Dr. Molle, and Father Lambert, remained confined to traditional motivations, which in the 1930s were to be fanned by the economic crisis, the events of Palestine, and Arab nationalist propaganda themes broadcast on the waves of Radio Bari, and Radio Berlin and Radio Stuttgart.

The anti-Jewish riots of Constantine (August 3–5, 1934), which pitted the two "Semite" communities of the city against each other, were hardly different in style and in substance from the pogroms of the precolonial era. These riots were triggered by the insulting attitude of a Jewish soldier toward some Moslems at prayers. Some mild incidents followed, but twenty-four hours later there was an explosion of violence, which, in the presence of surprised police forces little inclined to do their duty, ended in the pillage and arson of shops and in the massacre of dozens of Jews.[2] We present here two opposite interpretations culled from the various explanations of these tragic events. One is by Malek Bennabi, a reformist Moslem, and the other by R. Zenati, a naturalized French Moslem. Bennabi, the author of *Mémoires d'un témoin du siècle*, describes the state of mind of the Moslem population of Constantine:

> Anything that had remained in the hands of the former bourgeoisie of Constantine had been liquidated in these shops between the years 1920 and 1925. It is there also that peasants who still owned a bit of land in the areas of Sétif, Guelma, or Bône were stripped of their property. . . .
> In Constantine, the bourgeois for a wedding and the peasant of Sétif for a Citroen and for cash to go out on the town in Rue de l'Echelle needed money. The Jew was always ready to lend it to them at 60 percent interest, and the debt cumulated at this rate automatically caused their property to pass, after a year or two, from their hands into those of a settler. (Bennabi 1965:135–36)

Algerian Anti-Semitism

Why was the August 5 outbreak directed against the Jewish "middleman" and not against the European settler, the real beneficiary of native pauperization described by Bennabi? Why did the anti-Jewish riot break out only after the rekindling of anti-Semitic agitation? To these questions, to which Bennabi gives no answer, we must add the following comments by R. Zenati:

> Since August 5 there is much talk about the resentment of the natives against the Jew. It is put forward that the outbreak was a result of the resentment provoked by the traditional arrogance of the newly rich Jew, by his pretentious attitude since becoming a French citizen. . . . We must point out that this resentment could have been found only among city dwellers. However, the perpetrators of the August 5 attacks on people and property all, or almost all, came from rural areas. These people come into contact with the Jew only when they go to town to shop or to ask him for money services. In this situation, the man from the outbacks looks upon the Jew with the sort of consideration one has for the rich man whom one might need someday.
> As to the privileges of citizenship, there are only a few native intellectuals, particularly those who understand the value of a voting ballot, who reproach not the Jews who were able to take advantage of a moment of confusion to suit their interests, but instead France, which agreed to what is truly a social upheaval in Algeria. The rest of the Arab population is incapable of comprehending the significance of the Crémieux decree and has not included it in its grievances. At any rate the natives, who have shown no taste for the citizenship available to them since the Senatus-consulte of 1865, do not have the right to be jealous of the Jews for an advantage that they themselves still shun after a century of contact. (Zenati 1938:121–22)

According to Zenati, the riots would have led to "no more than the destruction of a few shops" if the Arabs "had been confronted with an armed force and mostly if they had not thought they were acting with the consent of the French."

This opinion was widely shared in the Jewish population even though some community spokesmen had the tendency, which now appears to have been erroneous, to consider the Constantine Arab outbreak as an anti-French insurrection.[3] In fact, despite the real importance of the immediate causes of the confrontation and of the effects of groundless rumors[4] on the overexcited crowd's behavior, it appears almost impossible to dissociate the macabre free-for-all of Constantine from the anti-Semitic agitation that, at the time, was widespread in Algeria. This agitation was cleverly kept up by the French local press, which, with the support of influential political personalities, succeeded in rekindling the anti-Jewish flame that had lost much of its intensity after World War I.

Men and an Idea

Just as it did at the end of the nineteenth century, the political elites and the notables occupied as prominent a place in the anti-Jewish offensive of the 1930s. Father Gabriel Lambert in Oran, Deputy Emile Morinaud in Constantine, and Lucien Bellat, the mayor of Sidi-bel-Abbès, championed this movement whose objectives were to be fulfilled with Pétain's accession to power and the success of his National Revolution.

The anti-Semitic itinerary of these three characters merits some attention here. Father Lambert was a clergyman who even though expelled from the church never stopped wearing the ecclesiastical dress; he was also a water prospector who caused the city of Oran to be equipped with an abundant but salted water supply. He began his political career by confronting the anti-Semitic municipalities of Dr. Molle and of his assistant and successor-to-be, Ménudier. Thus, Father Lambert felt it necessary to preach the union of the races and the condemnation of anti-Semitism against Dr. Molle's *Unions Latines* and its daily, the *Petit Oranais*.

And so he created the organization Amitiés Lambert to which adhered indistinctively Jews, Moslems, and Catholics. Thanks to his ecumenical program, Father Lambert managed successively to become a member of the municipal council and then mayor of Oran in 1933. Then, during the elections of May 1936, Lambert was defeated; the victory went to the Section Française de l'Internationale Ouvrière (S.F.I.O.)[5] candidate, Marius Dubois. Dubois had pulled in all the votes of the Popular Front while the mayor of Oran had had to cope with the competition of the candidates representing the various "nationalistic" parties such as the Parti Social Français and the Parti Populaire Français.

Without really believing it himself, Father Lambert accused the Jews of having betrayed him by casting their ballots for the Popular Front candidate.[6] His principal aim, however, was to fill the void left by the Unions Latines, which had fallen into near oblivion since 1933, and thus he became the ardent apostle of the anti-Jewish cause. On the day after the local elections of October 1937, he organized the Amitiés Latines, which became his means of accession to the leadership of the Rassemblement National created through the fusion of all the organizations whose program was the fight against Jews and Communists.

The Amitiés Latines was uncontestedly the anti-Semitic organization with the most ambitious organizational and recruiting set-up. Having inherited Dr. Molle's administrative apparatus and probably being inspired by contemporary totalitarian parties, Father Lambert gave his movement a Central Committee and a Political Bureau. Adherents were grouped into neighborhood sections as well as into electoral districts sections. For instance, the central district of Oran was divided into a grid of twenty-five subsections each having its own headquarters, where members could "go relax and soak up the Latin atmosphere."[7] Besides these subsections, the Amitiés Latines also comprised three departmental sections for the recruitment of women, Moslems, and youth (Jeunesse Latine). The means of propaganda consisted in the publication of pamphlets and newspaper articles,[8] and in organizing public demonstrations, cocktail parties, meetings, balls, distribution of food to the needy, parades, sports events, and so on.

The case of Father Lambert is in some respects reminiscent of that of Emile Morinaud. Morinaud had led the anti-Semites in 1898 but afterward developed kinder feelings toward his district's Jews thanks to, it seems, the influence of his friend Narboni, this "good Jew" who had provided efficient help for his electoral campaigns since 1904. *Le Républicain*, newspaper of the deputy mayor of Constantine, explained Morinaud's "electoral philosophy" as follows:

> In fact, the aim, in Oran as well as in Constantine, has not been and is not now to wage war against all Jews without exception. The gist of this matter is simply to stop letting ourselves be bullied by Jewish mass voting, to unite one and all for our defense against the Jewish masses who wish to take over everything in this country.
>
> Our program is the rigorous defense of the French majority.
>
> Our fight will only stop, as it stopped forty years ago in Constantine, when the revolting cause that gave it birth shall disappear. Let a Narboni stand up, as in 1904, against the scandal of twenty-three hundred Jews storming the ballot boxes against three thousand French voters, in other words, against the greater part of the French population, and there will be no more Constantine!
>
> And, as in 1904, our campaign shall no longer be necessary and thus will desist.
>
> In the meanwhile, as Frenchmen, we aim to know only Frenchmen here. Only with them shall we live, only them shall we help make a living![9]

Occurring sometime after the victory of the Popular Front, Morinaud's new anti-Semitic turn had as a background the deputy's defeat in the municipal elections of spring 1938.[10] Blaming the Jewish electorate for his defeat, he organized, with the help of some of his friends, the grouping Amitiés Françaises, whose avowed aim was to "organize the defense against the Jews of Constantine."[11] However, with the coming of the supplementary elections of December, Morinaud, believing that Jewish support would be indispensable, offered, during a secret meeting with the notables of the Jewish community, to stop his anti-Semitic campaign if they would ensure him of a favorable Jewish vote. The head of the police department wrote in his report:

> The Jewish representatives, however, expressed some objections. According to them, the mind-set of the mass of Jewish voters had changed in the past five years. It was no longer possible to make them obey to the letter instructions given by the consistory. They had progressed and intended to show their feelings of independence in political matters.[12]

As could be expected, these negotiations failed but they had the unforeseen consequence of the Radical-Socialists joining the "anti-Semitic league." They had been defeated in the December vote and they blamed their troubles on the "Judeo-Morinist" reconciliation, even though it had been aborted, but mostly they put the blame on the "treason" of Lellouche, an electoral kingmaker who "had promised [the Radical-Socialists] a certain number of Jewish votes."[13]

Lucien Bellat had been mayor of Sidi-bel-Abbès since 1929. He was the leader of the local section of the Unions Latines and openly flaunted his Fascist sympathies. In October 1937 he was even directly implicated in the kidnapping of a former consul of Republican Spain in Algeria (Esquer 1946:44–45). A few months later under the guise of the Lambrech law of 1871, which required Algerian Jews to prove their Algerian native origins before they could take advantage of the Crémieux decree, Bellat arbitrarily crossed out of electoral and recruitment lists the names of hundreds of Jews who had not been able to produce written proof with their declaration of the native status of their ancestors. This affair caused a lot of turmoil. It was brought up in the French cabinet and finally caused Albert Sarrault, the minister of the interior, to issue a decree on January 16, 1939, annulling the action of the mayor of Sidi-bel-Abbes.[14]

These three men and their like-minded rivals in Algiers, Tlemcen, and Mostaganem attracted the more visible local representatives of *pied-noir* society. The electoral committees of a Morinaud or a Lambert, which, to suit the needs of the moment, had rapidly transformed themselves into anti-Semitic action committees, included members of municipal councils, lawyers, medical doctors, wealthy settlers, and businessmen,[15] whose anti-Jewish gut feelings were devoid of philosophical, ideological, or pseudoscientific trappings.

Besides this circle of anti-Semites with electoral ambitions, there was also a core of individuals who derived their ideological inspiration and financial support from extreme right-wing groups of France and occasionally even of Germany and Italy. Among these, we should list Doriot's Parti Populaire Français, of which the Algiers section was headed by Victor Arrighi; Colonel de la Rocque's Parti Social Français, whose newspaper *La Flamme* was edited by Stanislas Devaud and Claude Martin, two professors of Constantine[16]; Commandant Jean Renaud's organization, the Faisceau Français, whose Algiers representative was René Barthélemy, editor-in-chief of the paper *Libre Parole*; the Front de la Jeunesse, whose leader J.-C. Legrand made a stormy visit to Algeria during the summer of 1938; Henri Lautier and his Algiers paper *l'Eclair*, which sought the role of organ of French national-socialism; the Amitiés Jacques Bainville; the local sections of Action Française; those of the Dames Royalistes; and the Centre Culturel Espagnol (Spanish Cultural Center), which was particularly active in Oran and in Sidi-bel-Abbès.

The Parti Populaire Français (P.P.F.) and the Parti Social Français (P.S.F.) occupied the first ranks of the Algerian extreme right, but up to the victory of the Popular Front and up to the drafting of the Blum-Violette project[17] the "Jewish problem" had been for them only a secondary concern. Furthermore, as had happened in France itself, some Jews had even joined the ranks of the Croix de Feu and then of the P.S.F. These two organizations completely joined the anti-Jewish bandwagon only on the eve of the local elections of 1938.

During Doriot's visit to Algeria in May 1938, Victor Arrighi expressed the P.P.F.'s position on the Jewish problem as follows:

> These are people who are French because of a seventy-year-old unjust decree, and they have not become part of the great family of France. In France we have quite distinct provinces: Corsica, Provence, Brittany, the Basque country. Each province has maintained its uniqueness, its customs, its traditions. Is there on that account a Breton problem, a Corsican problem, a Basque problem? Only Jews are kept out. They have adamantly preserved their autonomy. They have chosen to be Jews first and French second and to rule the French while remaining Jews. They have voted in bloc for one side or another according to the dictates of their leaders and for the interest of the family of Judaism. Foreigners they are, foreigners they shall remain. We shall give to the 450,000 Jews of France and to the 200,000 Jews of Algeria a special status like that of British subjects living in France. We shall put everyone back in their places and we shall leave the French person on his rightful one: the first place.[18]

As for the position of the Parti Social Français, it was defined by Devaud on the eve of the Constantine elections of December 1938:

> The Jews have become French without asking for it through the Crémieux decree. We, members of the P.S.F., are not anti-Semitic, but we do find it strange that the chosen people, chosen according to biblical tradition, has now become a "choosing" people who makes the electoral balance lean in favor of the Marxists and the "red kerchiefs." The Jews lack individual feelings, they have only collective goals, gregarious instincts, and they vote like sheep. Therefore it is they who are racist toward us who are resolutely hostile toward them.[19]

Waxing in the same vein, Colonel de la Rocque himself declared in the same newspaper:

> I find it stupid to yell "down with the Jew" and to be satisfied with this. . . . What I propose to you is more difficult: as long as the Jews of Constantine maintain this attitude you must . . . completely ignore them in the social, business, and industrial spheres. In short, you must act as if they didn't exist and have no contact whatsoever with them.

The economic boycott of the Jews was the favorite weapon of every anti-Semitic grouping. It was the first step taken by the Amitiés Françaises, which advised its members to stop hiring Jews, even as servants.[20] But, in Algiers as well as in Oran, there were very few firings of Jewish employees before the Vichy regime's promulgation of anti-Jewish directives. On the other hand, many Jewish shops experienced drastic drops in business volume while, in the small urban centers, Jewish sales representatives did not dare visit their customers for fear of being molested by the inhabitants.[21]

The Administration and Anti-Semitic Agitation

After being accused of incompetence and even of sympathizing with the Arab rioters of Constantine in 1934, administrators seem to have paid special attention to the evolution of the anti-Semitic movement in the five prewar years. Thus, at both the departmental and municipal levels, all police departments received the order to draft reports on the matter at regular intervals, first every three months, then monthly, and finally weekly. These form an invaluable source for the study of anti-Semitism, and they also provide first-class material for an analysis of the state of mind and the worldview of the civil servants whose task it was to maintain the public order and to enforce the laws of the republic.

Even while viewing anti-Semitic agitation as dangerous, particularly when there was a risk of it spreading to native milieus, there were many police officers and inspectors who, in trying to explain this phenomenon, gave vent to their own anti-Jewish convictions. They thereby gave credibility to the most extravagant rumors that were to weigh heavy on public officials' decisions in the months and years to come. This tendency was to be most noticeable after the rise to power in France of the Daladier administration, and much more so in Constantine than in Algiers and Oran.

Thus, the chief of the special police forces of Constantine, aligning himself with the "nationalist" parties, in a report on the elections of December 1938, explained how "Jewish attitude" had provoked a split of Constantine society into a "French" and a "Jewish" party. In his view, it was this that provoked the rise in anti-Semitic agitation: "Undoubtedly, the Jews made a serious mistake by voting in bloc for Mr. Massieu, the socialist party candidate."[22]

Refusing to attribute to the Jews any other motivations besides gregarious ones and pretending to ignore that Massieu had been the only non-anti-Jewish candidate the author of the report attributed this "massive" Jewish vote to the influence of the city's concillor-general, Lellouche, who "leans toward Marxism, mainly because his boss is Mr. Léon Blum, and only for this reason rather than out of political conviction." He thus accused Lellouche of having succeeded in "arousing a general hostility toward the Jews; the Jews will some day repent having challenged general opinion, which has given a vote of confidence to the Daladier administration and wants an immediate recovery for France."[23]

Without adopting the equation Jews = Socialists = anti-French that was implied by this analysis of the situation, R. Bouffet, the *préfet* of Constantine, nonetheless attributed the origin of the anti-Semitic movement to "the traditional method of Jewish voters to support in bloc the program of a single party and to the arrogance of a minority of Jews . . . who far from showing modesty in victory are, through their attitude and their sarcasms, exasperating those whom they take to be their enemies. . . ."[24]

However, just like his colleagues in Oran and Algiers, Préfet Bouffet opposed any potential direct attempt by governmental agencies to tone down the issue. Louis Boujard the *préfet* of Oran, explained this stance as follows: "Overly specific measures by public officials in favor of the Jewish demands would be interpreted as further proof of Jewish influence on those in power."[25]

As it was soon to become clear, the noncommittal stance of governmental officials resulted in giving free rein to anti-Semitic propaganda while any show of support for the Jews was systematically discouraged because officials felt that "these could only lead to a resurgence of anti-Semitism."[26]

After the declaration of war, anti-Jewish agitation became more strident and Jewish soldiers became the butt of serious and specific accusations that put in question their loyalty and their willingness to serve in fighting units. In this instance as well, official response was equivocal, and the evidence leads to the conclusion that, at least at the departmental administrative level, most of the accusations were taken at their face value.

Thus one could read the following in a report on the situation in the military hospital of Constantine:

> The nursing staff is in the main composed of Jews and these men have no qualms about offhandedly thinking themselves in conquered territory, in an annex of the ghetto. The patients are complaining of: (1) The repelling filth, the "Jewish" filthiness of the dormitories . . . , (2) The insufficiency of the food portions, even though the food is well prepared. . . . The only occasional exception to this occurs when a French sergeant-nurse personally oversees the food distribution.

And the author concludes: "I wanted to inform you myself of these complaints because by the time a neutral person gets out of the hospital he has become fiercely anti-Semitic. He then returns to his family, spreads anti-Jewish criticism, and the problem grows little by little."[27]

Of much more serious import is a report on Jewish attitudes toward military service issued by the Center of Information and Research of the Oran Préfecture. After having described "the rumors circulating among the natives and among the Europeans" according to which "Jews will eat soap so as to be found sick and exempted from the draft" and with the qualification that "the intent of this report is not to judge the soldierly valor of the Jews as a whole," the author nonetheless concluded his report by noting with seemingly more objectivity:

> However, besides these more or less unverifiable rumors, the president of the Commission for the Control of the Postal Services of Oran . . . notes himself that the general tone of censored mail could be summarized as follows:
> Letters from natives: excellent morale
> Letters from Europeans: good
> Letters from Jews: many letters show a dubious morale where the main concern is to avoid the common duty of military service.[28]

Finally, in Philippeville, the police learned that a Jewish military doctor, Dr. Jonathan, "might be having his fellow Jews exempted in exchange of payment" and as if to give a better idea of the type of person involved, the report adds that "before the war this doctor was one of the most active supporters of the Popular Front. . . . Possibly, it is the same Dr. Jonathan who has in Philippeville taken care of the Communist Avril and recommended him for an exemption. Avril had been acquitted on January 30 by the military tribunal of Constantine of the charge of making "defeatist statements." [29]

Moslem Population and the Jewish Problem

There is a recurrent theme, almost a given, that is present like a filigree in all the reports of the Algerian police. It is that of the tenseness of the relations between Jews and Moslems after the Constantine events. It was felt that any kind of provocation brought about the risk of a general outbreak that would pit the two communities against each other. Consequently, police organizations were watchful of the slightest incident, even as benign a one as a fight that broke out in a Constantine swimming pool and turned out to be a common brawl between drunken Jews and Moslems. They were alarmed by the faintest rumor such as false accounts of confrontations between Jews and Moslems that "eyewitnesses," European soldiers on leave, were spreading around town, or such as the one attributing the closing of a Moorish café of Oran to Jewish maneuverings. Governmental officials were also very sensitive to the slightest act that might be taken by Moslems as a further proof of the favoritism enjoyed by Jews. Thus the local press was discreetly advised not to divulge any information on the campaign undertaken by several Jewish groupings for the retrial of H. Zaoui, condemned to death for the murder of the disabled war veteran Aubertin:[30] "These goings-on seem particularly prone to nurture anti-Semitic feelings among the Moslem population." The reason given for this being: "The Moslem population . . . is the more heatedly in favor of the death penalty for Zaoui because two natives were decapitated in Oran a few days ago for a crime that was no more odious than this one. Justice must be the same for the Jews as for the Moslems. . . ."[31]

But, in contrast, public officials, normally quick to respond in this sort of circumstances, showed the greatest of restraint toward initiatives by right-wing organizations that aimed at supporting the creation of anti-Jewish groupings within the Moslem population or at the least tried to nurture a permanent hostility toward Jews in Moslem milieus.

Father Lambert and Emile Morinaud were very active in this field. The mayor of Oran had had the idea of adding a Moslem section to the

Amitiés Latines and he gave this section's leadership to Taleb Ahmed, who was in charge of the sanitorial services at city hall and who, between meetings, would write and have published "Appeals to the Moslem people" in which the Jews, "destroyers of religions," were pictured as the "worst enemies of Islam." In all likelihood, the creation of this section under the sponsorship of such an important man as the mayor aroused the interest of many Moslems who had up to then resisted anti-Jewish propaganda. "Natives assume that governmental bodies are approving or at least tolerating this section and that; thus the struggle against the Jews has taken on a legitimate character."[32]

In the meanwhile, Morinaud, the deputy from Constantine, had the newspaper *Le Républicain* print substantial excerpts from the Middle Eastern Arab press on the Palestinian events and letters of dubious authenticity from Moslem readers inviting their Algerian brethren to follow the path of their Palestinian brothers "crying under the Zionist yoke." Like the *Petit Oranais* and other publications of similar tendencies, the Constantine paper allocated much space to the various anti-Jewish themes generated by German and Italian propaganda agencies and aimed at the Arab populations of the Maghreb. At the same time, these newspapers deleted any mention of the violently anticolonial and anti-French aspects of this same propaganda, for the extreme rightist press was maligning the leadership of the Algerian nationalist movement by accusing them of being Jewish sympathizers because of their struggle for the adoption of the Blum-Violette project. The rejection of this project and the abrogation of the Crémieux decree were thus to become the two complementary themes of the propaganda of the anti-Semitic movement: "The Jews must be thrown into the sea, their French citizenship must be taken from them. . . . [The Moslems] must stop listening to the Jews who instead of helping them get work and bread want to get them the vote, which will be useless to them."[33]

On many occasions, militants of the Algerian nationalist movement denounced the schemings of anti-Semitic organizations. The Communist militant, Ben Ali Boukort, wrote in *La Lutte Sociale*: "One of the battle techniques used by the enemies of our cause is to stifle the demands of our movement by redirecting it onto the path of anti-Semitism. Could a truly conscientious Moslem be as naive as to not be aware of the criminal purpose of these anti-Semitic Arab haters?"[34]

As to the Palestinian events so often mentioned by the extreme right-wing press, "the struggle there is not between Arabs and Jews anymore" but "between the Palestinian Arab people and British imperialism along with Zionism, its accomplice," explained K. Belkaïm.[35]

From the point of view of the Algerian Moslem reformists, the aim pursued by the leaders of the Amitiés Latines seemed to be "a replay of the tragedy of Constantine," or according to Sheikh Zahiri: "They hope that thanks to the troubles, a state of emergency will be declared and that war councils will come into operation so that all our militants can be jailed, all the Arab movements crushed, and our schools closed. . . ."[36]

Were those stances inspired by Jewish personalities or by organizations such as the L.I.C.A. (Ligue Internationale contre le Racisme et l'Antisémitisme) whose representatives in Algeria tried to slow down the expansion of the anti-Semitic movement among the Moslem population? The police reports answered this question with a flat no, but public officials stuck with their viewpoint and as much as possible discouraged any campaign against anti-Semitism. The head of the Center of Information and Studies of Oran clearly explained this policy after the censoring of an article by a Moslem writer that was to have been published in the *Oran Républicain*:[37]

> The Jewish elements, very numerous in this newspaper, had been insisting for the last few days that something should be done. They want to fight against anti-Semitism of which they complain. For instance, they had asked Sheikh Zahiri to write some articles so as to specifically calm down the Arabs. *It is upon my own advice that the Sheikh has refused because I feel that, at this time, this sort of publication can only lead to a recrudescence of anti-Semitism.* The censoring officer must have felt the same way when he stopped the publication of the incriminated ariticle.[38]

Algerian Jewry in the Face of Anti-Semitism

Because the consistories were forbidden by law to participate in political matters, they showed little response to the anti-Jewish agitation. The initiative then passed into the hands of local organizations, such as the tailors' union of Constantine from which emerged a group of about forty Jewish workers ready to fight against the schemings of Morinaud's Amitiés Françaises. The initiative also passed to organizations that stood outside the Jewish community such as the Comité d'Etudes Sociales (social studies committee), which had been revived in 1937 under the leadership of the medical doctor A. Levi-Valensi, and as well to interdenominational organizations such as the International League against Racism and Anti-Semitism (L.I.C.A.).

"Truth must stand up to lies and reveal the hidden motives of the troublemakers and of those who fund them" (cited in Ansky 1950:78). This was the wording of the motion adopted in 1937 by the Comité d'Etudes Sociales, and it summarized the political line that the leaders of the Algerian Jewry were to adopt in the course of the following years.

Their responses to the incendiary invectives of the anti-Semitic movement were always toned down and were punctuated at regular intervals with pathetic appeals to justice, law, and above all to reason.[39] In answer to the "calomnies" and to the accusations of Jewish lack of patriotism by J.-C. Legrand, G. Lambert, and V. Arrighi, the Jews brandished the macabre statistics of World War I and made special reference to the *Livre d'Or du Judaïsme Algérien* (golden book of Algerian Judaism) in which was printed the number and the names of Algerian Jews killed, wounded, or imprisoned during the war.

The leaders of the Algerian Jewish community resisted any kind of action that might be labeled racist by their adversaries. They opposed the extremist and spectacular projects advocated by a small group of young Oranese militants belonging to the Beitar[40] and preferred to set their struggle within the frameworks of political or humanitarian organizations of national scope. In this way, they were more comfortable in denouncing the "antirepublicanism" and the "anti-French" aspects of the anti-Semitic discourse than in condemning its particularistic character openly directed against a specific segment of society.

The debate that led to the creation in May 1938 of a "Comité de Vigilance,"a watchdog committee for the defense of the moral interests of the Jewish community in Oran, is a good illustration of this state of mind.

The initiative for organizing this committee came from the president of the Oran consistory, A. Smadja, who in front of an assembly of 150 notables of the community explained that the aim of the committee would be to collect substantial sums for the defense of the republic against those who wanted to destroy it and to pay for the travel cost of committee members who were to visit the General Office of the Government (Gouvernement Général) and the Ministry of the Interior in Paris to denounce the anti-Semitic danger.[41] The speakers were far from unanimous on the desirability of this plan. Some of them pointed out that the L.I.C.A. was already working for the same goal and was in contact with the government; others were bothered by the leftist political orientation of the L.I.C.A., while the watchdog committee "not beholding to any political party would simply defend the republic against those who would sabotage its laws."[42] Other speakers felt that the republic should be defended by creating a "coordinating committee" who would support, that is, subsidize, newspapers and political parties remaining faithful to the Popular Front.[43]

Finally, the watchdog committee was organized according to Smadja's wishes who nonetheless declined its presidency. Its thirteen members were all notables respected in the community: businessmen, doctors, lawyers, and journalists.

This Oranese committee was an organization with purely local aims, and it does not appear that it coordinated its actions with other similar committees that simultaneously sprouted up in other Algerian cities — not even with the Social Studies Committee of Algiers, which, because of the intellectual stature of its members, appeared to be speaking for Algerian Judaism. The Algiers committee's discussions with French officials on the repression of the anti-Semitic campaign did not bring any positive results. In June 1938 the committee sent to Paris a delegation of four members[44] to meet with the premier and with the minister of the interior. Again, this attempt proved to be less than satisfactory; the cabinet directors of Daladier and of Sarrault were empowered only to offer them vague appeasing promises. At this point, it bears mentioning that besides the demands pertaining to their own community, the Jewish envoys also asked for the freeing of Shaykh al-'Uqbi, leader of the reformist Algerian movement, who had been set up and arrested by the police in June 1936 for the murder of the mufti of Algiers.

Besides its obvious humanitarian character, this demand manifested the desire for a rapprochement with the Moslems, desire that had been expressed by some influential members of the Social Studies Committee ever since the events of Constantine. This was to lead, a few months after the Paris visit, to the creation of the Union des Croyants Monothéistes (union of monotheist believers) led by the shaykhs Ben-Badis and al-'Uqbi, and, on the Jewish side, by P. Benichou, A. Valensi, and E. Gozlan. The Jewish leaders preferred to collaborate with the "reformist Ulama,[45] whose nationalism was more spiritual than political and who considered the taking up of French nationality apostasy" (Julien 1972:102–6). In contrast, they kept their distances from the other elements in the Algerian nationalist movement, particularly from the assimilationists. Thus they maintained a cool attitude toward Dr. Benjelloul because of his ambiguous role during the Constantine riots and particularly because of his barely veiled complaints about the "injustice" of the Crémieux decree.[46]

"To maintain themselves in the French family" was to be the first priority, the summum bonum of the political outlook of the Jews of Algeria during these crucial prewar years. Having adopted a cool attitude in the face of the attacks on their religion and their property of which they were the victims, they were, in contrast, extremely sensitive to any threat to their French citizenship and to any questioning of their attachment to the motherland. We can thus fully understand the grief that overtook the Algerian Jewish community in 1940 upon the repeal of the Crémieux decree. The blow was to be the more painful in that it came from the "French of France," which they had so painstakingly dissociated on the affective plane from the "French of Algeria," who were the ones possessed with anti-Semitism and racial hatred.

2

Moroccan and Tunisian Jews in the Face of the French Extreme Right and German and Italian Agitation

The situation of the two protectorate's Jews faintly echoed that of the Algerian Jewry. Both Morocco and Tunisia were the locus of the birth of similar movements of anti-Jewish xenophobia and, as in Algeria, these movements came out of the collusion of the French extreme right, Arab nationalism, and German and Italian propaganda. However, because the elements of this triad took on differing appearances from one country to another, each area ended up producing its own brand of anti-Jewish agitation.

The Extreme Right

French extreme rightist organizations were never as widespread in Morocco and in Tunisia as they were in Algeria. This difference can be explained not only by the proportionately smaller size of the European element and by the specific juridical status of the two protectorates, but also, and more particularly regarding Tunisia, by the relative "open mind" of European settlers, many of whom had been active members of the local sections of the C.G.T. (Confédération Générale du Travail) or of the Socialist or Communist parties. For these reasons the anti-Semitic organizations at play among the French population were in Morocco as well as in Tunisia pale emanations of the anti-Jewish movements of metropolitan France and of Algeria. Among these organizations we can list Jean Renaud's Faisceau Français, the Mouvement Franciste, which appeared in Fez as early as 1934; the sections of the P.P.F. (Parti Populaire Français) organized during the same year in the French zone of Morocco and in Tunisia, Les Croix de Feu, the P.S.F. (Parti Social Français), the Union Latine d'Action Française, the Alliance raciste Universelle, the Rassemblement anti-juif de

France, and Father Lambert's Amitiés Latines. These groupings generated intensive propaganda mostly through newspapers, tracts, and pamphlets.[1] After 1936 these organizations' anti-Jewish campaign was reinforced by large circulation dailies such as the *Dépêche Tunisienne*, the *Presse Marocaine*, the *Soir Marocain*, the *Soleil du Maroc*, and the *Voix Française*, whose adamant opposition to Léon Blum and to the Popular Front transformed them into more or less conscious admirers of Franco, Hitler, and Mussolini (Julien 1972: 142; Cohen-Hadria 1976: 127).

Maghrebian Nationalism and German and Italian Propaganda

Even though it is impossible to ascertain precisely the influence of this propaganda, it is obvious that its diffusion worsened the tension between Jews and Moslems, a tension mostly fanned by the news of the Palestinian conflict, pan-Islamic propaganda, and the nationalist awakening of the population of both protectorates. In Morocco, nationalism had for a long time been oriented toward Islam; in Tunisia, Bourguiba and the neo-Destour movement had given a strong secular imprint to their anticolonial struggle. And thus, in September 1934, precisely one month day for day after the Constantine riots, the Destourian militants who took to the streets to protest Bourguiba's deportation used among other rallying cries: "Jews are our brothers!"[2]

Meanwhile, in Morocco's major cities, Jewish neighborhoods were overtaken by a psychotic sense of insecurity through the spreading of the rumor that Yom Kippur 1934 (September 19) was to be the St. Barthelemy of Moroccan Jewry. In this country, the pan-Islamic Congress of Jerusalem (1931) had heralded a turn for the worse in Jewish-Moslem relations as shown by a series of incidents in Casablanca, Rabat, El-Ksar, and Tangiers,[3] and their echoes were amplified by the local nationalist press. This press was mainly inspired by the "Syrian Palestinian Committee" of Shakib Arslan who, from Geneva, was pulling the strings of pan-Islamic agitation in the Maghreb. Mixing anti-Zionist with anti-Jewish complaints, the Moroccan followers of Shakib Arslan ('Abd al-Khaliq Torrès, al-Hajj 'Abd al-Salam Bannuna, Muhammad al-Wazzani, and al-Makki al-Nasiri) reproached France for the emancipation of Moroccan Jewry in "flagrant violation" of the Protectorate Treaty[4] and for the favoritism enjoyed by Jewish schools as well as for the freedom of action of the Zionist associations that were working in Morocco.[5]

This propaganda first affected the masses and then gradually reached the Moslem level of the government. In October 1934 the grand vizir[6] pointed out to the French authorities the incovenience of Jews and Arabs jointly living in *medinas* (Moslem neighborhoods). The following year, the pasha[7] of Casablanca forbade Jews to settle in the new *medina* and in 1937 the pasha of Marrakech tried to prevent Jews from hiring Moslem domestic help (Coidan 1974:27). Following instructions by the nationalists who were accusing Jews of financially supporting the fight against Islam in Palestine with their business profits, many Moslems came to limit their business transactions with Jews. Many craftsmen stopped hiring Jewish helpers and some Moslems even came "to refuse to use the services of the Jewish barbers settled in the *medina*" (Coidan 1946:26).

Without minimizing the role of both traditional and modern internal factors around which this propaganda was articulated, there is no doubt that it was at least in part of foreign inspiration, primarily of Middle Eastern–Islamic and secondarily of German-Italian origins.[8]

Even while abandoning the Mediterranean area to Italian ambitions and despite his contempt for the Arab "race," Hitler did not fail to take an interest in the nationalist movements of the Maghreb and of the Mashreq. Free from the sin of colonialism and, putting to good use the prestige enjoyed by Germany in the Islamic world since the time of Wilhelm II, he understood the advantage of mobilizing Maghrebian nationalism against France thereby hoping to inflict at the opportune moment troubles and uprisings that would paralyze that country's North African holdings.

The influence of German propaganda was anything but negligible. Besides al-Amin al-Husayni, the Mufti of Jerusalem; besides Shakib Arslan and other Syrian, Iraqi, and Egyptian personalities, there were many Maghrebian nationalists (mostly Moroccan) who took an active part in the success of German agitation, which was centered almost exclusively on anti-Jewish and anticolonial themes. The leader of the Islamic community of Berlin, who was of Moroccan origin, generated the connection between the Islamischer Kulturband of Vienna (al-Rabita al-Taqafiyya al-Islamiyya) and the leaders of the Moroccan nationalist movement (al-Nasiri, al-Wazzani, and Bannuna). In 1938 a Committee for the Defense of Tunisia was established in Berlin besides the Committee for the Defense of the Arab Maghreb and the Committee of African Political Refugees. On the eve of the war, the Germans intensified their efforts by adding to the number of news broadcasts in Arab and Berber languages to the three Maghrebian countries and even by providing military training to a group of Algerian P.P.A, (Parti du Peuple Algérien) militants who were to adopt the name: Comité d'Action Révolutionnaire nord-africaine (C.A.R.N.A.).[9]

In the Maghreb itself, Ceuta, Tétouan, and Tangiers served as relay for German propaganda. The Arab expert, Adolphe Langenheim, had for a long time lived in the international city. He had in 1932 brought to Morocco the anti-Semitic agitator Karl Schlichting, member of the pan-

German association Fichte Bund. After Franco's secession, German ships used the Spanish ports of Morocco to unload thousands of leaflets urging the people of the Maghreb to initiate pogroms: "The Jew feeds off you as the vermin feed off the lamb. France protects him. He is the agent of France, he is its henchman. Germany locks up and hunts Jews down and takes away their property. If you were not the slaves of France you could do the same" (Julien 1972:141). Among other accusations, the Germans were circulating the rumor that the French authorities had agreed to let hundreds of German Jewish refugees into North Africa.[10]

As to the Italian role in the anti-Semitic agitation, it turned out to be as ambiguous as it was ostentatious. Up to 1938 anti-Semitism, at least officially, had practically been absent from Fascist ideology, and in Italy and Tripolitania as well as among Italian settlements in Tunisia and Morocco, many Jews became active members of local Fasci and actively participated in the Mussolinean recovery effort.

Undeniably, there were some clashes between the Blackshirts and the Jewish element in Libya after 1923. However, neither these incidents nor the coercive measures forcing Jews to open their shops and send their children to school on Saturdays could be interpreted as manifesting a racist policy. The representatives of the Mussolini regime were well aware of the Jewish role in the Libyan economy and were very much concerned with maintaining the prosperity of their colony. Thus, at least till 1940, they were to avoid applying in all its rigor the 1938 anti-Jewish legislation promulgated in Rome, which in principle applied equally to Libya (Felice 1978: chaps. 5–6).[11]

However, when it came to the French Maghreb, Mussolini was free from the economic constraints that forced him to an amount of restraint toward Libyan Jewry. He had taken the title of Sword of Islam in 1937, and although his territorial ambitions for Tunisia were well known, he imparted a strong anti-Semitic imprint to Italian propaganda directed at the French Maghreb. Relayed by the *Unione* in Tunis, the *Vedetta* in Tangiers, and the *Action Marocaine* in Rabat, Radio Bari and the Italian consular services pictured Moroccan and Tunisian Jews as the agents of French domination in North Africa and their Palestinian brethren as the henchmen of British imperialism in the Middle East. In addition, because of the relatively weak effect of this written and broadcasted propaganda on the masses, dozens of Italian "tourists" took to traveling around the Moroccan and Tunisian countrysides with the aim of directly preaching the Fascist gospel.[12] Finally, in conjunction with this campaign, Italian businesses and cultural agencies operating in Tunisia and in Morocco were ordered to let their Jewish agents go[13] while, from 1938 on, Italian schools in

Tunis, Rabat, and Tangiers closed their doors to Jewish children (Bessis 1981:189-92; Coidan 1946).

Jewish Response

The Jewish population of the two protectorates did not remain passive in the face of this agitation. Although in the synagogues solemn prayers and days of retreat proceeded at the rhythm of anti-Semitic persecutions in Europe, Jewish businessmen systematically boycotted Italian banks and products of German and Italian manufacture.[14] This movement began in 1933 with Hitler's rise to power[15] and occasionally led to incidents between Jews and Moslems, as in Tétouan, Casablanca, and Rabat.[16]

These shows of solidarity were applauded in both communities by the Zionist mainstream establishment, which, faithful to the Herzlean dialectic, welcomed the rise in consciousness triggered by anti-Semitic agitation:

This is one of the primary and indisputable benefits of this collective hatred (religious hatred in the past, racist hatred today, and perhaps tomorrow hatred on a yet unknown plane) without which Israel would have disappeared a long time ago. . . . Thus we feel no inclination to become indignant or to protest against a tidal wave that overtakes and often destroys the most powerful barriers. Let others howl at the moon. This ridiculous role does not tempt us.[17]

Considering hope the only reasonable attitude and abandoning to their conscience "those who dishonor themselves" by crying "death to the Jews," Zionist organizations, like the notables of both Jewish communities, vehemently condemned "the excesses" of a part of Jewish youth[18] influenced by the revisionist Zionist current and preferred to opt for direct action.[19] Except for a few soothing speeches on the necessity of preserving "Jewish-Moslem friendship," the initiative for responding to anti-Jewish agitation was left almost exclusively[20] to noncommunity organizations such as the L.I.C.A., the Ligue des Droits de l'Homme, the Libre Pensée, the Fédération des Anciens Combattants Républicains, and the S.F.I.O. (Section Française de l'Internationale Ouvrière) party.

In 1935 the governmental authorities of the Moroccan protectorate denied Bernard Lecache's request for permission to organize sections of the L.I.C.A. in the French zone. The following year, however, he was allowed to tour the main cities of Morocco where he advised his Jewish audiences to build closer ties with their Moslem compatriots.[21] This suggestion was to make immediate headway and led to the organization in

July 1936 in Fez of the Union marocaine des Juifs et des Musulmans, composed of young Jewish intellectuals and some Moroccan nationalists. This organization, however, lasted but a brief time, not surprisingly in view that its ideals matched neither the wishes of the Moslems nor the hopes of the Jews who almost unanimously had eyes only for France.[22]

And thus as soon as war appeared inevitable, hundreds of Moroccan and Tunisian Jews belonging to all levels of society made known their wish to enlist in the French army.[23] Committees of would-be volunteers were organized in all the major cities of both protectorates.[24] They were expecting the promulgation of a special law and in its absence there were only a few isolated cases of actual enlistments. The fear of Moslem discontent and the rise of anti-Jewish feelings within the European population settled the hesitancy of the French authorities, who were to reject the military help of the Jews of Morocco and Tunisia, even going as far as to censor newspaper articles that made mention of Jewish volunteers.

3

Toward Pétain's "National Revolution"

France's entry into the war brought the patriotism of North African Jews to the point of paroxysm. Their movement of solidarity with "liberal and peaceful France," with France "the protector of the weak and of the oppressed,"[1] was total and sincere: "It is Israel as a whole rather than each Jew as individual that must help France and its allies in gaining victory over the common enemy" (*L'Avenir Illustré*, December 30, 1939).

Everything contributed to this way of thinking: the horror of Hitlerism and the hatred for Germany, "the most inexorable enemy of the Jewish race (*L'Avenir Illustré*, December 30, 1939)," the rekindled affections for the emancipating country, "the France of Father Grégoire" threatened by an enemy "who has lost all sense of proportion and who plans on dominating the world after first ruining it,"[2] and finally the deep impulse, in the face of a common danger, of wanting to close ranks with the "adoptive and protective motherland." And thus, while, the grand rabbi of Tunisia was beseeching the faithful to turn their savings into arms bonds,[3] nights of prayers and days of fasting for the success of France and its allies were organized in Tunis, Nabeul, and Beja.[4] In Beja, the Jewish community, "wishing to contribute its utmost to France's victory," beseeched the authorities "to enact without delay a decree requiring the obligatory and immediate drafting of all Tunisian Jews of arm-bearing age into the French army."[5]

Similar responses were noted in Morocco: "The Moroccan Jews who were prevented from enlisting in the armed forces . . . have also contributed their francs to the National Defense fund, and we have noted large sums usually coming from important businessmen."[6]

However, the authorities of both protectorates were irritated by the Jewish population's outpourings of solidarity. In Morocco, Tunisia, and

Algeria, those who had hoped that "the fraternity of war" would bring anti-Semitic agitation to an end had to face the bitter truth: the anti-Jewish front was gaining strength as the defense lines against the German invader crumbled and the forewarning signs of the collapse mounted.

In Morocco, from the first days of May 1940, official reports began to mention the recrudescence of anti-Semitism among the European and Moslem population of the large cities.[7] These mentions became more and more numerous and specific on the eve of the armistice and immediately after. In Salé, the pasha decided to forbid Jews to employ Moslem domestic help,[8] in Meknès Moslem tradesmen of the Suq-al-'Attarin market demanded that Jews be expelled from it,[9] and in several other Moroccan cities swastikas were drawn on the walls of the *medinas*. However, in official circles it was believed that these gestures "reflected more a manifestation of anti-Jewish feelings than the expression of Germanophilia. [Moslem] intellectuals who have become Anglophobic through anti-Semitism are close to German concepts for the same reasons."[10] This anti-Semitic agitation, however, was labeled "serious" by the authorities and it was exacerbated by shortages of goods and rises in prices attributed to the Jews. The Jews were accused of willfully benefiting from the war that their European brethren were said to have themselves provoked. In cities with a large European population such as Casablanca, Oujda, Port Lyautey, Rabat, and Petit-Jean, extreme right-wing actions were decisive.[11] Elsewhere, "the anti-Jewish collusion of the European and the Arab populations" noted in the official reports took the form of "punitive actions" by French and Moslem soldiers in Jewish neighborhoods. In the *mellah*[12] of Fez, a Jew was killed and six others wounded during an operation of this type executed by native and French legionnaires.[13]

In Tunisia as well, a greater participation by the Moslem population and its more active role in the recrudescence of the anti-Jewish campaign were noted. While pamphlets calling for the massacre of the Jews were distributed in Tunis, La Goulette, Hammam-Lif, Monastir, Nabeul, and Gafsa, Jewish houses and shops were set upon and plundered in various areas of the Cap Bon and the Sahel.[14] The authorities attributed these events to "the natural anti-Jewish tendency of the natives of Tunisia" and to the influence of the anti-Semitic campaign conducted the preceding months by the European press.[15] However, these explanations skirted an essential aspect of the new situation: at the time that the "national revolution" was taking only its first steps, France's image to its overseas subjects was one of a giant whose infallibility and invincibility had just been cut to shreds by the German army. This weakening of the colonial power in itself generated ethnic conflicts that had been sublimated for a long time,

Toward Pétain's "National Revolution"

and it revived the desire for independence in the Moslem population. The latter, encouraged by the waning of French power, began to direct its blows toward the weakest and unprotected segment of the colonial society: the Jew, whose social promotion had specifically been one of the most objectionable aspects of colonialism in the eyes of a part of Moslem public opinion.

The situation presented itself differently in Algeria where, despite France's defeat, the colonial power maintained an appearance of strength credible enough to not encourage yearnings of independence in the Moslem population. All official reports concur that the Moslem population showed an unflinching loyalty and went as far as to condemn, along with almost all the French people, the "cowardly" attack on Mers-el-Kebir by the British fleet (July 3, 1940). This condemnation was colored by the fact that Great Britain had never found "much sympathy with the Moslems, who reproached it for its attitude toward their Middle Eastern brethren and particularly its policy favoring Jews over Arabs."[16] The Mers-el-Kebir event probably did inflame the animosity of the Moslems toward the Jews;[17] however, one fact does stand out: neither the Mers-el-Kebir affair nor the anti-Semitic agitation kept up by the extreme right-wing press and encouraged by German and Italian agents[18] led to incidents comparable to those occurring at the same period in Morocco and in Tunisia.[19]

The anti-Semitic campaign that broke loose after the armistice and after the repeal of the Marchandeau decree[20] remained predominantly European. Thus nothing new compared with the prewar years except for a more marked convergence of the outlook of traditionally anti-Jewish elements and of a part of the public administration.

Jews were for obvious reasons favorable to the continuation of the war against Nazi Germany and thus they were perceived as Britain's allies because they shared a common goal. Their leanings placed them outside the national community, which for the most part had become convinced of the legitimacy of the viewpoint that had led Marshal Pétain to ask for the armistice. From this, there was only a short step, easily taken by the authorities, to considering the Jewish population antigovernmental or even antinational.

Thus, the police *commissaire* of Nemours (Oranie) was to note that although "the real French" were enduring the pangs of defeat "in silent meditation," certain Jewish elements "were neglecting no occasion to celebrate, to indulge in noisy partying . . . coming close to indecency itself. This behavior astonishes and surprises more than it irritates the other elements of the population, who perhaps do not have the same reasons to rejoice."[21]

In Algiers, according to another report, Jews were showing toward England "feelings that seem to go beyond the platonic,"[22] while in Oran, the Jewish community "was thought to use funds to attract airplane pilots who were urged to enlist in the British armed forces."[23] In Constantine, moreover, Jews were accused of having incited the city's two hundred Communist railroad workers to damage the rails and to disturb rail traffic: "Wealthy Jews are ready to provide subsidies to the railroad workers' families in case the workers were to be pursued or imprisoned."[24]

Among the European population, anti-Jewish agitation was colored by the spreading of rumors of the imminence of pogroms in the large urban centers and by the circulating of threatening fliers and leaflets blaming the Jews for France's defeat and demanding their expulsion[25] and particularly demanding the repeal of the Crémieux decree. This latter theme was brought up at every meeting of the P.P.F., which, in this summer of 1940 took the forefront in the anti-Jewish campaign. Toward mid-September about twenty Jewish shops in the center of Algiers were plundered. The official report published the morning after this incident avoided condemning the anti-Semitic motives of the aggressors. Instead, it primarily reproached them for having taken over the role of the state:

> Dissatisfied with the measures for the general order taken by a government dedicated to social health, some people believe they can, without any risk, substitute themselves for the responsible authorities in a domain whose total elements and infinite complexity they are unaware of. It seems clear that while wanting to further a cause they are using methods that only hinder and complicate it. The spectacular acts of violence perpetrated in such a way as to lead to the belief that one can with impunity defy the police . . . lead in final analysis only at perturbing a set of events that cannot at this time be discussed in the public domain. (*La Dépêche Algérienne*, September 18, 1940)

The public authorities believed that the maintenance of the public order was an ineluctable necessity. They worried that these incidents would lead to uncontrolled rioting, which would be cleverly exploited by all kinds of anti-French elements. Given the highly charged emotional atmosphere prevalent in Algeria, this factor, and not any feelings of compassion on the part of the authorities, was to prevent anti-Semitic organizations from carrying out their threats.

PART TWO

North Africa on Vichy Time

4

The Maghreb after the Armistice: Attempts at Resistance and Militant Pétainism

On June 19, 1940, as France's fate was definitely sealed, Franco presented Hitler with a memorandum in which he demanded that Morocco be reunited into a Spanish protectorate. The caudillo also demanded the Oranie region of Algeria as price for entering the world conflict. Five days earlier, he had had the international sector of Tangiers occupied while Mussolini, a latecomer to the war against France, made no bones about his claims on Tunisia and the Constantinois region of Algeria.

In Bordeaux, French premier Paul Reynaud had vainly tried to convince the ministers of his cabinet of the necessity of transferring the institutions of the republic to North Africa. He favored pursuing the war effort and disliked the idea of an armistice with Nazi Germany. The premier had the support of the high-ranking administrators and military of Morocco, Algeria, and Tunisia, who were unanimously of the opinion that, with its resources and navy and air force divisions, North Africa was perfectly capable of resisting the onslaught of the Axis powers and contributing to the Allies' efforts to free metropolitan France.[1] But in the face of the opposite stance so staunchly defended by incredibly prestigious personalities such as Marshal Pétain and General Weygand who favored the armistice, what possible weight could the arguments of a Noguès[2] or a Le Beau[3] have? On June 17, the very day that Pétain formed his government and asked French troops to cease fighting, General Noguès let Weygand know that he was ready to continue the struggle "to save honor and to keep Africa for France" (Weygand 1950, vol. 3: 243). On June 18 Le Beau beseeched the government to take refuge in Algeria "to continue the fight on African soil at the side of France's allies" (Soustelle 1947:58). Noguès's and Le Beau's opposition to the armistice was shared by Admiral Estéva, a commandant of the Mediterranean fleet at Bizerte and by Marcel Peyrouton, the *résident-général*. However, one after another and "with brows blushing with shame" the overseas generals all came to accept Pétain's policy. Only immoderate German conditions for the armistice could have opened up a last chance for the plan of evacuation of the chambers of parliament and of the cabinet to North Africa as well as to the continuation of the armed struggle.

In these circumstances, the final decision was left to Hitler, who in consenting to a "generous" armistice put an end to the last thoughts of resistance in the French cabinet, which was relieved to learn that neither the fleet nor the empire were to be the butt of devastating German demands. Convinced of Great Britain's imminent fall, Hitler talked Mussolini and Franco into setting aside their claims on French overseas territories until the end of the war in western Europe.

It seems that the caudillo was the most difficult to persuade; as late as June 25 the German ambassador in Madrid expected an imminent Spanish attack on French Morocco. This project was given up definitely only after the Mers-el-Kebir affair when the Germans gave in to French wishes by softening the conditions of the applications of those clauses of the Armistice Convention pertaining to the defense of French possessions on the southern side of the Mediterranean.[4] However, this did not prevent the Spanish, at a later date, from putting pressure on Mawlay al-Hasan b. al-Mahdi, the khalifa of Tétouan, by promising him the sultanate of the whole Moroccan kingdom if he would initiate an invasion of the French zone.

The German policy was motivated by more than the strategic reasons of fear of dissidence and of the rallying of the French empire to Great Britain. The führer had already expressed in *Mein Kampf* his disdain of any southward expansion; Germany's vital space was to be sought in Europe and, to begin with, in Russia. Hitler was very little attracted to the Mediterranean[5] and thus he relegated the essential military tasks of this area to Mussolini and intervened only as a last resort, more often than not to help extricate his Italian ally from a tricky situation.

Consequently, the Armistice Convention, which amputated France of its capital and of two-thirds of its territory, at the same time guaranteed to it the entire possession of its empire and the preservation of its colonial boundaries. Neither at Wiesbaden nor in Torino did the German and the Italians arrogate to themselves any rights over French colonies except for that of a minimal inspection of the armed forces stationed in Morocco, Algeria, and Tunisia. This check as a rule was an Italian task, for in principle only the Atlantic shoreline of Morocco was to have been inspected

The Maghreb after the Armistice

by German observers. However, up to February 1941, the Germans sent only two civilian inspectors, Klaube and Auer, to the port of Casablanca.[6] In June 1940 French North Africa had been eager to pursue the war. A few weeks later it was completely won over to the Pétain mystique.

From the standpoint of many French of North Africa, if the National Revolution had not existed, it ought to have been invented. Gnawed by clan, race, and caste hatred, fertile during prewar years in minidespots such as Father Lambert in Oran or Bellat in Sidi-bel-Abbès, opened to Fascists' undertakings in Tunisia, to phalangist activity in Oranie, far removed from the suffering in metropolitan France and from direct contact with the enemy, our North Africa offered an ideal ground for the marshal's propaganda. Nowhere else, in France or in the empire, could one see it flaunting itself so shamelessly; huge slogans covering entire walls, gigantic portraits of the good dictator. Nowhere else was the legion, then the S.O.L. (Service d'Ordre Légionnaire), able to make so many recruits, their chests showing off the fateful "pressing iron,"[7] parading to the sound of ritualistic cantatas. Nowhere else in unoccupied territory did informing, snitching, and repression flower to such a large scale filling up, in the process, the concentration camps of the southern territories. (Soustelle 1947:419)

True, it is only natural and even expedient to seek in the *pied-noir* mentality and in the peculiarity of North African circumstances the causes of the Pétainist passion that overtook the French inhabitants of North Africa after the armistice. However, this is overlooking that the cult of the hero of Verdun was the lot of almost all the French people. They saw in Pétain, of whom Léon Blum said in 1939 that he was "the noblest and most human soldier of France" (cited in Paxton 1973:45), a savior and a redemptor who was to cleanse France of the blemishes and of the political, social, and cultural vices that had let it to disaster and humiliation.

No more here than in France did the advent of the "new order" of the National Revolution require the purging of any political and administrative personnel. Except for the forced bailing out by Darlan of a few idle admirals, the top ranks of the hierarchy remained on the whole intact. The few "new men" who appeared there, such as Châtel and Ettori in Algiers or Monnick in Rabat, came from the social milieus and the manpools from which all French governments had traditionally recruited their high-ranking colonial civil servants. These men, who were to carry out without demurring even the most abject of Vichy's orders, were neither "Doriotists" nor even opportunists. Without exception they were all excellent French patriots who harbored an implacable hatred for the German warlords; in other times, under other laws, they had rightfully deserved their superiors' confidence.

General Noguès provides a perfect example of this continuity in the French colonial administration. Known as a "republican general," he was named *résident-général* of Morocco by the Popular Front government, but he was kept in his post by Pétain who forgave him his hesitations on the eve of the armistice.[8] Showing an unflinching loyalty to Vichy, Noguès was to oppose fiercely, despite all the American entreaties, the Allies' "aggression" of November 8, 1942.[9] Marcel Peyrouton, his colleague in Tunisia who had preceded him at his Moroccan post, had behind him a long career as a high-ranking civil servant of the Third Republic when he was sent to Tunisia on June 6, 1940. He had opposed the armistice along with the rest of the empire's chiefs, but this did not prevent his appointment in July to the post of Sécretaire d'Etat (secretary of state) and on September 6, 1940, he became minister of the interior. This man, who was to have to his credit the promulgation of the first racial laws elaborated by the Vichy regime as well as the December 13 "coup" against Pierre Laval, was to resurface on the North African scene after the American landing. Admiral Estéva, who had been in Bizerte up to that time, succeeded Peyrouton in Tunis on July 25, 1941. He was a devoted man of "high moral values" and prey to endless internal debates with his conscience. Yet this did not prevent him from enforcing Vichy's anti-Jewish laws or Darlan's collaborationist directives. Darlan relied on the sacrosanctity of military hierarchy and on the navy's esprit de corps to put pressure on Estéva's decisions as well as on those of Admiral Abrial, the governor-general of Algeria.

Abrial had taken over his post after Governor Le Beau's retirement in July 1940. Before becoming one of the staunchest enemies of the Anglo-Saxons, Abrial had brilliantly distinguished himself during the evacuation of the Allied Expeditionary Forces from Dunkerque, an act that earned him military honors from the British armed forces. Upon his return to Cherbourg from London, he was taken prisoner by the Germans, who freed him only through the intervention of the Vichy government. After about a year in the post of governor, Admiral Abrial had to give up his position to General Weygand, who had been in Africa since October 1940 in the position of general delegate of the Vichy government.

The former commander in chief, who had been sent away from Vichy by Pétain, was to occupy a unique slot among Maghreb administrators. An unrelenting critic of Laval's and Darlan's pro-German policies, Weygand at the same time vehemently attacked de Gaulle's "Free France" and was unfalteringly loyal to Pétain. Nonetheless, Weygand became one of

The Maghreb after the Armistice

the "ideologists" of the National Revolution. Weygand was accompanied to North Africa by Yves Châtel, who had served many years in Indo-China. Châtel started out as the delegation's secretary-general. He became adjunct governor-general in July 1941 and succeeded Weygand in November 1941 as governor-general of Algeria and retained this post till the Allied landing.

Châtel was a cynical and intelligent man of few ethical scruples (Aboulker 1945:72; Esquer 1946:52–53) but Weygand was fully confident in him:

> The liveliness of his mind, his experience of human beings, his administrative capabilities made of him a precious collaborator in all matters. We only worked side by side for a year, but I keep of those months of intense work a memory that is the more grateful and faithful because he died in disgrace far away from his country. (Weygand 1950:353–54)

The body of *préfets*, directors, and secretaries-general was to have, no more than the echelon of the governors and the residents, "new" men of different backgrounds inserted in their ranks. Any government, regardless of its nature, could be only too happy to have at its service such competent civil servants of such high administrative abilities, and in this context, one of their most useful qualities was their ability to repress their previous political leanings to the point of oblivion. Thus, Boujard, the *préfet* of Oran, was to carry out the orders emanating from Vichy with the same thoroughness as he once carried out those received from the Popular Front administration to which he owed his job. His colleague from Constantine, Max Bonnafous, who was a Socialist and held an advanced degree in philosophy, was noticed by Pierre Laval, who made him, in 1942, minister of food. As to Charles Ettori, he had been a member of the Conseil d'Etat on a mission to North Africa when Weygand appointed him in 1941 to the post of secretary-general of the government of Algeria.

All these men looked upon themselves first as servants of the state, which they conceived of as a "good in itself" that neither the defeat nor the change of regime could or should affect in its supporting structures and functions. As soon as the ethical quandary caused by the armistice was set aside, most of them saw no reason to question orders or to judge the ethical implications of the new regime's actions. Moreover, these men's military and administrative background made them receptive to the political philosophy of the National Revolution, which assigned a primary role to the state viewed as protector of the nation and seat of all power and also propounded a strictly hierarchized view of authority. As in the military, from now on to govern meant to transmit orders from the top of the hierarchy down to the various levels of the social body "and by degrees down to the very foundations of the state and of the nation (Aron 1956: 156–57). Thus, for instance, after anti-Jewish actions perpetrated in Algiers in September 1940, Admiral Abrial, "the sole repository of the thinking and plans of the government of Marshal Pétain," condemned the perpetrators because they thought "they could without risk substitute themselves to the authorities in charge"; however, "the state has ceased to tolerate any substitution of itself. From now on it intends to guide and not to follow as in the past. . . . There will be no room for the unpredictability of those who persist in believing themselves to be more powerful or wiser than the state" (*La Dépêche algérienne*, September 18, 1940).

To implement the "revolution from the top," the new regime created the Légion Française des Combattants aimed at spreading the principles of the new order through the words of the "nation's best," that is, war veterans. In North Africa where the legion was put under the authority of General François, Weygand instructed him "to stick to, in the realm of propaganda, commenting on governmental informations to let people know the reasons for the decisions taken and to rectify the untruths so often broadcast from external radio stations" (Weygand 1950:497). The legion was organized into different sections for each of the three Maghreb countries, and it was instructed to collaborate with local authorities to facilitate "certain aspects of their task" such as the overseeing of food supplies and the repression of the black market. Having excluded Jews from its ranks, the legion in contrast came to be opened to all the supporters of the new regime including those who had never seen any military action (Esquer 1946:48–50; Gosset 1944:46–54). Thus it was to number, in Algeria alone, about 150,000 members from all social backgrounds out of a European population of one million.

> At the top of the legion's hierarchy were the high-ranking officers who held the presidencies and who, even though retired, received their full active duty pay. Every month, Vichy lavished a small fortune on the legion to amply cover the cost of propaganda, of various projects, and even the hours spent in the various sections' quarters in spacious premises, in fine locations, and often luxuriously appointed.
>
> Besides these material advantages, the members of the legion as well as those of the P.P.F. enjoyed being granted an authority that put them above the common run of mortals who were not part of the hallowed organizations. The exclusion of the Jews alone imparted to simple *légionnaires* the conviction that they themselves were the salt of the earth. (Esquer 1946:50–51)

The Maghreb after the Armistice

On the initiative of Pucheu, the minister of the interior who was to make a resounding trip to Algiers in 1942 (Aboulker 1952:84–85), Vichy decided toward the end of 1941 to recruit from the body of the members of the legion an elite corps of "revolutionaries," the Service d'Ordre Légionnaire (S.O.L.), the French equivalent of the Nazi S.S., which under Darnand's leadership was to have as oath of induction: "I swear to fight against democracy, against Gaullist dissidents, and against the Jewish scourge" (Aron 1956:300). In North Africa, S.O.L. members were prominent among those putting up a last-ditch resistance against the Allied landing in Algeria and Morocco. In this task as well as in many others, they received the strong support of the P.P.F., which, of all the extreme right-wing parties, had been the one whose foundations gained the most strength, this thanks to the more or less secret ties developed by its leaders with the German Armistice Commissions and with prominent members of the governments.[10] Its self-confidence strengthened by this, the P.P.F. conspired in September 1942 to attempt a coup against Noguès in Morocco. Noguès, who barely escaped an attempt on his life with a bomb, obtained from Laval the recall to France of one of the leaders of the Moroccan section of the Doriotist party.[11]

Besides this party and other similar French organizations, there were Fascist Italian organizations in Tunisia and the Phalangist party in Morocco and in the Oranie region of Algeria. These organizations were openly banking on Italian and Spanish occupation subsequent to the German victory. The Phalange, an organization with a Spanish majority, had attracted many French individuals into its ranks, among them L. Bellat, the mayor of Sidi-bel-Abbès (Esquer 1946:67).

The proliferation of these organizations was not the only means of adhesion to the National Revolution and to its policy of collaboration with the Axis powers opened to the Europeans of North Africa. Other means included purged left-wing—or Jewish—newspapers, which for twenty-eight months were to indulge in an ieological shelling in perfect harmony with the directives of Vichy's propaganda office. North African papers did not limit themselves to the printing of censored and standardized information.[12] They gave free rein to their most collaborationist and Pétainist editors such as André Nicolai and César Filori of the *Dépêche Tunisienne*, Pierre-Louis Ganne of the *Dépêche Algérienne*, and Alex Delpeyron and Stephanle Lanzanne of the *Echo d'Oran*.[13]

As for the Moslem population, it was split between the loyalism of its notables, who were attracted to the paternalistic and traditionalistic aspects of the new regime[14] and the pro-German activism of its nationalistic elements. In between these two extremes was the more or less indif-

53

ferent mass of urban dwellers and peasants, who at first, surprised by the magnitude of the French defeat, held for a moment the hope to be freed by "al-Hajj Hitler" before becoming more and more concerned with worsening material problems.[15]

The authorities were deeply preoccupied by this situation; they were obsessed during the course of the war with the possibility of a popular revolt in all three Maghrebian countries. Hence the effort directed toward persuading the United States government to effectuate the delivery of sugar and English tea, the national drink of Morocco, for the use of the native population.[16] Hence as well, Weygand's concern with the success of his negotiations with Murphy. He explained repeatedly to the American diplomat that Germany alone would benefit from the economic breakdown of the Maghreb as well as from the political turmoil that would follow and would irremediably endanger French presence in this region.[17]

German propaganda was to be another source of worry to the French authorities. After a break that lasted several weeks after the armistice, German subversive propaganda, stronger than ever, took up again in the Maghreb through radio, press, and even the subsidy of small extremist groupings.[18]

Relayed since the defeat by *Paris-Mondial*, German emissions aimed at North Africa, whether in French, Maghrebian Arab, or Kabyle, multiplied their funerary orations of French power while simultaneously carefully avoiding any incitement to revolt. Concentrating mainly on the acceptance of the idea of the very near victory of the Third Reich, the campaign's principal targets were the Jews and the British, presented as the common enemies of both the Arab-Islamic world and of Germany. Influenced by these broadcasts, scores of popular songs were composed in the North African countryside. These songs bedecked Hitler with titles such as "lion," "son of a lioness," "victorious and generous," and called upon him to "free the suffering peoples from oppression."[19]

At any rate, the Germans did free several hundred North African political prisoners held in France since the beginning of the war. In prisoner-of-war camps (where there were sixty thousand North Africans in June 1940), the Germans published an Arab paper, *Lisan-al-Asir* (the prisoner's voice), aimed at Maghrebian soldiers. But news of the guards' harsh discipline imposed on the prisoners, the deprivations and the ill-treatments endured at the hand of their German guards, made its way back to the Maghreb. In this regard, the administrator of Marnia was to note that this information unfavorable to the Germans "brings perplexity to our administrees, who had gotten used to, without too much difficulty, the idea of coming under the authority of the anti-Semitic German warriors."[20]

The Maghreb after the Armistice

However, despite its ambiguity caused in part by the evolution of the relations between Vichy and Berlin, German propaganda did nonetheless succeed in attracting nationalist North African elements ranging from the militants of the P.P.A. (Parti de Peuple Algérien) and religious reformists in Algeria, the members of the old Destour and of the new Destour in Tunisia, and even to members of the entourage of the Moroccan sultan[21] as well as the nationalist parties of Spanish Morocco, which, under the leadership of Ibrahim al-Wazzani and of 'Abd al-Khaliq Torrès, were openly working for the Axis powers. The Germans were publishing in Paris a journal in French and in Arabic called *al-Duniâ' al-Jadîda* (the new world) aimed at these elements and at the Maghrebian political elites, and was circulated at the same time as the Berlin weekly *al-Jahir*.

Besides these parties, which saw Hitler's Germany as the spearhead of the anticolonialist struggle, there were also elements that were primarily collaborationist or pro-Nazi such as the Comité Musulman de l'Afrique du Nord founded by the Algerian Muhammad al-Maadi Lakhdar[22] or the Union des travaileurs nord-africains founded by his fellow citizen 'Ammar Khider, as well as other organizations that were the works of agents of the German secret services or were simply outshoots of pro-Hitlerian groups in Paris such as Marcel Déat's Front Social du Travail or Doriot's P.P.F.

These extremist elements were hounded by the French police and were victims of the contradictions in Hitler's Arab policies and of his reticence regarding North Africa. In fact, they were to exert little influence on the Moslem masses, whose pro-German feelings were as harmless as they were widespread. In these circumstances, neither Algeria, nor Morocco and Tunisia had produced leaders of the same character as al-Amin al-Husayni or Rachid 'Ali al-Galayni, who, thanks to the political circumstances specific to Palestine and Iraq, had turned these same feelings into a powerful lever for the uprising against the Jews and the colonial presence. But, regardless of its limitations, the state of mind that predominated in the Moslem population of North Africa did nonetheless congrue with the openly collaborationist atmosphere that permeated this part of the French empire. Privileged territory of Vichyism, Algiers was thus to give a few days before the Allied landing a rousing welcome to Admiral Darlan (Pétain's designated successor), who showed up with General Vogh, the president of the Wiesbaden Armistice Commission, at his side.[23]

5

Vichy and the Jews of North Africa

Ideological Background

Vichy's anti-Jewish laws were no more "carried in by the German tanks" than was the National Revolution conceived or demanded by Hitler. P. Baudouin, the minister of foreign affairs, declared in July 1940:

> The total revolution that France is now initiating has been in incubation for the last twenty years. The present evolution has been freely chosen and is not in the least aimed at pleasing our victors. . . . We shall adopt a solution that is a French one, corresponding to our character, our needs, our best traditions. . . . The pre-1940 world has been definitely buried. (*L'Echo d'Alger*, July 19, 1940)

In fact, there was German pressure on Pétain neither to impose the promulgation of racial laws in the fall of 1940 nor to extend them to North Africa, and even less to repeal the Crémieux decree, a demand that for decades had been the rallying cry of the anti-Semites of France and Algeria. The German "alibi," which was to be often spoken about during postliberation trials, was never invoked by the men in Vichy, at least not before summer 1942, to explain the anti-Jewish policy of the French state. On the contrary they were all at pains to emphasize the specifically French nature of this policy and the complete independence of the Pétain regime in the drafting of legislative texts regarding the Jews.[1]

Before the Final Solution was to be entered into the world of facts, the Germans gladly lent themselves to Laval's and Darlan's game, which was to turn the Jewish question not quite into a bargaining asset but at least into a bait in the discussions with the occupying power.[2] Kept informed of all the anti-Jewish measures in preparation at Vichy and of the French leader's frame of mind regarding this matter,[3] the Germans contented themselves during this first stage with lavishing their encouragements and advice to the Vichy authorities, who with their own hands were to weave the juridical and administrative net into which the Germans when the time became ripe would trap the Jews of France.

As a result, the Statut des juifs (Jewish statute), elaborated in complete freedom by Alibert, then justice minister, was strictly racist and was of such rigor that it outdid the corresponding text published a few days earlier by the occupation administration in Paris. The Germans had defined the Jewish status in religious terms only, but the French used the notion of race to the point of including in that status certain categories of "Jews," such as the Karaites, which had been spared by the German edicts.[4]

At the beginning of March 1941 the Germans suggested to Vichy the creation of a Commissariat Général aux Questions juives (commissariat-general for the Jewish questions), which would oversee the enforcement of the anti-Jewish laws with those enacted by the French state, ensure the compatibility of these laws with those enacted by the occupying authorities in northern France, and would put the final touch on the new legislative measures pertaining to the Aryanization of the economy.[5] On March 29 Marshal Pétain named Xavier Vallat, an anti-Semite of long standing, to head the new agency, which was first put under the authority of the prime minister, then under the authority of the minister of the interior (Billig 1955:73–84), and then again under that of the prime minister. The commissariat-general was by no means a simple organ for the execution of German orders. Instead, it was given its own juridical identity, an administrative personnel that was entirely French, and it took upon itself tasks supplementary to those demanded by the Germans. This was so with the North African Jewish question. Without the Germans intimating the slightest wish in that direction, Xavier Vallat came to consider that it was his agency's responsibility to take care of this "complex"[6] problem and to present "projects for its solution" with the aim of eliminating Jewish influence from this part of the French empire, an influence "which has shown itself to be so nefarious to the national interest."[7]

And it was thus that just as the defeat had served as a "providential" stepping-stone to the proponents of the National Revolution, the Final Solution was to offer to French anti-Semites the opportunity to finally put into action ideas they had advocated since the Dreyfus affair.

The essence of Vichy's anti-Semitism was more cultural than racial and it was rooted in the French assimilationist tradition. On the eve of the promulgation of the Alibert law, La Rocque defined its rationale as follows:

> All citizens, once they have been adopted and assimilated, become subject to the general law: Jews who have been naturalized for several generations belong, as a matter of principle, to the great civic family. It is unconceivable that preventive sanctions would be taken against them, sanctions that the most exacting national vigilance would not have had recourse to before our defeat.[8]

This pertained to metropolitan France where assimilation—and consequently the right of French Jews to naturalization—was to be handled "on the basis of objective personal considerations applied a posteriori." The North African case was seen as altogether different. According to the leader of the P.S.F., the Jewish problem there was different:

> The Jews of Morocco, Algeria, and Tunisia have lived close to one another in their *mellah*. Their local groupings have taken on and preserved all the particularistic attitudes of clans obeying their religious chiefs, not only in confessional and social matters but also in political ones. . . . These are the facts. And this is why, in North Africa, the solution to the problem could only be reached through collective measures, applied a priori: abrogation and revision of the Crémieux decree and of similar types of legal instruments, immediate suspension of the citizenship rights that resulted from this decree, and general investigation for the authorization of individual exceptions to be justified by proven military or civic contributions.

The Vichy men labeled themselves "state anti-Semites," the contrasting category to "passional" or "gut anti-Semite" of Maurras's old dichotomy. They thus presented their anti-Jewish measures as an action defensive and protective of the French organism against "the bacteria that was driving it into a deathly anemic condition," or as a surgical operation aimed at curing "this French soul suffereing from a sickness that has led us to our present situation."[9] The Jew revolutionary, the Jew "controlling the French soul and French interests," the Jew "foreign agent," or, more simply, the Jew usurer were the principal targets of Vichy's anti-Semitism, an anti-Semitism that at any rate remained very classical and in the mouth of certain dignitaries of the regime seemed even downright confusing:

> The Jews have been admitted into the great house of France and Algeria as tenants with the same rights as the others. But they have tried

to destroy the house. Thus they should not be surprised that the other 98 percent of the tenants are balking.[10] This 98 percent of the French people I ask to behave in a French manner, thus without violence. Do not harrass the two tenants on the top floor.[11]

In a similar vein, J. Barthelemy beseeched the French people to discuss the Jewish problem "in friendship" and "in fraternity" while Xavier Vallat himself was to declare to a group of Algerian Jewish war veterans that "he did not want that someday it could be said that through his actions he had reduced a single Jew of this colony to famine" (C.D.J.C., 80–11b).

These men's sincerity cannot be doubted and neither can one deny that Vichy's anti-Semitism contained some humaneness, which sharply differentiated it from Nazi racial hatred. Nonetheless, the fact remains that once the juridical machine constructed by Vichy was set in motion, it gained an infernal momentum that was rhythmically prodded onward by the German authorities' demands and, when these were lacking, by the impulses of public opinion and the bureaucratic zeal of the agents of the state.

Anti-Jewish Legislation and Its Application in North Africa

Of all France's overseas possessions, Algeria was uncontestably the one that attracted Vichy's attention the most regarding anti-Jewish legislation. As an integral part of France, it had the right to a multitude of laws, decrees, and edicts that put the members of its Jewish community in a juridical situation almost identical with that of the Jews of the Free Zone of France. The status of this colony does not adequately explain the treatment of Algerian Jews because Vichy pursued no less the Jews of Morocco and Tunisia even though they were not French citizens. Despite this difference, the three Maghrebian countries had in common their proximity to metropolitan France and the substantial size of their Jewish population. This population was awkwardly wedged between a Moslem majority with ambiguous feelings toward it and a European minority that had turned anti-Semitism into its sole, or almost sole, political creed.

Besides the fact that this fitted perfectly with the ideological orientation of the regime, the extension of anti-Jewish laws to North Africa was motivated by the aim of satisfying the long-standing wishes of the European population of the Maghreb and, incidentally, of gaining the support of the native population of the three colonies. Better than any other avenue, the abrogation of the Crémieux decree was to go a long way toward fulfilling these twin goals.

The abrogation of the Crémieux decree (October 7, 1940). Even though it was enacted chronologically later than the law pertaining to Jewish status (October 3, 1940), the abrogation of the Crémieux decree preceded the promulgation of this law in North Africa (J.O.A., October 8, 1940).

In the same way as the recently settled Jews in France had been denaturalized in mass by the Vichy regime, the Algerian Jews lost with a stroke of the pen the French citizenship that had been collectively granted to them in 1870. However, they remained French subjects because their civil rights remained under the jurisdiction of French law and, in contrast with the status of the Moslems on which the new legislation claimed to model the status of the Jews, they could not regain their former juridical autonomy because their private and civil laws continued to be subsumed by the French civil code.

To maintain French citizenship individually, it was required to not only have belonged to a fighting unit in 1914-18 or in 1939-40 but also to have earned the military distinctions of the Légion d'Honneur, the Médaille militaire, or the croix de guerre. Moreover, neither the ascendants nor the descendants of the victims of either wars nor war widows or even prisoners of war would henceforth enjoy French citizenship unless special exceptions were made.

By putting Algerian Jews on an equal footing with the Moslems, the new texts were theoretically offering them the possibility of becoming French citizens under the same conditions as their Moslem compatriots, conforming to the *senatus consulte* of 1865. But having noted this possibility, Vichy, on October 11, promulgated an addition to the law of October 7, which "suspended the Jews of the Department of Algeria" (J.O.A., October 13, 1940) from the usual procedure of attaining French citizenship as set in the law of February 11, 1919.[12] The authorities went even so far as to take away the citizenship of Algerian Jews living in Paris. Those among them who expressed the desire to retain it not only were to be faced with an absolute denial but also their names were entered in a special list subsequently given to the Germans (C.D.J.C., V88).

Hailed by Maurras as "the end of a seventy-year-old scandal,"[13] the abolition of the Crémieux decree aimed, according to official commentaries, to "indirectly appease Moslem demands" because this decree had clearly favored the Jews over the natives.[14] Consequently, the officials in charge of Moslem affairs in Algeria were called upon to assess the native population's responses to the adoption of this measure.

The responses in rural areas, at least as they were reported by the authorities, were said to be very positive. Thus according to the administrator of the mixed commune Palestro, the repeal of the Crémieux decree "has caused a wave of rejoicing clearly noticeable among every one of the central localities' natives, who are aware of the implications of this happy return to an earlier state of affairs."[15] In Tablat the news was greeted "with a deep satisfaction and a contained inner joy. In this period of Ramadan, it is favorably commented upon."[16] In the mixed commune of the Eulma "the reaction is considerable even though the natives do not yet comprehend all its importance. Some, however, believe that the rights of citizenship that will still be enjoyed by Jewish war veterans decorated with the Légion d'Honneur, the Médaille militaire, or the croix de guerre should also be granted to Moslems who have earned these same distinctions."[17]

In Sedrata, in contrast, the abolition of the Crémieux decree did not lead to any outward response: "The Jews saw it coming and the natives have greeted it with a kind of indifference that, however, does not exclude a certain satisfaction."[18] There was the same indifference among the Biban "where there has been no show of feeling"[19] and in Takinount "where the only recorded comments are those of the European population."[20]

In contrast with urban centers, even though the repeal of the Crémieux decree had "a considerable effect on the masses,"[21] it did not trigger any response in the "westernized" urban milieus. Dr. Bendjelloul and Dr. Smati of Sétif asked their brethren "not to take side in the present Jewish affair and to keep their distance from it as much as possible."[22] This disaffection by elected officials was greatly deplored by the authorities, who tended to see in it a result of Jewish propaganda. Indeed, according to some police reports, the Jews were trying to persuade the Moslems that "the Crémieux decree has been abolished to avoid granting rights to Moslems" and, from a "reliable source," it was even foreseen that "because of their resentment, some Jewish leaders were going so far as to offer funds to nationalistic Moslem groupings."[23]

The police were soon to "uncover" various indexes of this connivance. For instance, in Sidi-bel-Abbès, Moslem cloth tradesmen did not have to wait very long to get the merchandises ordered from the Jewish wholesalers of Oran. The chief of police noted: "We have to assume that the Jews want to win the goodwill of the Moslems of Sidi-bel-Abbès (a very large Communist center) in case of a pro-English movement that, it is said, would be largely financed by the Jews."[24]

As to the Algiers Jews, they were suspected of advising their Moslem domestic help to set aside their salary "because life is going to become more and more difficult. French rule will not last much longer in this country. They will get kicked out by the British."[25]

In fact, even though these new circumstances undeniably colored attempts at a Judeo-Moslem rapprochement, this rapprochement never went beyond the platonic stage of "monotheist fraternity." Algerian nationalism had a long time ago acquired its own identity and its own dynamics and had no need for the support, tenuous at best, of Algerian Jews who, from their side, even after having lost their citizenship, nonetheless considered themselves genuine French patriots.

And it is thus that while Admiral Abrial had troops assigned to the important buildings of Algiers and had them set up machine guns to shoot Jews that were expected to manifest their anger (Eisenbeth 1945:64), Jewish notables felt that their duty was "to avoid doing anything that would add to the present difficulties." They limited themselves to address Marshal Pétain a solemn protest signed by the presidents of the consistories and the grand rabbis of Algiers, Oran, and Constantine. Making theirs the notion of "baptism through blood" so dear to the war veterans presiding over the fate of the French state, the Jewish leaders took pains to voice their protest in the name of their dead and "glorious wounded" as well as in the name of their prisoners: "Until now French citizens, we remain totally French at heart. Long live France! Long live French Algeria!"[26]

To the text addressed to the marshal was added a long report that restated the various positions of French and Algerian personalities who had demanded the naturalization of Algerian Jews since 1847. After pointing out how important a role the Algerian Jewish community had played in the economic and intellectual development of Algeria, "which today is rightfully one of the glories of the French empire," the authors of the report then examined in detail the clauses of the law of abrogation of the Crémieux decree. They argued that the exceptions authorized by the law "lead to the splitting up of families, to the differentiation of a brother from a brother, a son from a father, even though they have received the same moral education and the valor of one is the product of this common upbringing." Finally, alluding to one of the three pillars of Vichy's ideology, they asked this surprising question: Does this division within a single family not go against the policy that aims at consolidating the family and family sentiment?

Naive or blind, it took for the Algerian Jews the publication a few days later of the law on the Jewish status to grasp that the loss of their citizenship rights was only a first step toward a more awful situation that was to appear to them as the realization, in almost every minute detail, of the ideas propounded earlier by the likes of Max Régis, Edouard Drumont, Emile Morinaud, and Dr. Molle.

The "Statut des Juifs." As in metropolitan France, the Jewish Statute in its versions of October 3, 1940 (the Alibert law), and June 2, 1941 (the Vallat law), was to be the corner-stone of anti-Jewish legislation in the Maghreb. This statute had general applicability and affected Jewish citizens, subjects of and under the protection of France, as well as foreign Jews living in French-controlled territories. Its application to North Africa was neither the result of an automatic bureaucratism nor a simple reflex of administrative centralism. Carefully adapted to the juridical stituation of each of the three territories, it was to be rigorously applied, the only moderating modifications being those imposed in Morocco and in Tunisia through the intervention of local non-European authorities.

The Alibert law, applicable without modification to Algeria, defined the status of the Jews solely from a racial standpoint. The first clause stated: "A Jew is: any individual issued from three grandparents of the Jewish race; any individual issued from two grandparents of the Jewish race if his/her spouse is also Jewish."[27]

Regardless of which religious denomination they belonged to, individuals were considered to be Jews by birth if they had at least three Jewish grandparents or became Jews if, having two Jewish grandparents, they married a Jew. They remained Jews so defined even if they converted to Christianity or Islam and, inversely, a Christian or a Moslem even if converted to Judaism remained a non-Jew in the eye of the law. Even the Germans did not dare impose such drastic notions in the Occupied Zone.[28]

In Morocco and in Tunisia, the French authorities exercised more caution and took religious denomination into account, but only for native Jews; foreign Jews (French, Algerian, or others) who lived in either of the protectorates were submitted to the racial criteria established in the original version of the statute.[29]

Thus in Morocco and Tunisia a Jew was defined as (1) any Moroccan or Tunisian Jew and (2) any non-Moroccan or non-Tunisian individual living in Morocco or Tunisia and issued from three grandparents of the Jewish "race" or from two grandparents of Jewish origins if the spouse was Jewish as well.

In contrast with Algeria and the Free Zone of France, these conditions precluded the existence of "non-Jewish" Moroccan or Tunisian Jews. Once converted to Islam, the Moroccan or Tunisian Jew was no longer a Jew as far as the law was concerned, even if he had four grandparents of the Jewish "race." On the other hand, all Moroccans or Tunisians belonging to the Judaic denomination were considered Jews, even if they had only two or even one grandparent of the Jewish "race."

However, Vichy neglected to coordinate the legal texts promulgated in the protectorates with those applying to metropolitan France and Algeria. The result was that one could be simultaneously a Jew in Morocco and Tunisia and a non-Jew in France and Algeria, or inversely, a Jew in France and Algeria (in the case of a convert to Islam or Christianity) and a non-Jew in the protectorates. The French lawmaker perpetrated a similar type of omission regarding the beylical decree (Tunisia) and the Moroccan *dahir*: by not stating that any Moroccan Jew would be considered a Jew in Tunisia and vice versa, an individual could be a Jew in one of the two protectorates and a non-Jew in the other if he or she had not had three Jewish grandparents or two Jewish grandparents and a Jewish spouse.

The three legal texts inflicted on Jews various derogations from common and civil laws. They were almost identical with those applying in France and they affected all Jews. In Algeria they even affected the Jews who had retained their citizenship after the abrogation of the Crémieux decree.

Thus, barring certain personal exemptions, the access and the exercise of every public function was forbidden to Jews. The law of October 3, 1940, specifically forbade them political mandates and positions, administrative positions other than the lowest-ranking ones, all diplomatic and consular positions, teaching (other than in Jewish schools), all colonial and military positions and employment in businesses of public interest and in those benefiting from concessions or subventions granted by public bodies.

Low-ranking civil service positions could be filled by Jews if they held a war veteran certificate for 1914–18 or had earned a military citation in the course of the 1914–18 or 1939–40 campaigns or if they had been awarded the Légion d'Honneur for military services or the Médaille militaire.

Exhibiting more flexibility than the French (and Algerian) law, the Moroccan *dahir* and the beylical decree allowed Jews to continue to hold jobs in institutions and organizations of the Jewish community. Despite the *numerus clausus*, Tunisian authorities were to broaden this clause and to permit Jewish medical doctors and disbarred lawyers to continue to take care of sick Jews and to represent their brethren in front of rabbinical courts.

Like the French law, the texts promulgated in each protectorate allowed exceptions in favor of certain Jews and for specific functions. Thus in article 4 the Moroccan *dahir* provided privileged treatment for Jews who had obtained a military distinction in the Moroccan armed forces or had been awarded the Ordre militaire. But because they had never served in the army, Moroccan Jews had little opportunity to avail themselves of these privileges.[30]

As to the beylical decree, it provided exceptions in favor of all Jews or Tunisian origins — whether French or Tunisian citizens — who had given exceptional services to France or to Tunisia:

Jews of Tunisian nationality or Tunisian Jews who have become French through their own naturalization or that of their ascendants will moreover have right to the same privilege if they can fulfill one of the following conditions:

1. Have received a military citation or hold a veteran's card for war service in external war theaters before November 11, 1918[31]
2. Had either their father or a son die for France during the 1914–18 war, the 1939–40 war, or during action in external war theaters
3. Acquired the war veteran status during the 1939–40 war through voluntary enlistment for the duration of this war
4. Is a nonremarried war widow drawing a war pension[32]

Tunisian leniency was to manifest itself as well in other domains: Thus though in Morocco the *dahir* barred Jewish membership from every elected, professional, or representative assembly (chamber of commerce, chamber of agriculture, and the like), in Tunisia, Jews could have access to mandates in elected assemblies as representatives of the Jewish Tunisian population. Furthermore, the beylical decree authorized the Jews to maintain their own press organ, which would bear the subtitle: *Journal israélite de Tunisie* (Tunisian Jewish newspaper) and in which they would speak up for their own interests.[33]

Interdictions, stemming from the derogations from civil law, applied to all Jews, regardless of their citizenship or war veteran status. Thus several professions were to become completely closed to them (journalism, radio broadcasting, theater, and film industries) while the principle of a *numerus clausus* was established for the liberal and independent professions.

The second Jewish Statute (June 2, 1941) was the work of Xavier Vallat and of the Commissariat-General for the Jewish Questions established by Vichy on March 29, 1941. The new text restated the main clauses of the Alibert law but it was all the more severe, for it aimed at filling the loopholes left by the older text. Thus the definition of a Jew, as stated in the first article, took into account the religious factor besides the racial one established by the October 3 law. From then on a Jew would be:

1. A person, belonging or not belonging to any denomination, issued of three grandparents of the Jewish race, or of only two if the spouse is issued of two Jewish grandparents. The grandparent who belonged to the Jewish religion is considered a member of the Jewish race.
2. A person who is a member of the Jewish religion or was one on June 25, 1940, and who is issued of two grandparents of the Jewish race.

Nonadherence to the Jewish religion is established by showing proof of the adherence to one of the other denominations recognized by the state before the law of December 9, 1905. The disowning of a child or the annulment of the acknowledgment of a child considered a Jew are without effect in regard to the preceding dispositions. (J.O.A., June 27, 1941)

In Morocco and in Tunisia no change was brought to bear on the previous definition given the native Jew.[34] The new criteria were only applied to foreigners, thus leaving unresolved most of the paradoxes and problems raised by the first statute.[35]

The new statute expanded the already long list of jobs forbidden to the Jews. In its French and Algerian version, even though it still made some allowance for the ascendants and the orphans of the military who had died in the field of battle, it now required of Jewish war veterans that they had been decorated for heroic deeds of war—a simple military citation not being sufficient anymore—if they wanted to maintain access to low-ranking positions in public administration.[36]

As had been stipulated in the October 3 law, the functionaries affected by the new text were to be fired within two months if not sooner. Only the ascendants, the spouses, and the descendants of war prisoners could temporarily keep their jobs. The descendants, along with their close kins, were to be subjected to the common rule two months after their liberation. In Algeria, in November 1941, the total number of lost jobs came to 2,169 (out of a total of 2,638) for civil servants, 232 for employees of commercial services, and 130 for employees of service concessions.[37]

Besides the purging of administrative bodies, the June 2 law aimed at expelling the Jews from French economic life and more particularly from the banking and stock market sectors. On November 17, 1941, the list of business professions forbidden to Jews grew to include advertising, insurance, real estate, trade in grain and livestock, trade in antiquities and paintings, the lumber industries, gambling concessions, and others.[38]

In Morocco, the August 5, 1941, *dahir* pertaining to native Jews forbade them borrowing any form of capital but, on the other hand, it allowed them free access to the crafts and to the retail trade. These activities were generally shunned by the French settlers, who, thanks to the laws of the protectorate, were able to engage in large wholesale trade from which they wanted to eliminate Jewish influence. As it was understood and practiced in Morocco, economic Aryanization was a handy way to get rid of a bothersome competition.

At the same time as the new statute, Vichy on June 2 promulgated a law requiring a Jewish census, and its application was extended to Algeria,

Morocco, and Tunisia. It required Jews to provide within two months[39] information as complete as possible on their civil status and that of their parents, spouse, and children as well as precise details on their level of education, their profession, the amount of capital they might be possessing, the value of their real property holdings, their participation in business enterprises, and a host of other details that were to be subsequently used for the Aryanization of Jewish property.[40]

In the meanwhile in execution of article 4 of the Vallat law, several decrees and directives were to establish a *numerus clausus* in the liberal professions, a project already mentioned in the first statute.

The first profession to be affected was that of lawyer. According to the decree of July 16, 1941, published at Vichy, the proportion of Jewish lawyers could not remain beyond 2 percent of the total non-Jewish lawyers in each jurisdiction. To be maintained in priority even if their numbers exceeded 2 percent were the lawyers who held a war veteran's card or had received the croix de guerre in 1939–40, the Légion d'Honneur or the Médaille militaire for combat accomplishments, or held the status of *pupille de la nation*—were, for example, the ascendants, the widows, and the orphans of military personnel who had died for France. Those who did not meet these conditions could benefit from an exception "based on the eminent character of their professional merit" provided the Bar Association so requested. This measure was applied to Morocco with the viziriel order of August 8, 1941 (B.O.M., September 26, 1941), to Tunisia by order of the Resident's Office on October 9, 1941 (J.O.T., October 16, 1941), and to Algeria with a decree enacted November 5, 1941.[41]

A *numerus clausus* of 2 percent was also set for medical doctors through a decree enacted August 11, 1941. As for lawyers, exceptions were granted to war veterans and war victims. Moreover, only those doctors belonging to these categories could practice in public hospitals.

The exclusion of Jewish doctors was in force as early as October 16, 1941, in Tunisia where, however, the *numerus clausus* was raised to 5 percent (J.O.T., November 6, 1941). In Algeria the terms of the decree were rigorously applied from November 5, 1941, on (J.O.A., November 18, 1941); in Morocco, the text became effective only on February 24, 1942.[42]

Neither in Morocco nor in Tunisia did the residents-général deem it necessary to promulgate the execution orders for the decrees aiming at regulating Jews' access to other liberal professions. This contrasted with the situation in Algeria where local formulations of all the texts put out by the Commissariat-General for the Jewish Questions were to be enacted with the exception of a December 26, 1941, Vichy decree pertaining to Jewish pharmacists.[43] Thus, as for lawyers and doctors, a *numerus clausus* of 2 percent was put in force for the professions of midwife,[44] notary public,[45] architect,[46] and dentist.[47] Finally, of the three territories, only Algeria was to have a "Special Department for the Control of the Jewish Problem." As stated in the August 14, 1941, order signed by General Weygand, this department was charged with applying the Jewish Statute "according to the government's directives and in function of the problems stemming from the specific ethnic, political, and economic Algerian circumstances."[48]

The number of people affected by the clauses of the Jewish Statute varied from one North African country to another. But, whether they were Moroccan, Tunisian, or Algerian, the Jewish victims all had in common their adoption of the "French ideal." Having gone through the French educational system and often being the brilliant products of France's "civilizing mission," these men and women were sent back to their prior status of "natives" and were, as well, deprived of their means of livelihood. This happened because they had reached out to France and its culture. It is not surprising, then, that the Jews least affected by the Jewish Statute were those — more numerous in Morocco than in Tunisia and Algeria — who had distanced themselves from Western civilization or had ignored it, in short, those whose way of life and behavior had remained the most traditional.

The Aryanization of education and of the Youth Service Corps. In accordance with the October 3, 1940, statute, all Jewish teachers, except those of the Alliance Israélite and other denominational institutions, lost their jobs within two months in all three North African territories. However, neither this statute nor that of June 2, 1941, dealt with Jewish students. This "loophole" was to be promptly remediated with a law, dated June 21, 1941, that "regulated the conditions for the admission of Jewish students to institutions of higher learning." Vallat's office explained with implacable logic that it was setting a limit of 3 percent on the number of Jewish students allowed to enroll in universities to prevent them from obtaining diplomas that would be "empty titles" now that the liberal professions were closed to them (Lubetzki 1945:61).

The new law was applied to Algeria[49] through a decree dated August 23, 1941 (J.O.A., September 19, 1941). However, the possibility remained open for the excluded students to take the set of final examinations required for graduation. At the joint instigation of G. Hardy, rector of education and member of the Algiers Academy, and of the president of the Students' Association of Algiers, this text was replaced by a new one dated November 5, 1941, which stipulated that "the number of Jewish students admitted to enroll or to graduate in each year (that is, take the year-end final examinations) in any given faculty, school, or institution of higher

Vichy and the Jews of North Africa

learning cannot exceed 3 percent of the non-Jewish students enrolled or graduating on the same day of the preceding academic year" (J.O.A., November 18, 1941).

The zeal of Algerian university administrators was also to be directed against secondary and elementary school children by limiting their numbers in public schools. The initiative for this measure, which even Vichy had not dared take against the Jewish children of the Free Zone, came from Rector G. Hardy, who submitted it to Admiral Abrial. Abrial approved the rector's proposal but because he soon had to leave Algeria, General Weygand and his assistant Yves Châtel took pains to make it applicable, after first consulting Xavier Vallat during his August 1941 North African tour.[50]

Consequently, a *numerus clausus* of 14 percent was established for secondary schools, affecting both new and already enrolled students. The same 14 percent ratio was set for new students in elementary schools, while it was decided to spare those presently attending "only temporarily" till January 1, 1942 (Ansky 1950:123-24).

After further elaboration by the rector's office, the new measure, which, it must be remembered, totally lacked legislative basis,[51] was executed in the following terms:

> The ratio of Jewish students to be admitted in each class cannot exceed 14 percent of the non-Jewish students enrolled November 5 of the preceding year.
> The ratio established for each school year shall thus be definitive and unalterable.
> As a result, those classes attended solely by Jewish students shall be eliminated. Those mostly attended by Jewish students might end up with too low an enrollment; these classes will be dealt with later as the need arises. . . . French citizenship does not enter in the determination of Jewish status. Only those factors mentioned in article 1 of the law of June 2, 1941, will be taken into account.
> Any Jewish student excluded from a class because of the *numerus clausus* shall absolutely not be allowed, immediately or later, to request admission to another class or to another institution. The pronouncement of eviction is definitive regarding the current school year. . . . In those boys' educational institutions where girls are occasionally admitted, female Jewish students shall, starting with the current school year, not be henceforth admitted.[52]

At the start of 1942–43, the *numerus clausus* in secondary schools was reduced to 7 percent. This new measure, which was announced in the *Journal Officiel* only on October 24, had nonetheless already been put into execution by the Algerian Rector's Office by the end of September. This gives one reason to believe that the measure was originally initiated by this department.[53] Morover, Jewish students who had been evicted from the secondary schools were forbidden to try the secondary cycle diploma examinations; only access to the elementary cycle diploma examinations remained opened to all.

The result of the elimination of Jews from public institutions has been established from official sources; see tables 5.1 and 5.2.

After being denied access to public education, North African Jewish students were soon to find themselves barred from the civic youth works instituted by Vichy, while those among them who still held French citizenship were expelled from the Youth Corps.[54]

This rejection had not been initiated by the Commissariat for the Jewish Questions but was originally the work of the general commissariat of the Youth Corps. In a letter addressed to Xavier Vallat, General de La Porte du Theil explained that the recruiting of Jews in the metropolitan territory posed less of a problem than that of their Maghrebian brethren. This was so because even though "Jews are little opened to the benefit of the moral education dispensed by the corps and they can contribute nothing of value, their presence has so far not caused any inconvenience. Recruiting calls distribute them over the forty-six sections of the Youth Corps in the Free Zone. This splits them up sufficiently so that we are only dealing with individuals."[55]

In North Africa, however, the incorporation of Jews was considered to be "dangerous" for two reasons: (1) The verification of the French citizenship status of the would-be Jewish recruits was "very complicated and almost impossible there." (2) Because of the more limited number of North African sections (only five compared with forty-six in metropolitan France), there were many more Jews in the North African sections of the corps than in France. Thus, while in France "the few isolated Jews within the sections can only be a passive element, on the contrary in North Africa a regrouping of several hundred Jews[56] is incompatible with the national recovery work undertaken by the Youth Corps. Surely these Jews can gain nothing from the corps and they might spread the seeds of disunity within it."

Xavier Vallat readily approved his colleague's initiative and suggested to him that he also eliminate the Jews of France from the corps.[57] However, the barring of the Jewish recruits came into effect only after Vallat's replacement by Darquier de Pellepoix as head of the Commissariat for the Jewish Questions. The decree dealing with this matter was published on July 19, 1942, and was without further ado put into effect in North Africa.

TABLE 5.1
HIGHER EDUCATION

	Start of 1942–43 School Year				
	Law	Medicine	Science	Arts & Letters	Total
Jewish candidates	300	151	99	102	652
Remaining Jewish candidates	34	24	22	30	110

TABLE 5.2
SCHOOLING OTHER THAN HIGHER EDUCATION

	Start of 1941–42 *Numerus Clausus* 14%			Start of 1942–43 *Numerus Clausus* 7%	
	Total non-Jewish students as of October 5, 1940	Jewish students maintained	Jewish students eliminated	Jewish students maintained	Jewish students eliminated
Secondary . . .	10,000	1,000	765	549	1,314
Secondary cycle of elementary & complementary courses . . .	13,693	1,100	530	550	1,000
Vocational . . .	764	71	8	35	43
First cycle of elementary . . .	223,282	10,658	10,234	5,529	16,583
Agricultural . . .	238	7	4	3	7
Business . . .	118	6	7	3	10
Navigation . . .	70	2	0	1	1
Arts . . .	3,600	225	414	112	526
Total . . .	251,765	13,069	11,962	6,782	19,484

Source: Eisenbeth 1945: 41.

The Aryanization of property. Article 5 of the June 2, 1941, law promulgated in the three North African countries excluded Jews from the following professions: banker, money changer, canvasser, intermediary in transactions in the stock or futures markets, advertising agent, real estate or capital loan agent, dealer in businesses, dealer in real estate, business, and similar types of properties (marchand de biens); broker, trustee, forester, gambling operator, publisher, director, manager, administrator, copywriter even if only as a local correspondent for newspapers or periodicals except strictly scientific or religious publications, owner, manager, every type of job in the film industry from producer to scriptwriter and pertaining to the production, printing, distribution, and presentation of movies; play producer, and owner, director, or administrator of any enterprise connected with radio broadcasting. However, it seems that the elimination of Jews from these targeted professions was effective only in Algeria where the terms of application of article 5 were to be set the same way as in France.

According to the decree of October 20, 1941,[58] Algerian Jews had to relinquish forbidden professions before December 15, 1941.[59] Businesses and other property had to be either voluntarily transferred or liquidated by that date and these transactions were subject to the authorities approval. Otherwise, the properties were to be assigned to a temporary trustee charged with their transfer or liquidation. Any infraction of this decree was to be severely punished, "the *préfet* having the right to impose internment in a special camp."

Behind these measures lurked the threatening shadow of the July 22, 1941, law, which had the confiscation of Jewish property as sole aim. Applied to Algeria through the decree of November 21, 1941,[60] this law stipulated in its first article that "to eliminate all Jewish influence from the national economy," the governor-general could assign a temporary trustee to any industrial, commercial, real estate, or craft enterprise, to any building, to any right in furniture, or right in any kind of lease as well as to any kind of movable property or right thereof, belonging in part or in totality to Jews. This measure did not apply to structures and apartments used for personal lodgings. Furthermore, according to comments in the Algerian press, only Jews who in managing businesses not covered by article 5 were guilty of some sort of infraction were at risk of having their business put into the hands of a temporary trustee (*Echo d'Alger*, December 1, 1941). This did not change the fact that the governor-general could dispossess Jews of their property anytime he found it opportune, because the letter and spirit of the law authorized him to do so.

Furthermore, Algeria was also given an Office for Economic Aryanization. It was made up of three sections, one for each departmental division of Algeria, set up respectively in Algiers, Oran, and Constantine. This office was entrusted with executing the economic laws promulgated by Vichy and with extending to the colony the means devised for the appointment and compensation of temporary trustees[62] and the determination of the conditions for the trusteeship and appropriation of Jewish property.[63]

The governor-general directly appointed the temporary trustees, who could pay themselves from the business proceeds a compensation not to exceed six months salary. However, few temporary trustees were willing to let go of this unexpected source of income. Consequently, they tried to postpone for as long as possible the sale of the businesses under their care, not realizing that, thanks to their greed on the one hand and to the Allied landing on the other, they were to rescue Jewish property in Algeria from liquidation.

In parallel to economic Aryanization, Algerian Jews, like French Jews, were forbidden to purchase retail businesses or to buy buildings without authorization.[64] According to the law of November 17 that regulated the access to real property,[65] Jews could not possess any other structures than those to be used for their own lodging, for that of their ascendants or descendants, or those used exclusively in the exercise of their profession. Finally, as if this arsenal was not enough, the Algerian Office for Aryanization ensured the adoption of two other legislative texts that were nonexistent in metropolitan France. The first text forbade Jews from managing or owning drinking establishments;[66] the second forbade them from transferring to another party the license for any drinking establishment they might be owning.[67]

There was no such bombardment of economic laws in Morocco and Tunisia. Public authorities in both protectorates contented themselves mainly with the prohibitions stipulated in article 5 of the June 2 law. In Tunisia, in addition to and in the spirit of Vichy's laws, one text was promulgated limiting Jews' access to landed property[68] and a second one forbidding unauthorized acquisitions of retail businesses.[69] Furthermore, the beylical decree of March 12, 1942, established procedures for the assignment of temporary trustees to any Jewish enterprise whose economic activities had become forbidden to Jews. However, Admiral Estéva postponed for a fairly long time the publication of the required executive orders of enforcement. Under pressure from Xavier Vallat, who was giving vent to his indignation in the face of the admiral's delays,[70] the Tunisian *résident-général* finally decided to spread out the various deadlines for the eviction of Jews from each of the forbidden professions: public service, medicine, law, insurance,[71] armaments,[72] banking,[73] advertising, journalism, publishing, performing arts,[74] real estate,[75] and the purchase of businesses.[76] Despite this, there was no promulgation of a text establishing procedures for the designation of temporary trustees, and only movie theater owners endured the confiscation of their property.

Moroccan economic legislation was the sketchier of the three. Outside the general *dahirs* pertaining to the Jewish Statute and outside the viziriel decree of August 19, 1941, which forbade Jews to live in the European neighborhoods of urban centers,[77] the elimination of Jews from the economic life of the country was left to the initiative and discretion of business groups and professional unions. Thus the film industry association, under the pretext of applying the interdictions of article 5 of the June 2 law, laid off all Jewish personnel, from the projector operators to the cashiers, of Moroccan movie theaters (*Le Petit Marocain*, October 2, 1941). Besides the film industry's action, various import associations, such as the one for oil and the one for textile, expelled from their organizations all their Jewish members. The latter were thus deprived of means of continuing to do business[78] and forced to let go their employees, who further swelled the large and growing numbers of the unemployed.

As if all these legal and semi-legal measures were not enough, Jewish businessmen and tradesmen in all three territories were the everyday butt of all manners of police harassment, arrest, and judicial pursuits for "black market activities" or illegal business speculations.[79] A Vichy personality thought to be "particularly knowledgeable" was to explain the hidden philosophy underlying these persecutions in the following terms:

> We must bear in mind that the complexity of the laws and regulations has in the economic domain brought forth a black market as well as a host of illegal trafficking. These are dangerous activities but they bring in a handsome profit to those who do not get caught. These temptations are too much for the Jew. . . . But the legislator's duty—his Christian as well as his civic one—lies not only in the protection of the nation but also in protecting the Jew against himself by keeping him from his own instincts of which he has perennially been the victim.[80]

North African Public Opinion and the Jewish Statute

Despite its remaining in the shadows, there is no doubt that a part of North African public opinion rebelled against Vichy's racist policy. But in circumstances where the means of expression were stifled and the police throughly observed every motion and gesture, it would certainly have required much courage and probably an equal amount of blind optimism to try to rip through the quasi-mystical veil of conformism surrounding Pétain and his regime.

Because of this, opposition to the Jewish Statute left few traces, most individuals choosing to ponder in silence[81] their sorrow and frustration in the face of measures that, in the words of an Algerian European writing to Xavier Vallat, had striked such a painful note "in the heart of all true French people" in the eyes of whom France had betrayed "its rational genius" by importing the "horrifying racist scourge" to the colonies. The letter writer further pointed out that the humiliations inflicted upon Algerian Jews can only slowly wear out France's colonial prestige. No . . . the Moslems have not gladly welcomed the stringent measures taken against the Jews; on the contrary, they were surprised by them. They were astounded by the revelation that France, breaking its commitments, harbored leanings toward throwing back to their previous miserable existence those whom it had called forth to its civilization, those who had had faith in it, and this after seventy years. . . .

Germany can indulge in racism; lacking a colonial empire, its population is composed of a homogeneous race. But Algeria, the jewel of the French empire, is doomed to perdition in the absence of perfect racial harmony. . . . Algerian Jews who contributed invaluable help during the conquest, who helped permanently solidify French authority in Algeria, who insisted on fighting, struggling, suffering, and dying for the motherland did not deserve this downfall. (C.D.J.C., 371–5, June 1941)

From time to time, the administration took pains to take polls and conduct inquiries to monitor the pulse of public opinion. From the mass of internal documents we were able to consult, it appears that the type of ideas expressed in the document just cited were those of a minority characterized indiscriminatingly in our sources as "Communist" or "Gaullist." It is true that the various departments charged with keeping track of public opinion had the regrettable tendency to try at all costs to present a comforting image of public opinion to their superiors.[82] Nonetheless, initiatives of the type taken by the Algerian rectorate or by Moroccan business associations would have been unthinkable if their authors had had the least doubt as to the public's response.

Even though it is practically impossible to draw a picture of the North African population's attitude toward racial laws, it is nonetheless easy to make out nuances and even different degrees of stringency in the execution of racial legislation in each of the three Maghrebian countries. Thus, the Jewish Statute was relatively less rigorously applied in Tunisia than in Algeria and Morocco.

These variations were pronounced enough to catch Xavier Vallat's attention. They stemmed from two kinds of factors. The first kind, which we will label the human factor, pertained to the personality of Admiral Estéva and of some of his associates at the residency. The second kind of factor pertained, on the one hand, to the moderating role played by Ahmad Pasha Bey and Moncef Bey during this period and, on the other hand, to the presence on Tunisian soil of a sizable Italian settlers population that drew the hatred of French rightist circles as much if not more than the Jewish community did.

Labeled pro-Jewish by Radio Stuttgart, Estéva has left the memory of a deeply religious man, torn between his loyalty to Marshal Pétain and his Christian faith, which forbade him from perpetrating the excesses required by the racial laws. His attitude reinforced by the influence of several highly placed civil servants of the residency, the admiral was to show little zeal in executing anti-Jewish decrees, as evidenced by his waiting till March 1942 to promulgate the main decrees of application of the Jewish Statute.[83] At the same time, he also showed caring for the Tunisian Jewish community by visiting the ancient synagogue of Ghriba at Djerba (*Petit Matin*, May 22, 1941) and by making donations to Jewish indigents on the eves of the Pessah celebrations of 1941 and 1942 (*Petit Matin*, April 12, 1941, and April 1, 1942). Admiral Estéva's concern was also shared by Vice Admiral Derrien, who was in charge of the Bizerte naval base. On July 28, 1941, Derrien wrote Moïse Borgel, president of the Jewish community, to warn him that at Vichy's request he was forced to let go before December 31 all the Jewish employees at Tunisian arsenals.

> I am writing to you to spare them from an abrupt layoff and its consequences and so that you might as soon as possible see to their finding jobs in the private sector. As the laying off will be gradual, I plan to let go around October 1 all those easily replaceable specialties such as clerks, sail makers, carpenters. As to the rarer specialties, I will let them go last; but of course if they should be offered other positions before December 31 they will be free to take advantage of them. As to the apprentices, it would be deplorable to let them go before the end of their training. I propose to keep them on, even after the deadline, as free apprentices, that is, unpaid ones. They can remain till the end of their regular training and the completion of their final vocational project.[84]

This show of concern by the vice admiral had no parallel in Morocco and even less in Algeria where the authorities instead tended to worsen the anti-Jewish measures imposed by Vichy.

As to the beys' attitude,[85] they were well aware that the protectorate's constitution was giving them little freedom of choice and that they were in fact only carrying out the orders given them by the Resident's Office. However, article 11 of the first Jewish Statute promulgated in Tunis stipulated that the bey had the right to grant exemptions to native Tunisian Jews who had given exceptional service to the the regency. Indeed, it turned out to be Ahmad Bey who selected the only two individuals to benefit from this favor.[86] His successor Moncef Bey found it important to express his concern for "all the population of the regency" immediately

Vichy and the Jews of North Africa

after coming into power.[87] Faithful to an old beylical tradition, the new monarch consistently maintained relations with several Jewish notables, and, at a time when the downgrading of Jews was the rule, he found it opportune to award the highest Tunisian distinction, the Nishan Iftikhar, to about twenty Jewish personalities, among whom were businessmen and doctors.[88]

Without meaning to diminish the importance of Admiral Estéva's ethical qualms and Moncef Bey's shows of sympathy, these would not have softened the virulence of the anti-Jewish legislation without the effect of the Italian factor, which tangibly helped hinder the application of racial laws.

From a German souce, we thus learn that the Italian Armistice Commission operating in Tunisia opposed the application of Vichy's racial laws to the five thousand "Livornese" Jews holding Italian citizenship and living in the regency. As a result, the Italians were to sabotage the policy of economic Aryanization, for the Livornese included the most "Aryanizable" situations.

Alfieri, the Italian ambassador to Berlin, explained the reasons for his government's opposition in a note handed on September 2, 1942, to E. von Weizsacker, Germany's secretary of state. Alfieri argued that through racial laws and decrees pertaining to the Aryanization of Jewish property, the Vichy government aimed at fulfilling a long-sought goal of France: the weakening of the Italian position there by hurting Italian economic and political interests in the regency. Alfieri further pointed out that during the negotiations with Vichy, the French delegates had explained that their policy resulted from German pressure for the immediate application of racial laws in North Africa. Thus Alfieri concluded that "considering the importance for Italy of a satisfactory solution to this problem, we hope that the government of the Reich will agree to give appropriate instructions to its agents, asking them not to consider the application of racial laws in North Africa an urgent matter and if possible suspend their application in French Tunisia."[89]

The Italian request put the German authorities in an awkward position. While von Weizsacker was coming close to the conclusion that this whole business was nothing but a French intrigue aimed at sowing discord between the two Axis partners,[90] Otto Abetz, who had discussed this matter with Laval and Bousquet in Paris, was very critical of the Italian attitude. He had declared a few weeks earlier to General Gelice, the secretary-general of the Italian Armistice Commission, that "it is not in the interest of Italian colonial policy that the French should appear as the persecutors of Jews in Tunis and Algiers while the Italians appear as their protector."[91] Even while emphasizing the need for uniform application of anti-Jewish measures in the territories occupied by Germany or located within its sphere of influence, the Nazi authorities finally decided to leave the Italo-Tunisian Jewish problem on the back burner and not to intervene one way or another in Vichy's policy.[92] This problem was to come up again after the entry of the Axis troops in the regency.

In a surprising convergence of viewpoints, neither were the Tunisian French keen on the Aryanization of Jewish property. The Italians worried that this property would be taken over by the French, but the French in turn feared that "non-French people," for example, Italians, would possess it. This worry is clearly evident in a letter to Admiral Estéva written by the president of the Légion Française des Combattants de Tunisie on March 25, 1942:

> It is likely that the Jews who have been subjected to various restrictions and interdictions regarding some professions before the promulgation of the new texts have concluded that their actual status is not definitive and that other, yet more stringent, measures await them in the future. . . . In these circumstances many Jews will feel the need to liquidate those properties of which they still have free use to turn their wealth into goods that are easy to hide (cash, bearer bonds, perhaps even jewels). This is not in principle contrary to the spirit of the Jewish Statute. In metropolitan France this liquidation will benefit French persons. But this could not be so in Tunisia unless the liquidation is watched and controlled. More often than not, the sales would be to foreigners as the French make up only about one twenty-fifth of the total population and despite their role in the country's economy, they are mostly civil servants. Moreover, Jews will certainly prefer to sell to non-French. . . . Under these circumstances it appears necessary to prepare a measure that would slow down the move toward massive liquidation and ensure that it profits the French community, which cannot take over rapidly such an important patrimony. (Sabille 1954:167–69)

Thus, this representative of Tunisian Vichyst milieus did not ask for the slowdown of the liquidation of Jewish property because of ethical concerns or in the name of some ideal. The Jewish Statute and the economic Aryanization of Jewish patrimony had in his eyes for sole aim "to stimulate the increase of French influence." And so, far removed from German *Diktats*, Vichy's anti-Jewish policy in North Africa was conducted "in the name of France" and for the sole and exclusive benefit of the North African French. It was to be more stringently or more lightly applied according to the interests of this part of the population.

Let us consider now the situation that prevailed in Morocco, where it seems that General Noguès did not experience ethical conflicts and hesitations as Admiral Estéva did. Noguès very strictly enforced Vichy's directives. He showed himself more concerned with getting his prearmistice "mistakes" forgotten than in living up to his former reputation of "general of the left."[93]

As to Sultan Muhammad V, public rumor gave him credit for helping his Jewish subjects by interposing himself between them and the resident's administration.[94] Reality was somewhat different. Like the Tunisian beys, the Moroccan sovereign had no other alternative than to put his seal on the *dahirs* and edicts that were submitted to him by the Resident's Office. However, he was more timorous than Moncef Bey and did not take the liberty to hold a position or to act publicly in any way that might be interpreted as a criticism of Vichy's policy. The only gesture recorded by history was the warm welcome the king gave to Moroccan Jewish delegations that in May and June of 1942 came to discuss with him the serious consequences of the application to the Moroccan kingdom of the Jewish Statute.[95]

Although Moroccan Jews had little reasons to hope for help from the Resident's Office or from the palace, Franco's Spain initiated a move toward their defense. The Spanish press on several occasions criticized the treatment of French Morocco's Jews and contrasted it with their brethren's treatment in the Spanish zone:

> Moroccan Jewish settlements for the most part poor and toiling do not serve the aims of international Judaism. We do not perceive in Morocco a racial problem nor even a political problem of infiltration of the state's administrative apparatus or invasion of the liberal profession that can cause concern to European states. It would be a grievous mistake to bring to Morocco and to a population we are protecting measures that at any rate are inadequate. On this occasion again, Spain in its relation with other peoples has been able to hold original ideas imbued with a deeply humane meaning.[96]

French authorities were irritated by this lesson in tolerance. They were particularly worried by the rise of Spanish influence in Morocco, a rise that was happening through the intermediary of Moroccan Jews who were acutely aware of Spain's concern for Sephardic Jews and Sephardism. This worry was expressed in the following report by the French consul in Larache (Morocco):

> We note the start in Spain of a campaign in favor of Spanish Jews, who are scattered all over the world. As with Moroccan Jews, there is an at-

tempt at dissociating them from international Judaism to which, it is claimed, they were never incorporated. This pro-Semitic tendency of a peculiar type can only be explained at this time by Spain's desire to arouse the sympathy of Spanish-speaking Jewish groupings of North Africa, of the Orient, and even of North America, to make use of them at an opportune time to further imperialistic ends (C.D.J.C., 54-1; August 22, 1941).

We do not have much information on the effect of this sort of warning on the behavior of the protectorate's public authorities, but the French consul in Larache certainly had good reasons to advise the resident's administration to be more careful to avoid pushing the Jews "into the arms of fishermen in troubled waters." In this regard he advised the agents of the French state to use more "tactfulness" in carrying out their racial task by showing "less aggressivity toward the Jewish elements." Even though we do not know what kind of reception greeted this sort of advice, it is nonetheless clear that the Spanish factor in Morocco was of a nature different from that of the Italian factor in Tunisia. This, added to the already mentioned differences between the highest officials of the two protectorates, made for a lack of an external brake mechanism, lack that could only harm Moroccan Jews, who indeed were to be the butt of a harsher enforcement of racial laws than their Tunisian brethren were.

In Algeria, where the impediments encountered in Morocco and Tunisia were completely lacking, the application of the racial laws was to be done on an extremely fertile terrain, all the more so in that it had been worked for so many years by successive waves of anti-Semitism. Even with setting aside racist slogans, there was not a single anti-Semitic measure—whether the abrogation of the Crémieux decree, the Aryanization of education, or the liquidation of property—that had not been conceived and advocated by the ideologues of Algerian anti-Semitism, from Max Régis to Dr. Molle and Father Lambert. It is not surprising that in those circumstances the Commissariat-General for the Jewish Questions became the focus of a part of the Algerian population that believed its duty was to inundate Xavier Vallat's and Darquier de Pellepoix's office with letters filled with comments and advice on the best way to resolve the Jewish problem in North Africa.

There were those who thought that Xavier Vallat was "too indulgent"[97] or reproached him for having added a measure of equity to the Jewish question "as if surgeons engraved the pretty words Justice and Fraternity on the blades of their scalpels." These rabid "enthusiasts" did not admit the possibility of the existence of two categories of Jews—good ones and bad ones — "because from the wealthiest to the poorest, the most educated to the most ignorant, they all, without exception, obey only the international synagogue."[98] Then there were also those such as this "good Frenchman, an old soldier who for fifty years has struggled against the Jews" and who felt disgusted at seeing so "many" Jews retained "in the bosom of the French motherland." He wrote to Xavier Vallat that "you are aware the Jew is very prolific and if my fears are realized, you will see this race spread out like an oil spot, again invade our country, and again grip it into its vulture's claws."[99] L. Bonzon, former *ministre-délégué* (special minister representing the national government) to the *resident-general* in Tunis, advocated that, to slow down this proliferation, separate living quarters should be assigned to Jewish men and women younger than fifty years.[100]

Darquier de Pellepoix's appointment to the directorship of the Commissariat-General for the Jewish Questions seems to have drawn cries of joy from North African anti-Semites. You are "the right man," wrote Marcel Bellier, one of his Oran friends, who proceeded to give him the following didactic advice:

> The solution to this delicate and very complex Jewish question not only requires a vast historical and theoretical knowledge of Judaism but also a mental outlook, a state of mind if you will, that cannot be acquired overnight. One must have come close to them, particularly, one must have fought them for a long time, to know Jews well, to be aware of the threat they represent, of their intelligence when it comes to evil deeds, and their inability to foresee the future, even their own. Just as caterpillars in the garden do, they move about blindly, throwing themselves left and right, guided by a ferocious instinct for pleasure and domination, rotting and destroying everything that stands in their way . . . but without ever believing the fatal arrival of the pest control man. (Oran, May 6, 1942 [C.D.J.C.,35])

Father Lambert was among those who congratulated Darquier de Pellepoix after his appointment: "You are now where you belong, in a position you have well deserved by your civic and military courage." Had not de Pellepoix, just like Lambert in his book *Allemagne 38*, been opposed to the war?[101]

The Commissariat-General for the Jewish Questions did not always trust in the judgment of the zeal of the Algerian authorities and so found the veterans of Algerian anti-Semitism ideal informants and occasionally even secret advisers. Thus, Dr. Lucien Costa of the Faculty of Medicine of the University of Algiers was regularly consulted by René Gazagne, director of the Statut des Personnes (status of individuals) office at the commissariat-general regarding requests for exceptions sent him by Jewish medical doctors or members of other liberal professions.[102] Dr. Costa in particular put in much effort during the expulsion of the Jewish students from the University of Algiers:

> The French students of Algeria have painfully accepted the 3 percent ratio. What they really wanted was a 0 percent one. The students have indicated that 3 percent was a reasonable figure only because they are afraid to be seen as extremists by the people in metropolitan France who are completely unaware of the Jewish menace and who lack "a feel" for Jews. . . . We have already grievously lost face in the eyes of the natives because of our military defeat; it is crucial not to lose it again by letting them see the lack of consistency of our new state, which despite its national essence has not dared tell the Jew that he is but a simple foreigner.[103]

Dr. Costa, who went so far as to engage Jérôme Carcopino, the education minister, in a heated discussion was backed in his campaign by Rector G. Hardy and by F. Gillot, the president of the Students' Association of Algiers.

It is more than likely that other factors besides ideological considerations entered into the frenetic anti-Jewish behavior of these people. At a time when to be labeled a Jew was cause enough to lose one's property, many Algerians did not resist the temptation to denounce colleagues, neighbors, or old rivals to easily get rid of a bothersome competition and even possibly acquire the temporary trusteeship of a Jewish enterprise that had caught their fancy.[104] This was the course of action taken by the lawyers of the Oujda Bar in Morocco and those of Sétif in Algeria, who in their haste to get rid of their four Jewish colleagues accused them of using their profession "as a means for pursuing financial disputes."[105] This was also the case with the Wheat Cooperative of Oran, which, wanting to take over the Jewish flour mills of the city, invoked the need for an ethical clean-up of the profession to be achieved by expelling "the lazy ones, the undesirables, the parasites," and "the Jew who will by definition always be a parasite."[106]

At the close of this description of the juridical, political, and social frameworks of Jewish life in North Africa, we still need to look at Jewish communities' responses to the new situation. This will be the theme of the next section. In the meanwhile we must point out that racial legislation was only one aspect, though undoubtedly a fundamental one, of Jews' relations with society as a whole. Living to the rhythm of the publication in the *Journal Officiel* of decrees and orders aimed at them, North African Jews also had to face the threats and the generally hostile atmosphere kept by those organizations close to the regime, mostly the P.P.F., the Légion des Combattants, and the S.O.L. Anti-Jewish propaganda channeled through the press, publicity posters, and the radio[107] reached a climax on the eve of the Allied landing. On November 7, 1942, *La Vigie Marocaine* published a pamphlet written by the Service d'Ordre Légionnaire (a department of the Légion des Combattants), which, claiming to purify Morocco of the Jewish pollution, hinted at upcoming pogroms.

Finally, the picture would not be complete without mention of the police spying, investigations, and surveillances of which Jews were the victims. They were held in suspicion and they were accused of having transformed their synagogues, their restaurants, and their drinking establishments into Gaullist or Communist meeting places. Their rabbis were accused of holding prayers for Britain's victory and of organizing fundraisers to make possible the departure for England of Jews and other militants.[108] Their women were even accused of taking advantage of the long lines in front of shops and grocery stores to utter "stupid" comments discrediting the new regime in natives' eyes.[109] As to the parents who, because of the effect of the *numerus clausus* in schools, had been driven to enroll their children at the American Methodist Mission school in Algiers, they were accused of having done so with the sole aim of "rapproching themselves to the Anglo-Saxons."[110]

Every aspect of Jewish behavior raised the suspicion of the police and excited the hatred of a part of public opinion. In the small town of Aumale a general confrontation was almost triggered when two Jewish spectators left a movie theater before the projection of the news, an act immediately interpreted as a show of hostility toward the regime.

The climate of suspicion was so acute that on at least two occasions the leaders of the Algerian Jewry were threatened with being made hostage if their brethren kept on uttering comments hostile to public authorities and the regime (Eisenbeth 1945:24-25).

The Internal Life of North African Jewish Communities under Vichy

Despite the insinuations of the police reports mentioned in the preceding section, we can safely state that even after losing their French citizenship and even while affected in their possessions and their work, North African Jews never put into question their loyalty toward the "motherland" or their faith in "French conscience," which at all times had been "humankind's guide."[111]

From the notable to the simple citizen, from Casablanca to Tunis, they all were reluctant to believe that the recial legislation of which they were the victims had been freely generated by "humane and generous France."[112] Instead, they were convinced that the Jewish Statute was a scourge imposed from the outside and was in fact solely the tribute exacted by the occupant from Marshal Pétain. Thus many of them did purchase the Secours National (national help) bonds put up by the new regime[113] and, if it had been only a matter of choice, their war veterans would have flocked by the hundreds into the ranks of the Légion Française des Combattants. Reluctant to take into account the ideological and emotional underpinnings of Vichy's anti-Semitism as well as its authentic French traits, leaders of the three communities did not give up the hope that French public authorities would realize and redress the error of imposing upon Jews a status that "was as unjust as it was undeserved."[114]

The argumentation propounded in their petitions and protestations consisted essentially of three points: (1) inhabiting the region long before the arrival of the Arabs and the French, they could not be considered foreigners; (2) as an autochthonous group, they were worthy of partaking of the spirit of the National Revolution in the light of their attachment to the institution of the family, their hardworking habits, and their loyalty to France; (3) attached to their traditions and almost all of modest means, they could not be accused of dominating French economic and political life and even less of being in any way responsible for the military disaster. How absurd, indeed, to lay such a blame on Moroccan Jewry, which came to know France only in 1912!

However, in the face of the intransigence of public authorities and their refusal in any ways to soften the effect of the anti-Jewish laws, and in the face of the indifference, even the hostility, of public opinion, North African Jews were led toward a "self-rediscovery," a turn all the more remarkable in that it affected the most assimilated individuals of the three communities. I. Shapiro, president of the university organization Qol Aviv, expressed the new "act of faith" of Algiers Jewish youth as follows:

> We are French and we state loudly that even though it is possible to change a juridical status, there is no power in this world that can affect the deep feeling that unites us to our country, to its culture, to its dead. But we are also Jews. We must admit: for many of us it is only since we have been so marked that we know it; and this attribute of Jewishness has appeared at first as an undeserved burden imposed on us, a bother-

some label. Forced by circumstances, we have been led to introspection. We have wondered if behind these more or less arbitrary classifications there was not something else. We have wondered if we should content ourselves with rejecting the label, with showing only that we are French or, on the contrary, we should look for lost roots and, to give a deeper answer to unjust accusations, find in Jewish culture the possibilities for spiritual enrichment.[115]

There were within the North African Jewry and in particular the Algerian one individuals labeled by their brethren "ashamed Jews," "Jews in spite of themselves," or "neo-Marranos," who aspired only to their own survival "even at the expense of the group" and were severely criticized by Arnold Mandel, Armand Narboni, Elie Gozlan, and others.[116] However, in the main and judging from the opinions published in the *Bulletin de la Fédération des Sociétés Juives d'Alger* this renewal of Jewish consciousness led the new generation to be more receptive to Zionist theses. Thus, although in Algiers the *Bulletin* referred more and more often to the rebuilding of Palestine and emphasized particularly the importance of agricultural work,[117] and although also in Algiers, Qol Aviv organized series of lectures on Jewish history and culture, in Tunisia and Morocco Jewish youths by the hundreds flocked to the courses in modern Hebrew offered, often in precarious conditions, by Palestinian envoys (*shlihim*), who had gotten stuck in North Africa because of the war.[118]

However, the Jewish communities of the three countries had to face more urgent social problems. First of all, help was needed for the thousands of heads of households who, from one day to the next, found themselves without work or income. Then, some sort of solution was required to solve the problem of the hundreds of university, secondary, and elementary school students who had been expelled from their schools starting in the fall of 1941.[119] The Algerian community, which had for several decades been integrated with French society, was the least equipped of the three to cope successfully with these tasks. It lacked the required charitable organizations and, even more, the educational infrastructures, such as those organized by the A.I.U. (Alliance Israélite Universelle)[120] in Morocco and in Tunisia, which, despite its shortcomings, proved to be of such help and usefulness that the Aryanization of education had almost no effect in the two protectorates.

On January 9, 1941, Grand Rabbi Eisenbeth was granted permission to organize a Comité d'Etude, d'Aide, et d'Assistance (study, aid, and assistance committee) but, to prevent Jews from forming "a state within the state," the *préfet* of Algiers forbade him to give his committee a federational nature. In these circumstances each locality had its own mutual help committee,[121] whose resources came from gifts and monthly dues.

"Our ancestors were forced to share the bread of poverty during the time of slavery. Called as we are to be equal in the face of suffering, let us lighten the pain as much as possible." This was the motto of the campaigns undertaken by the leaders of Algerian Judaism who nonetheless were to be faced with the reticence of some "hopeless individuals blinded at once by gold and selfishness" (B.F.S.J.A., no. 70, June-July 1941). But aid committees were able to distribute help in kind and in money to the unemployed and to the laid-off civil servants and to organize programs of vocational retraining on their behalf. The "school" of Algiers, which had programs in carpentry, bookbinding, electrical work, and welding, offered courses from October 1941 to the end of January 1943 to some two hundred adolescents and adults.[122] However, the domain where the Algerian Jewry marshaled a genuine tenacity was that of education. Having resolved to save their children from ignorance, "the mother of intellectual slavery," Algerian Jews organized a system of classes and schools serving all the students excluded from public education:

> Israel has survived through the ages only because it has looked upon ignorance as one of the most terrible scourges among the many calamities that befell it through the centuries and because it is the struggle against ignorance that it has taken to heart. Ever since its exile, Israel has unceasingly maintained the divine flame of knowledge that ensures the supremacy of mind over matter. Consequently, our children must not remain ignorant and we have the duty to educate them broadly at every level.[123]

University students had been the first to be affected by the *numerus clausus*, and so Jewish university professors, who themselves had lost their jobs, organized for them during the fall of 1941 courses and lectures covering a broad range of fields—from Latin to medicine and including mathematics, physics, chemistry, French, and English. The subjects were taught in accordance with the regular programs at the faculties. Unfortunately, as the creation of a chemistry laboratory was being announced, the order came for the suppression of the "pirate university," which operated till December 1941.

In the meanwhile hundreds of students had been excluded from high schools and elementary shcools. A central office for private Jewish education was created. It was presided by Prof. R. Brunschvig and it opened its classrooms in haste to accommodate the expelled students.

More often than not, because of the lack of space, classes were offered only half time, either in the morning or in the afternoon. Sometimes a boys school alternated with a girls school in the same rooms in the course of a day. Classes were not held on Sundays and legal holidays. Moreover, barring a very few exceptions in the west, they were closed on Saturdays and on Jewish holidays. Thus in principle a child came to school only five mornings or five afternoons per week. But where possible this education was supplemented with walks, music lessons, physical education. The latter subject was particularly developed in Constantine. In Algiers, musical notation and choir were taught by a famous musician, a former orchestra leader of the theater of Paris who had had to return to his native city. (Brunschvig 1944:68)

Jewish schools adopted the same curriculum, schedules, and methods as public schools. They took pains to emphasize their French nature and this is why religious instruction was not obligatory in any of these schools.

This French patriotism, which did not accommodate any particularistic tendency, was expressed emphatically in the following comments of the president of the Relief and Assistance Association of Oran during the inauguration of a "lyceum of the banished" in this town:

> We want neither a national Jewish state nor separationism nor even any sort of particularism. Deeply and intensely French, we maintain the same attachment to the idea of France, to the French community. We find deplorable that the hardship we are enduring has been rationalized with the pretext that Jews cannot assimilate. We must do everything for assimilation, for a closer adaptation of the French Jew to the French motherland. We are certain that we will end up by being heard and by convincing.[124]

The attitude of public authorities toward private Jewish education was ambiguous. At first they were very favorable to it and Governor Yves Châtel went as far as to promise financial support from the state to Grand Rabbi Eisenbeth (Eisenbeth 1945:38). However, as soon as the project took shape, the administration hastened to put up all kinds of difficulties aimed at hindering the opening of Jewish schools. R. Brunschvig gives a fairly typical example of this type of harassment:

> This paternalistic administration, taking into its hands with a touching solicitude the interest of the families and of the Jewish children that it itself was persecuting, decided to be demanding on a specific matter: the question of the salubrity of the classrooms. Bear in mind, it was not a

question of the overall salubrity, which our committees would not have sacrificed, but of details one would have been justified in considering secondary in these difficult circumstances: playground, natural light, locations of toilets. Municipal public health inspectors and elementary school inspectors doing their job according to the ordinary standards of their professions often caused additional difficulties through their authoritarian remarks and negative reports. (Brunschvig 1944:67)

Indeed, Vichy did not intend to allow the development of a Jewish "cultural ghetto" free from all constraints and controls. On December 31, 1941, the text of a law pertaining to the "organization of private Jewish instruction in Algeria" was promulgated.[125] Expanded and made more rigorous in the executive order of June 8, 1942,[126] the new law excluded higher education from the realm of private Jewish education, which from then on was to be subjected to a tight control by the authorities. Not only did the opening of any new school first require the permission of the government but also the selection of curriculum, courses, schedules, and books was to be submitted to the authorities for approval. Moreover, although most Algerian Jews had lost their French citizenship, article 4 of the law required teachers to be French citizens. Finally, the governor general could order at any time the temporary or permanent closure of Jewish schools (article 6) or teachers' suspension (article 7).

At the start of the school year, in October 1942, when the *numerus clausus* in public schools was reduced to 7 percent, twenty thousand Jewish children were accommodated by private Jewish education, which had succeeded in opening seventy elementary schools in all Algeria and five secondary schools in Algiers, Oran, Constantine, and Tlemcen. But this exceptional success could not make the Jewish leaders forget the worrisome financial situation affecting most schools. This situation gradually worsened as the campaign of economic Aryanization cut off the income of the major donors and of many students' parents. Even though no school had to close down for financial reasons, nobody harbored any illusion as to the future of private Jewish education, which could not go very far under the circumstances. As Robert Brunschvig was to testify later, "collapse would have come before the Liberation."

After having pushed them away from the political, economic, and cultural life of the three countries and after having isolated them into their prior native status with the more or less explicit intention of locking them into specific vocational activities, Vichy then tackled the community structures and organization of the North African Jewry. The German Judenrat of which the U.G.I.F. (Union Générale des Israélites de

France) established in France was but a simple copy, was to serve as model also in Algeria.

On March 31, 1942, a decree pertaining to the organization of a Union Générale des Israélites d'Algérie was published by the French General Government.[127] According to article 1 of the law, the U.G.I.A. was destined to become an organ for the implementation of governmental orders, and it was supposed to ensure Jewish representation with the public authorities, particularly concerning matters of assistance, security, and social reclassification. Every Algerian Jew was to be affiliated to the Union Générale, which was to be substituted for all Jewish organizations in existence. It was to be headed by an administrative council made up of fifteen members appointed by the governor-general and it was to be financed with all the property and resources of the dissolved Jewish organizations, with obligatory fees paid by Jews and with money taken from the Jewish Solidarity account, which, in accordance with the law on the Aryanization of property, was the recipient of the money coming from the liquidation of Jewish enterprises.

Grand Rabbi Eisenbeth was notified by March 4 by Governor-General Châtel, who asked him to compile "after conferring with the grand rabbis of Oran and Constantine" a list of forty-five personalities fit to be appointed members of the administrative council to the U.G.I.A. (Eisenbeth 1945:56–57). Even though Yves Châtel made it clear that the law gave him the power to choose freely the candidates "even outside the list of persons that you will compile," Châtel nonetheless advised the grand rabbi to suggest "individuals chosen in terms of the role the union will fill, so as to ensure within this organization an equitable representation of the affected interests."

This official request caused serious turmoil in the Algerian Jewish leadership, which, faced with this "offer" of collaboration with the authorities, was torn between the wish to preserve their brethren's welfare, even as minimal as it was, and the fear, entirely justified because of the fate that befell the U.G.I.F. and the Judenrät, of having to carry out the administration's dirty work. But under the encouraging advice of an eminent Jew living in Marseilles[128] and in the face of the risk that the governor-general would appoint opportunistic and unethical individuals, the grand rabbi presented on May 5, 1942, a list of forty-five candidates for the administrative council. Showing an unexplained lack of zeal, the governor-general took his time to select the fifteen members of the U.G.I.A. council. Their identity was made public on September 3. To be led by Paul Stora, president of the Algiers consistory, the adminstrative council of the *union* was made up of the presidents or vice presidents of the other Algerian consistories as well as the leaders of the associations of Jewish war veterans. This, however, was not the end of it, as the designated president was to submit his resignation on that very same day. André Bakouche, the president of the Constantine consistory, was appointed in his place. However, he accepted the position only after the entreaties of the grand rabbi and after having obtained from Yves Châtel the assurance that "he would never have to associate with measures incompatible with his conscience and with the strictly constructive goals his colleagues and he "had assigned themselves in the interest of their brethren."[129]

However, the U.G.I.A. was not to function. At the time of the Allied landing, it had been in existence for barely forty days.

In Morocco and in Tunisia public authorities did not have to put up much effort because community organization was already very close to the model they wanted to enforce in Algeria. In Morocco the functioning of the Jewish communities' committees had been closely controlled since 1918 by the authorities, who guided as they saw fit the activities of these institutions (Bensimon-Donath 1968:87–90). Just like the leadership of the future U.G.I.A., the members of each committee were appointed by the administration on the basis of lists of candidates compiled by community notables. In Tunisia, in contrast, the community council was an elected body. According to the terms of the decree of August 30, 1921, Jews of twenty-one years or older elected sixty representatives who sat on the council and in their turn chose twelve councillors.

On October 5, 1939, this Council of Twelve became a "temporary administrative council" and was enlarged by order of the resident, who appointed the extra members. On September 29, 1941, the body was eliminated along with all the provisions of the 1921 decree. The Jewish population was henceforth represented by an administrative committee made up of eleven members appointed by the administration.[130] Just as in Morocco and Algeria, the Tunisian committee had to report only to the resident, who had more need of straightforward agents to implement its policies than properly elected delegates.

Jewish Refugees and Internees in North Africa

Internment camps both in North Africa and France were not one of Vichy's innovations. Most metropolitan French camps had been set up in 1938 east of the Pyrenees to shelter Spanish republicans and the "international" elements who had retreated to France after Franco's victory. After the declaration of war, every "individual posing a risk to national defense" was thrown into them. This included foreign agents, political suspects (Communist militants after the Ribbentrop-Molotov agreement, North

Vichy and the Jews of North Africa

African nationalists), and thousands of Jewish refugees from Germany and Austria who had migrated to France in the hope of escaping the Nazi menace. For the latter as well as for Czechoslovakian and Polish refugees whose numbers were gradually rising with the spread of Hitler's hegemony in central Europe, there was only one possible course of action to escape internment: to enlist under the French flag as volunteers for the duration of the war (E.V.D.G.) or as nonfighting auxiliaries if they were not of the right age to bear arms (younger than twenty or older than forty-eight). Until January 1940 some thirty thousand Jewish refugees enlisted in this manner in the French armed forces (*Contemporary Jewish Record* 3 [1940], p. 175). Most of them were assigned to infantry regiments of the foreign legion and after a brief training period in North Africa took part in all the campaigns of the Battle of France.

In keeping with the terms of the Armistice Convention, the foreign legion was disbanded and the voluntary enlisted men were crossed off the army's rolls. However, they did not all regain their freedom. Thus in North Africa only the individuals who held a French identity card, a job contract, or a pledge of shelter could be demobilized. The others, in fact almost all the Jewish and Spanish E.V.D.G.s and noncombat auxiliaries, were sent to work camps in the Moroccan and the Algerian south, where from the condition of soldier they passed to that of convict.

In France in the meanwhile, large successive waves of refugees made their way toward the line of demarcation and the unoccupied zone from which they hoped to reach the Spanish border. Until the end of summer 1940, the departure from France and the passage through Spain and Portugal were relatively easy. However, once Vichy overcame the chaos produced by the defeat and completed the organization of its administrative apparatus, a draconian control was set up along the border. Jews and foreigners "in excessive numbers" were thus arrested by the thousands and herded in the "transit camps," the "locked centers," and the "disciplinary camps" of Rivesaltes, Gurs,[131] le Vernet, Argelès, Barcarès, Agde, Brens, Rieucros, Recebedou, Noé, Saint-Cyprien, Milles, and others.

In November 1940 Vichy let the United States know that it was not opposed to freeing internees who were able to migrate to countries in the Western Hemisphere (Tartakower and Grossman 1944:201-4). The French government's good intentions were greeted with relief by the international agencies providing aid to the refugees, such as the J.D.C., or JOINT (American Jewish Joint Distribution Committee), H.I.C.E.M. (a Jewish emigration society), and the American Friends Service Committee (a Quaker organization). However, these intentions proved to be a sham; the Vichy administration soon piled up all sorts of obstacles to the obtaining of "exit visas." These obstacles were added to the already great difficulties in the obtaining of entry visas to the countries of immigration and of transit, as well as to the problems inherent to the growing scarcity of maritime traffic between Europe and the New World.

The refugees had usually embarked in Lisbon but from 1942 on, the Portuguese and the Spanish made the Jewish emigrants' passage through their territories difficult. They first closed their door to refugees of Russian origin, then ceased granting transit visas to citizens of arms-bearing age of any warring or neutral country.[132] Under those circumstances, the J.D.C. and the H.I.C.E.M. had to focus on the North African ports of Tangiers, Casablanca, and Oran where the ships headed for the United States, Cuba, and Mexico, where most of the refugees were heading, were still stopping.

Once they arrived in North Africa, the emigrants soon found that the fate awaiting many of them there was not very different from the one they had had to cope with in metropolitan France. The luckiest ones, those with all their papers in order, were taken under care by local committees of assistance to refugees until their departure. The others were interned immediately upon their arrival and taken to the "shelter centers" and the detention camps of Algeria and Morocco, where thousands of their brothers in misfortune had been forcefully assembled since the beginning of the war. As in France, the authorities nonetheless allowed the J.D.C., the H.I.C.E.M.,[133] and other local and foreign charitable organizations to help them.

It is to these acts of human and of Jewish solidarity that we wish to devote the following pages. But to remain within the scope of our topic, we will limit ourselves to the activities of the local committees set up in Casablanca, Tangiers, and Algiers.

The first committee was organized in Tangiers by the local Jewish community. It was followed in July 1940 by the creation of the Casablanca committee of Hélène Cazès-Benathar and, in 1941, by that of the Algiers committee led by Elie Gozlan.

These three committees made immediate contact with the J.D.C. and the H.I.C.E.M. They took on the task of easing the emigrants' transit and of helping the refugees unable to pursue their wanderings in search of a safe asylum. In the face of the threat of internment hanging over the refugees' head, the three North African committees succeeded in saving a number of them by spreading them through the Jewish communities of Morocco and Algeria, where they were provided with shelter and work contracts.

On the day after the Allied landing, the J.D.C. estimated that ten thousand Jewish emigrants had passed through Casablanca since January 1941.[134] If we add to these the five to ten thousand civilian refugees, camp internees, and "foreign workers" who had lived in French Morocco, Tangiers, and Algeria since the Armistice, we surmise that between 1940 and 1942 the three North African committees had to deal with about twenty thousand Jewish refugees.[135] The biggest share of the task fell to Hélène Cazès-Benathar's committee. Cazès-Benathar was a lawyer and the president of the association of the former students of the Alliance Israélite Universelle. She was forced to cope with the suspicion of the authorities only a few months after the organization of her committee. In April 1941, at the suggestion of the German Armistice Commission, her committee was dissolved. In principle it should have ceased all activities and turned over to the authorities the list of refugees demanded by the Germans. However, thanks to her powerful connections at the Résidence Général and at the Région Civile, Hélène Cazés-Benathar was left alone by the police. She thus continued with her task, in full view of the authorities to whom she had to report her movements to obtain special allotments for gasoline and the required authorizations to bring emigrants from the port of Casablanca to the reception centers set up on their behalf.[136]

Help for the emigrants. All the emigrants coming from Marseilles were automatically directed toward the reception center of Aïn Sebaa located a few miles from Casablanca. Made up of three large rooms, which had previously been used as a dancing hall and as housing for children's summer camps, this center sheltered up to six hundred refugees; for bedding, each refugee had to make do with a pallet consisting of a mattress made up of rough jute material stuffed with horsehair.[137] A sum of fifty francs per day was demanded of each resident to cover the cost of housing, food and transportation up to the day of departure. Because the refugees could not bring to Morocco more than two hundred French francs and five thousand Moroccan and Algerian francs they were supposed to pay in advance for the cost of their stay in Morocco (which in principle was not to last longer than ten days) and for their travel costs to their final destination at the Marseilles office of the H.I.C.E.M.[138] However, migrants often arrived in Morocco without the proper papers and the reservations required for the continuation of their journey. The self-appointed task of the Casablanca committee was to see to it that they were not left to fend for themselves by requesting visas for them from the United States consulate, requests that were to involve more and more fastidious formalities from June 1941 on,[139] and by getting them tickets on the few ships that commuted between the two shores of the Atlantic. In 1942 maritime traffic between Morocco and America consisted of five ships. Most of them had been chartered by the H.I.C.E.M., notably the Portuguese ships *Nyassa, Serpa Pinto, Guiné,* and *São Thome,* which at their regular stop in Casablanca were embarking refugees who had been brought there from France by the *Lyautey,* the *Ville d'Oran,* and the *General Cambon.* Until May 1941 refugees lacking Spanish transit visas still had the possibility of leaving France on board the *Winnipeg,* the *Alsina,* the *Wyoming,* and the *Monte Viso,* which went by way of Casablanca to Martinique where the emigrants could reach the United States directly or through Saint Thomas and Puerto Rico. However, in the wake of the capture of the *Winnipeg* on May 10, 1941, by the British fleet, the traffic between Marseilles and Fort-de-France was interrupted and the refugees on board the *Monte Viso* had to disembark in Casablanca. The same thing happened to the passengers of the *Alsina* who had been stuck for weeks in Dakar before being rerouted to Casablanca, where they were interned in the Moroccan camps along with the passengers of the *Monte Viso* (Wischnitzer 1956:169–74; *New York Times,* June 13, 21, and 26, 1941).

Despite all this, during the period that ended with Vichy's France forbidding all refugee departure (June 1942), a substantial movement of ships carrying emigrants was recorded in Casablanca. This attracted the German general consul's attention who, from March on, began to transmit to Berlin precise information on the number of immigrants their nationalities, and their destinations.[140]

We thus learn that on March 15 the *Ville d'Oran* brought 165 Jewish refugees from Marseilles; five days later they embarked on the *Guiné,* which had come from Lisbon and Cádiz, with 465 emigrants. On March 22, the *Lipari* stopped in Casablanca with 369 refugees from Marseilles. They were joined the next day by 443 passengers from the *Ville d'Oran* and together they embarked on the *São Thome,* which on the same day left for Havanna and New York with an additional 107 passengers in transit. Other emigrants' departures were on the *Nyassa,* the *Guiné,* and the *Serpa Pinto* on May 5, June 6, June 25, July 2, and July 6. One of the last large-scale departures was that of June 6 on the *Serpa Pinto;* coming from Lisbon with 176 passengers, it embarked with 502 refugees in Casablanca.[141] The emigrants were of all European nationalities; most were German and Polish Jews and there also were Czechoslovakians, Romanians, Russians, Dutch, French Belgians, Hungarians, Yugoslavs, Greeks, and even Turks and Palestinians.

Relief for the refugees. In September 1940 there were 731 refugees from eastern Europe registered with the relief committee of Casablanca.[142] This figure, which included only the civilian refugees in French Morocco, was to grow substantially during the following months and was to include besides the former enlisted volunteers and the auxiliaries all the male subjects of the British Empire who had been forbidden to leave the French territory after the Mers-el-Kebir incident.[143]

At the beginning of the war, the authorities had allowed the relief committees as well as the Jewish communities to take care of their foreign brethren to keep them out of the internment camps. Thus, five shelters were opened in Tangiers and Casablanca to house part of the refugees, and many others were taken in by private parties or by inland communities such as Marrakech, Fez, Mogador, Safi, and Mazagan. Each refugee was given a weekly allowance, the amount varying according to his or her needs, as well as medical care and help with school expenses, transportation costs, and so on.[144] In Algiers, where there were fewer refugees, the relief and assistance committee contemplated setting the amount of these allocations on the same scale as that adopted for the civil servants fired because of the Jewish Statute.[145]

The resources at these committees' disposal came from the H.I.C.E.M., which had two representatives, R. Spanien and J. Oettinger, in the field to keep an eye on the relief process, and from fixed dues from Jewish communities and individual donations.

In Casablanca a plan was afoot to set up a system by which regular dues were to be collected from the community's members; however, the plan had to be abandoned because the Benathar committee lacked a legal identity.[146] Because of the lack of enough resources, the budget could give only stopgap assistance to the refugees, whose material circumstances were to worsen from month to month.

The following, which was reported by the president of the community of Mogador in March 1942, clearly illuminates the nature of this situation:

> In November [1941] when I had questioned all the refugees to be informed of their situation . . . , almost all refused aid of any kind as most of them were expecting to leave shortly for the United States. However, their departure being indefinitely postponed and at present seemingly impossible, they are forced to exhaust their resources so that some of them are in difficult circumstances even though they state they were well-off in the past.[147]

Special attention was devoted to the refugees who had been interned. In each major city, shelters had been organized for housing internees and foreign workers on furlough. Besides trying to free the sick and the children from the camps, committees managed to give certificates of shelter and work contracts to a number of internees, who were thus able to gain their freedom. Moreover, regular help in money, food, and clothing was delivered every month to the internees.

Except foreign workers, most of the refugees were held in the following camps: Sidi al-Ayyashi (near Azzemour), which was the largest civilian camp in Morocco; Oued-Zem, located about 150 kilometers west of Casablanca; Missour, which, like Saïda in Algeria, mostly housed individuals unfit for work; Kasbah Tadla, Oued Akreuch, and Berguent, which was located near the path of the projected trans-Saharan rail.[148]

The trans-Saharan rail and the work camps of North Africa. The construction of a railroad connecting the two edges of the Sahara was an old French colonial dream. It had been debated by all the governments of the Third Republic ever since the end of the nineteenth century. Its construction was ordered by the Pétain government and the job given to the Mediterranean-Niger Company. This railroad was to serve, among other points, the coal mines of Djérada, Kenadsa, and Bou-Arfa from which Morocco and Algeria filled much of their coal needs. The rail was to reach Colomb-Béchar (Algeria) through Bou-Arfa, then, after passing through Beni-Abbès, to the south of the Guir valley, was to head for Adrar and Reggane in the Touat region before following the Tanezrouft and the "Adrar des Iforas" valleys to reach, at the end of the line, Gao (Mali) on the Great Loop of the Niger River.[149]

The Allied press and some American diplomats posted in North Africa were convinced that the Germans were behind this project, which fitted in perfectly with plans elaborated in Berlin for the future insertion of Africa into the new economic world order conceived by Hitler.[150]

Nonetheless, although it is not excluded that some French collaborationist elements did consider such a contribution, it seems more correct to view the trans-Saharan project as a large prestige undertaking launched by Vichy to fulfill purely internal aims. One could read the following on official posters put out by the French government:

> The trans-Saharan line is the indispensable connection of A.O.F. [Afrique Occidentale Française] to the Mediterranean. . . . The governments of the Third Republic debated it for more than fifty years without making a decision. One meeting of Marshal Pétain's cabinet council was enough to implement the immediate start of the project. Settler remember this! (Vanino 1952:303)

However, the Germans could but rejoice at Vichy's initiative, which, through the forced recruiting of hundreds of former voluntary enlisted soldiers and nonfighting auxiliaries for work on the railroad, kept them from joining the Allied forces.

This was, for instance, the case with the auxiliaries of the Foreign Work Company, which, up to the defeat, had been assigned to the British expeditionary forces in France. After the armistice, these auxiliaries were taken to Casablanca, whre they then requested to rejoin the British forces. This arose the suspicion of their officers, who immediately sent them to the camp of Boghar in Algeria.[151]

About thirty work camps were set up in Morocco and Algeria. The Moroccan camps were: Agdz (south of Marrakech), Aïn-al-Ouraq (fifty miles from Bou-Arfa, which served as a disciplinary camp), Berguent, Bou-Arfa, Bou-Denib (which served as a detention camp for autochthonous internees, both Jewish and non-Jewish), Djérada, Foum-el-Flah (another disciplinary camp), Fqih ben-Salh (near Settat), In-Fout, Mengoub (near Bou-Arfa), Midelt, Missour, Moulay-Bou-Azza, and Settat. In Algeria the camps were: Bedeau, Berrouaghia, Bidon V (South of Colomb-Béchar), Boghar, Bossuet, Crampas, Djelfa, Djenien-Bou-Rezk, al-Arisha, Fort-Cafarelli, Géryville, Hadjerat M'Guil, Kenadsa, Kersas, Relizane, and Saïda.

According to the terms of the contract that each individual working for the Mediterranean-Niger Company had to sign, the foreign workers were classified as *requis* (wartime labor conscripts) and thus were to be submitted to military discipline. Consequently, they were turned over to military authorities for any infraction of camp rules. The contact also stipulated that the foreign workers were to receive salaries and family allowances comparable to those of civilian employees, but, as we will see shortly, these were but empty promises.

Camp personnel consisted of former petty officers of the foreign legion, most of them of German origin and stridently anti-Jewish, and of Senegalese sharpshooters and Arab *goumiers*;[152] all three groups were under the jurisdiction of the Direction de la Production Industrielle (office in charge of industrial production) of Rabat and the Direction de la Main-d'Oeuvre et du Travail (office in charge of manpower and work) of Algiers. In January 1942 the Amicale des Anciens Engagés Volontaires Etrangers was organized in Casablanca with the aim of helping interned workers in any way possible, but it was dissolved four months later by order of the Resident's Office, which systematically refused to follow up on any complaints regarding the situation in the camps.

In every camp, internees were forced to work ten hours per day. In Berguent the work site was located two and a half miles from the camp; the workers were forced to walk this distance morning, noon, and night besides their working hours. In Bou-Arfa they were imposed tasks four times more strenuous than the Arab laborers. In In-Fout the former enlisted volunteers were paid 7.50 francs per day while Arab civilians received 12 francs for the same work. In Berguent the salary was limited to a daily loan of 1.25 francs plus 2 francs bonus if the work was deemed satisactory. Poorly fed and housed, the workers lived in terrible sanitary conditions. In Berguent each man was allotted only one quart of water per day; infested with vermin, lice, and fleas, half of the workers assigned to In-Fout fell ill daily. Tortures were inflicted for the slightest breaches of the rules: deprivation of food, rounds of beatings with sticks, "the lion's cage" where the prisoner was locked in a square cubicle with sides 6 feet long made of barbed wire and entered through a trapdoor, being tied to a post the whole day with one's head unprotected against the sun, the *pelote* (punishment drill) where the victim was made to carry a basket of stones on his head and run to exhaustion, and the "tomb ordeal" in which the victim had to lie down in a ditch 5¼ feet long and slightly over 2½ feet wide where he was immobilized for as long as eight to twenty-five days and continually tormented by the Arab and Senegalese guards, who threw stones at him and hit him with rifle butts. Several internees died from this torture in various camps, notably in Hadjerat M'Guil.[153]

Hadjerat M'Guil, which usually held about 150 inmates, was the disciplinary camp formed in October 1940 and spread out between Kenadsa and Colomb-Béchar. At the beginning, its group of prisoners was made up of 2,070 internees, among whom 250 were Jews and 1,300 were Spaniards. At the end of 1941 Jewish internees were split off from the group and sent to Kenadsa, where they were assigned to the coal mines.[154]

The treatment endured by the internees of Hadjerat M'Guil was to be subsequently described during the trial of the camp's staff held by the military tribunal of Algiers in February 1944:

> The internees were not treated as human beings. . . . The camp was literally starving; some would eat anything and because of this became seriously ill. Others died from this state of affairs. Despite their physical weakness, the men were assigned particularly strenuous work. . . . The guards, armed with cudgels, beat up the workers without any compunction, without any reason, just to hit. . . .
> The internees being disciplined were piled up in the cells and were forced to go to the bathroom in their mess tins. . . . Sometimes the interned doctors were forbidden to bandage their fellow prisoners, who having been grievously beaten by their guards were nothing but one open wound. . . .(cited in Vanino 1952:307)

Not far from Hadjerat M'Guil, between Aïn Sefra and Colomb-Béchar, was the camp of Djenien Bou-Rezq, whose population mainly consisted of European, Moslem, and Jewish political prisoners. Like the other camps, Djenien Bou-Rezq was commanded by openly pro-Nazi former officers of the foreign legion. In July 1941 de Ricko, the camp commander, had all the individuals undergoing punishment freed from their cells in celebration of a victory of the Wehrmacht over the Red Army (Moine 1972: 187).

The camp of Bedeau, located near Sidi-bel-Abbès, belonged to a different category because of its function of concentration camp for Algerian military personnel of Jewish origin. One yar after the armistice, Algerian Jews conscripted in 1939 and serving in various regular units were assigned to Bedeau to form a special unit called Groupement de Travailleurs Israélites (G.T.I.; Jewish workers group). In March 1942 they were given the same status as that of foreign workers; their military uniforms were replaced by civilian black outfits and they were assigned to the most strenuous tasks under the supervision of foreign legionnaires.[155]

Also in Algeria, the camp of Djelfa with its seven hundred to one thousand internees was probably the most populated and the most "cosmopolitan" North African camp. In operation since 1939 it contained Spaniards, Frenchmen, Britishers, Poles, Czechoslovakians, and Russians. In April 1941 the internees of the metropolitan French camps of Vernet, Gurs, and Argelès were sent there after a brief stay in Bossuet.

Located some 550 yards from the town bearing the same name, the camp of Djelfa was commanded by an individual named Caboche, who chose his aides from the common law prisoners and the Spanish anarchists. The aides were dubbed with the title of "camp chief" and they inflicted the worst atrocities upon the inmates who, upon their arrival, were grouped according to their countries of origin except for the Jews who were put together in a separate section. Until 1942 the internees were housed in cone-shaped military tents, twelve to twenty individuals per tent. Summer as in winter, with temperatures ranging from 140 to 50 degrees, the prisoners had to sleep on the ground on a thin layer of straw.

Besides maintenance work at the camp, the inmates were employed in a variety of tasks in the town of Djelfa such as the building of an auditorium, of a soap factory, of two brick factories, and a raffia workshop, established in the camp itself, where espadrilles, mats, baskets, and bags were produced.

Sanitary conditions were very rudimentary. During the summer of 1941, a serious typhoid epidemic caused the death of about thirty prisoners. Medical care was provided by interned doctors, but these were continually watched by Caboche and his helpers who severely punished doctors for the slightest show of "indulgence" toward their patients.

The usual punishment was detention at Fort Cafarelli, located one and a quarter miles from the camp. The prison was made up of about ten cells, each with a surface of less than ten square feet. This is the description provided by a former inmate:

> Often up to three prisoners were piled up in a cell. No straw mattresses were given and it was forbidden to bring in more than one blanket. Smoking and reading were forbidden. There was no lighting. There was no period for outdoor exercise. Food consisted of six ounces of bread per day and two measures of always meatless camp soup. In winter it was freezing and the more so as the panes of the windows beneath the ceiling were broken. . . . After a few days in a cell, the prisoners were directly taken to the infirmary or to the hospital.[156]

In Morocco, the camps of Missour, Bou-Arfa, Aïn al-Ouraq, and Foum-el-Flah looked like regular penal colonies. The camp of Berguent, which on the eve of the Allied landing held four hundred inmates, had an exclusively Jewish population made up mostly of former enlisted volunteers.[157] In Bou-Arfa and in Foum-el-Flah, the regulations provided for severe punishment to those who, "violating the law of hospitality and gratefulness, have, on French soil, engaged in any kind of political activity, work sabotage, or incited to strike or to revolt" (cited in Vanino 1952:305).

The disciplinary camp of Aïn al-Ouraq at the end of 1942 held about 100 inmates, many of whom had been interned for a variety of infractions ranging from political agitation to the refusal to work on a Jewish holiday. The ordeal of the "tomb," from which several inmates lost their lives, was the most common form of punishment (Tartakower and Grossman 1944:209–11).

How many foreign Jews were interned in North African work camps? The documentation now available makes it difficult to attempt any kind of evaluation, for the numbers given in the sources at our disposal are too fragmented and inconsistent. The number of voluntary enlisted Jews who were in Algeria at the time the camps were set up is estimated to be two thousand. To this figure should be added the unknown number of internees from southern France camps, of people grabbed during raids and sent as "volunteers" to North Africa, of a portion of the passengers of the ships *Monte Viso* and *Alsina*, and another indeterminate number taken from the ranks of the refugees housed at the "shelter centers" such

Vichy and the Jews of North Africa

as the one of Sidi-al-Ayyashi. At any rate, on the day after the Anglo-American landing, the New York weekly *Aufbau* provided the following figures for the census of the internees in the major Moroccan and Algerian camps, figures which added up to twenty-one hundred internees in Morocco and two thousand internees in Algeria:[158]

Berguent	400	Saïda	400
Mengoub	400	Colomb-Béchard	400
Bou-Arfa	200	Bidon V	200
Aïn al-Ouraq	150	Hadjerat M'Guil	200
In-Fout	500	Berrouaghia	200
Sidi-al-Ayyashi	450	Djelfa	600

PART THREE

A Difficult Liberation

6

Operation Torch and Its Consequences

Churchill had been contemplating a project for an Allied landing in North Africa ever since August 1941. This project became a reality at the beginning of summer 1942 after the lightning-swift advance of the Afrika Korps on Egyptian territory. The reservations voiced by American generals who leaned toward an operation in France were swept aside after the fall of Tobruk (June 21) and after President Roosevelt's decision to initiate effective military action before the end of the year to satisfy, at least in part Stalin's appeals for the opening of a second front. During discussions held in London on July 24 and 25, Churchill agreed that the supreme command should go to the Americans, and on July 26 General Eisenhower was appointed to that post. All that was left to decide were the date and place of the landing. These choices were to cause much controversy among the Allied command. The British, who wanted the operation to take place as soon as possible, were proposing a landing on the Mediterranean coast to progress rapidly toward the Tunisian border and attack Rommel's rear echelon. On the other hand, the Americans were satisfied with a limited landing in Casablanca from where they would later stage an offensive toward Tunisia by going through Algeria.

The plan for Operation Torch was definitely agreed upon on September 5. It consisted in taking Casablanca with a contingent entirely made up of American troops under the command of General Patton, in taking Oran with an American expeditionary force and a British naval escort, and in taking Algiers with a British-American task force under the command of the American, General Ryder.

On September 22 Roosevelt appointed Robert Murphy adviser to General Eisenhower for political affairs. The American president explained in his instructions to Murphy that changes in the French administration were not contemplated and that no Gaullist force would take part in the operation.[1] The Americans were perfectly aware of the state of mind that prevailed within the French army and French population in North Africa, and they felt that the participation of General de Gaulle might prevent French officers from eventually joining the Allied side, a move that both Washington and London felt to be absolutely necessary. Thus, while more and more numerous alarming rumors on the immediacy of German occupation of Tunisia and Morocco were spreading,[2] Murphy set out to find at any cost a prestigious French military leader who would be willing to be associated with Operation Torch and whose stance would win over the North African French army to the Allied cause.

Contacts had already been established long before with Weygand, Juin, Noguès, and even Darlan. But in the face of the failure of these discussions, Murphy turned to General Giraud, who in April 1942 had managed a dramatic escape from the German fortress of Koenigstein.

The American diplomat's frantic activities and the Allies' military preparations did not go unnoticed by the Vichy government and armistice commissions established in Algiers and Casablanca.[3] But up to the end of October, the Paris collaborationist press and German intelligence were persuaded that the Allies were planning to take Dakar.[4] As late as November 6, the German chiefs of staff thought that the American fleet observed around Gibraltar was aiming an offensive operation either on the Libyan coast or on the south of the Italian peninsula. On November 8, when Operation Torch actually began, Allied commandos who landed on the Algerian and Moroccan coast had to fight neither the Germans nor the Italians but French soldiers resolved to defend the empire "against all agressors" while, at the same time, French General Barré's soldiers let the Axis forces enter Tunisia.

The Allied Landing and the North African Resistance
We do not aim here to give a detailed account of the events of November 8, 1942, for many narratives and several reliable studies have been published on this topic. However, we cannot help concurring with Leon B. Blair and noting that probably no other modern military victory has been marked by so much unpredictability, poor timing, mistakes, and double dealings as Operation Torch (Blair 1970).

On October 23, 1942, during the intriguing meeting in Cherchell, General Clark described the main lines of the American plan to the representatives of the North African resistance movement. Colonel Jousse, one of the French participants, subsequently was to describe the main points covered during the meeting:

> General Clark explains that the Allies plan to take care of the Mediterranean problem by winter by occupying North Africa to prepare the necessary bases for the establishment of a second European front in the spring. They of course hope to get the help of the French army but they have resolved if necessary to overcome its opposition. They are not providing us with a specific date for this action and they give the impression that their preparations are "yet far from complete." The French delegation's report, drafted after the meeting, estimates that one month will be required for the completion of these preparations, the Americans' intention being to land as soon as these will be complete. . . . Considerable means are to be used. "Roosevelt and Churchill have a personal interest in this project." The American delegation cites figures: 500,000 men, 15 divisions of which several are armored, 2,000 planes. . . . (Jousse 1945: 204–6)

The French delegation insisted on the need to arm the North African Resistance, and the Americans promised them that a shipment of the arms necessary to the realization of their joint plan would be delivered to them before the landing. Bernard Karsenty, who along with José Aboulker was one of the main leaders of the Algerian Resistance, gives the following account:[5]

> Mr. Murphy had José Aboulker and I come to him one morning so that he could show us a Sten gun. He left it with us to see if we found the weapon suitable. The Sten gun truly being an extremely practical and easy-to-handle arm, we asked for 800 of them for Oran and Algiers. We also requested 400 handguns, 400 defensive grenades, 400 tear gas grenades, and 50 portable radios. . . .
> In mutual agreement with Mr. Murphy we selected November 2 as the date for the secret sea delivery of the weapons. The operation was to take place in Cherchell, on Jacques Tessier's property, where the meeting with Clark had been held. . . .
> Everything went as planned on our side but nothing was delivered. Early the following morning I went to see Mr. Murphy to let him know "the result" of our expedition. He seemed very surprised and had a cable sent to Gibraltar to ask for an explanation and to warn them that the Cherchell beach was not safe anymore as our three cars had drawn attention while going through the town the preceding evening. He received an

answer the next day, November 4: the boat had not been able to leave on time and its crew needed to know the new landing place. José Aboulker and Pierre Alexander[6] had spent the preceding night on a beach east of Algiers. . . . We asked the boat to unload the weapons on the fourth around 11:00 P.M. at this point, which was located very near Alma-Maritime, 18½ miles from Algiers.

Everything went as planned; we lit the agreed-upon signal at 9:00 P.M. and we waited a second time for nothing.

Again we returned to Algiers. Murphy seemed genuinely upset and sent a new cable to Gibraltar. The next morning, November 5, he received the answer: the boat will unload the arms on the agreed-upon spot that very evening around 11:00 P.M. . . .

This time again the American weapons did not show up, and, as the Algerian resistants were soon to find out, this "snafu" was to be the first in a series of mix-ups, the worst of which were to occur at the very time of the landing.

According to the terms of the Cherchell agreement, the mission assigned to the Algiers Resistance consisted in paralyzing the main strategic points of the city and in neutralizing those military leaders apt to organize resistance to the American landing. This time we cite from José Aboulker's account:[7]

The time set for the beginning of our operation was 1:30 A.M.; we were to be replaced by Allied troops two hours later or at the worst by 7:00 P.M. . . . Forty-eight hours before the landing the resources at our disposal were the following: (a) troops: 750 to 800 civilians organized quite a while ago into perfectly compartmentalized groups by young reserve officers; (b) transportation: 30 civilian cars put at our disposal by Mr. Louis Lavaysse, who was also in charge of putting them into shape; they run on gasoline that will be provided by the American consulate; and (c) weapons: 900 old Lebel guns and 25,000 bullets taken from the secret caches the army had hidden from the armistice commissions and the Algiers groups had, at Colonel Jousse's request, stashed three weeks previously in Mr. Lavaysse's garage. . . .

Our two-pronged plan, military and civilian, consists in causing the breakdown of communication, arresting leaders apt to organize resistance, and occupying headquarters.

Speed is of the essence for this plan to be successful. To reach this objective we are making use of the following factor: Military plans for the defense of the coast against an enemy landing provide for the transport of troops to the point under attack and at the same time for the recruitment from the Légion and the S.O.L. of civilian volunteers called *volontaires de place* [volunteers of a garrisoned place] who will wear arm bands with the letters V.P. on them and be charged with the maintenance of order. The presence at our head of Colonel Jousse, who is a V.P. commander, will enable us to use the plan for the maintaining of order for our own ends. Our own volunteers, bearing the arm bands and led by their own group leaders in uniform will relieve the watch points and occupy strategic emplacements.

On D day there were close to four hundred young men who executed within the allotted time and with astonishing precision the plan devised a few days earlier by their leaders. However, there were fewer American troops than intimated by Clark and they entered the city only at the end of June 8. When they should have been making the connection with the "putschists" they were still four miles from Algiers.

We had thus blocked the city, not from midnight to 2:00 A.M. but from midnight to 6:00 P.M. We held the town while gradually abandoning our positions during the day because we had no reasons to kill people gratuitously. We knew that the Americans had landed, we were in contact with them, and we were wondering why they were so hesitant.[8]

In fact, from the start of the insurrection another political and military game was being played out, from which the resistants were totally excluded.[9] The deus ex machina of this game was Robert Murphy, who, on the occasion of his visit to General Juin to ask him to join the Allied cause, had found himself face to face with Darlan, the representative of "legitimate power," with whom he soon struck a cease-fire agreement.[10] This had been accomplished by the evening of the eighth when General Ryder entered Algiers with his meager troops. As to General Giraud who had been supposed to arrive at the same time as the Allied troops, he had gotten held up in Gibraltar by unproductive discussions with Eisenhower. When he reached Blida the next day, he had no other choice than to accept Darlan's authority, who "in the name of the marshal" controlled the cease-fires in Oran and in Morocco where General Noguès, constantly in contact with Laval and the German armistice commissions resisted the American "aggression" till November 11.[11]

The Algiers Resistance had been double-crossed by Murphy and Darlan. The Oran and the Moroccan Resistance did not even have time to organize and even less to put on one good fight for honor. They were warned too late of the Americans' arrival, and thus their leaders were powerless to act or, even worse, they skirted their commitments in the face of the defense apparatus set up against the invaders.

The North African resistants were undoubtedly the great losers of these November days. The daring and heroism they had so brilliantly showed in Algiers were matched only by the disappointment of the following days when they found out that the "new" leaders of the empire were none other than Darlan, Noguès, Châtel, and Boisson, who, under the Americans' benevolent gaze, were to draw the claim to legitimacy of their power from the wellspring of their loyalty to Pétain and Vichy.

Vichyst Africa under American Protection

Darlan's manipulative ability, Giraud's lack of political experience, and Murphy's duplicity by themselves do not provide enough of an explanation for this failure. The North African Resistance was an odd assortment of widely different elements. It brought together a few militants who had solely in common the will to liberate France from German occupation. The immense popularity enjoyed by the marshal and the particularly positive welcome given to the National Revolution in North Africa doomed the Resistance to isolation, to individual action, and to the most stringent compartmentalization. The only elements that gave it a broader popular base were its Jewish members. Thus, of the 377 militants who participated in the taking of Algiers, 315 were Jewish. However, in view of the deep-seated anti-Jewish atmosphere prevailing in North Africa, it would have taken much naïveté to believe, even for a single instant, that the people of Algiers would, on the morning of November 8, rise up and follow Dr. Aboulker and "his Bab el-Oued[12] gangs," as General Giraud subsequently was to put it (Giraud 1949:31).

The history of the Jewish Resistance in Algeria has already been written (Danan 1963; Ansky 1950). Scions of the high Jewish bourgeoisie of Algiers and Oran, its principal leaders — Henri and José Aboulker, Raphaël and Stéphane Aboulker, Dr. Morali-Daninos, Roger and Pierre Carcassonne, Bernard Karsenty, Guy Calvet, and Armand and Pierre Alexandre — had acted as, and only as, French patriots. Without any hesitation, these young Jews had allied themselves with the "Committee of Five" composed of Lemaigre-Dubreuil, Jean Rigault, Henri d'Astier de la Vigerie, Van Heycke, and Tarbé de Saint-Hardouin, who were as Vichyst as they were anti-German. This group presided over the political preparations for the insurrection. Three of its members stand out with particular sharpness: Lemaigre-Dubreuil, Jean Rigault, and Henri d'Astier de la Vigerie.

Lemaigre-Dubreuil was a wealthy industrialist, a former *cagoulard* and an antirepublican who had transferred his factories from France to North

Africa. He was to hope until the very last moment that the liberation of North Africa by the Americans would occur under the aegis of Vichy whose internal policies he greatly approved of:

> As a man of action, he seems to have adopted, immediately after the armistice, a very sharp stance against collaboration with Germany. . . . His many business interests provided an ideal cover for the contacts he was making between Vichy and Algiers by constantly visiting Pétain and Weygand. His innate taste for intrigue and secrecy, his widespread connections in America make of him the ideal intermediary in a web of negotiations of which one pole is in Algiers in the person of Robert Murphy and the other one at Vichy in the marshal's closest entourage. (Richard and de Sérigny 1947:44)

Jean Rigault was Lemaigre-Dubreuil's right-hand man. He was also a former *cagoulard:* "He has a Machiavellian personality, intelligent, soulless, cruel, frightening, and icy. Until November 8 he is the general secretary, the underground archivist, and is perhaps trustworthy. . . . But on the day after the landing, he reclaims his freedom of action and deliberately betrays all his former allies" (Aboulker 1952:66).

Henri d'Astier, who from March 1942 on became the central character of the Algiers Resistance, was an entirely different breed of man:

> He had been a *cagoulard*; this is rumored and he doesn't deny it. He has a strong liking for intrigue, an urge to throw rocks at windows, a sort of need to act on the margin, to recklessly spend his inner energy—which makes him a quixotic character completely out of place in our century. This very blue-blooded aristocrat is the enfant terrible of his family. He thinks on the right, of course, but he makes no bones about the fact that he is more royalist than monarchist. His personal temperament drives him toward dedicating himself more to a man than to an idea. (Gosset 1944:61)

D'Astier had arrived in Oran in 1941 as an officer for the Deuxième Bureau (Intelligence bureau). He met here Father Cordier, "a priest in which right away one discovered the intelligence officer, an officer who never allowed one to forget the priest" (Soustelle 1947:425). He also met Van Heycke who commanded the Chantiers de la Jeunesse (youth corps) and was turning this Vichyst institution into the base of a Resistance group, and Roger Carcassonne, a young Jewish industrialist from Oran who soon put him in contact with José Aboulker. In August 1942 d'Astier met another Jewish leader of the Resistance. Raphael Aboulker, who had organized in the Geo-Gras sports establishment a commando made up of several dozens of young Jews. Finally, it is through the intermediary of police Commissaire André Achiary, whose job enabled him to keep track of the various clandestine groups as well as to protect them, that Astier, at the start of 1942, became one of the "Group of Five," which itself became the top council of the North African Resistance and from which the Gaullist elements represented in Algiers by René Capitan, Louis Joxe, and René Moatti were kept out up to the eve of November 8. This exclusion was no accident and Jacques Soustelle was quite right in perceiving it as one of the consequences of the political orientation given to the movement by Lemaigre-Dubreuil and Rigault.

> Their hostility toward Germany was matched by their hostility toward Free France. A "Free Vichy" was not a Free France, the National Revolution freed from the Hitlerian shackles and protected by Washington—this is what they wished for and this is what they almost got. . . . The two active and intelligent men supported by the wealth and power of the United States had no difficulty in imposing themselves to the leadership of the Resistance. . . . D'Astier and Van Heycke along with Achiary, José Aboulker, and Carcassonne contributed their combat troops and their intelligence-gathering organizaton. Lemaigre and Rigault contributed their American contacts. (Soustelle 1947:431–32)

Like the exclusion of Gaullists and Communists, the Group of Five's support of Giraud was not due to chance either. Instead, they shared with the general the same hatred for the "boche,"[13] the same admiration for the marshal, and the same disgust for the republic and its democratic institutions.[14] Giraud, who claimed to have a thorough knowledge of North Africa, harbored set opinions on the Jewish question in this region:

> In North Africa, particularly in Algeria, the Jewish question is still in the news. The Moslem looks down at and despises the Jew but he cannot do without him. Moslems and Jews are natives who are divided by religion and exhibit all the heated fanaticism accompanying this sort of split. Both groups have the same origin, the same life-style, eat the same food—but one has always been dominant, the other a pariah. The first are agriculturalists, pastoralists, above all brawlers; the second are tradesmen, craftsmen, usurers.
> The first are always prodigal, the second patient lenders. Normally after a few decades all the wealth of the first has passed into the hands of the second unless some "pogrom" or some "free gift" has returned to the sons of the prodigal ones, part of what their fathers did not know

how to save. The role of the protective imperial power is specifically that of ensuring a balance as just as possible among all its subjects. (Giraud 1949:30–31)

Consequently, the state should absolutely refuse to reinstate the Crémieux decree (Giraud 1949:122–23):

> Vichy had repealed the Crémieux decree and I certainly had no desire to reinstate it, despite American pressure. I have very good Jewish friends in France. I had chosen a Jew, Mr. René Mayer, to be my minister of public works in Algiers. I have seldom come across a man of more integrity and more capable of doing his job despite the ordeal of the death of his beloved son who fell heroically for France. But I felt I knew North Africa better than those who had just landed. I argue then, and I still do now, that North African Jews must not be treated differently from Moslems. They are simply natives practicing a religion different from that of their neighbors, that's all.
>
> Of course, if these natives, Jews, or Moslems show by their intelligence, their education, their diplomas, by the services they have given that they are worthy of becoming French citizens, I am ready to grant them this citizenship if they give up their personal status.[15]

As a result, and to the great disappointment of the Jewish resistants, neither the Group of Five nor Giraud were in a position to resist Darlan. In the atmosphere of Pétainist piety prevailing on November 9 among African generals, the admiral feared the Algiers insurgents less than he did General Noguès, who had been the last to be appointed by the old man of Vichy and almost managed to take away Darlan's henceforth mythical "function" of the marshal's representative in North Africa.[16] Because the Americans—Eisenhower, Clark, and Murphy—were interested only in the strictly military aspects of the situation, Darlan was not to encounter any difficulty in maintaining the men, the spirit, and the form of Vichy's power.[17]

Darlan set up an Imperial Council whose members were Noguès, Bergeret, Châtel, and Giraud. Upon American request Giraud was also to be assigned the function of commander of the armed forces. Darlan, who became *haut-commissaire* (high commissioner), appointed Jean Rigault, Lemaigre-Dubreuil, Tarbé de Saint Hardouin, and Henri d'Astier to important positions such as the secretariat of the ministry of the interior and the management of the police department. He decreed a general mobilization in response to the Allies' request. Algerian Jews were called up just as European Jews were, but their "military service" consisted in being assigned to "pioneer" units that did earthwork in the Algiers area and agricultural work in the Constantine area.

The Americans finally began to worry at the appearance of the Algiers regime. In the face of more and more pointed criticism in the Allied press regarding the "Darlan deal," Roosevelt qualified the Algiers agreement as a "temporary expedient." On November 17 he explained: "The temporary arrangement has made it possible to avoid a "mopping up" period in Algeria and Morocco which might have taken a month or two to consummate. Such a period would have delayed the concentration for the attack from the west on Tunis. . . ." And he added: "I have requested the liberation of all persons in Northern Africa who had been imprisoned because they opposed the efforts of the Nazis to dominate the world and I have asked for the abrogation of all laws and decrees inspired by Nazi governments or Nazi ideologists" (*New York Times*, November 18, 1942:4).

It took a long time for the American president's requests to be satisfied. And the fact that was no less indicative of the situation was that, at the instigation of Darlan's office, the North African press printed only a truncated version of Roosevelt's declaration and this after a long delay. But because American diplomats in Algiers did not voice any objection to this, the prevailing impression in the *haut-commissaire*'s entourage was that the "temporary expedient" had good chances of becoming permanent. On November 23 the admiral went even so far as to deny "rumors" according to which "the American military authorities would have presented French authorities with demands having no bearing upon military needs."

A few days later, L. Boujard, *préfet* of Oran, circulated an "orientation note" intended for the under-*préfets* and the mayors of the department, which gives a clear indication of the state of mind prevailing in Algerian administrative milieus at that time.[18] After praising the department's population for consistently "drawing" its patriotism and loyalty "from the appeals and advice given by Marshal Pétain," the *préfet* proceeded to explain the circumstances of the "liberation" of Oran by the Allies:

> The army, loyal to its traditions of honor and entrusted with the defense of the integrity of the empire, has lived up to its promise of defending the territories entrusted to its care to the point of exhaustion. [Our men] were inferior in numbers and clearly dominated by the mechanized armaments opposing them — and we must point out that this was the fault of the Axis powers, which, because of mistrust or aggressive aims, had taken away from us all possibility of arming ourselves. The members of

Operation Torch and Its Consequences

the division of the French army only ceased fire to avoid fights that could not have changed the outcome of the battle and would have uselessly added to the casualties and the destruction of property. The civilian population, through its loyalty and courage, has with dignity confirmed the troops' attitude.

Then, the *préfet*, commenting on the hostile responses to the general mobilization decreed by the *haut-commissaire*, attributed as principal motivation for the discontent the argument positing that "this war can only benefit the Jews." He elaborated on this by noting that "it is necessary to emphasize the following two aspects: (1) the meaning of President Roosevelt's recent declaration that indicates that the United States is pursuing exclusively military aims rather than political ones in North Africa; (2) the implications of the specific measures of mobilization, particularly of the fact that Jews . . . are assigned to work groups."

Thus out of all of Vichy's legacy, the maintainence of anti-Jewish legislation was to become the most eloquent symbol of the Algiers regime's independence from the Allies and at the same time the best proof, the most telling sign, of its Pétainist legitimacy. Consequently, only a greater Allied intervention in North African internal affairs and only the disappearance of Vichyst institutions were to ensure the juridical rehabilitation of North African Jews. The murder of Darlan on December 24 and his American-imposed replacement by Giraud were to trigger this double process, which was, from spring 1943 on, to be completed by the gradual restoration of the republic and the taking of power by the Gaullists.

7

The Germans in Tunisia (November 1942 to May 1943)

Toward midday on November 9, a German air squadron commanded by Colonel Harlinghausen landed at the airport of al-Aouina, near Tunis. This arrival preceded by a few hours Hitler's order to the Werhmacht to establish a bridgehead in Tunisia to stop Allied progress toward the west and, if possible, even to repulse them out of Algeria and Morocco. The Americans and British were not in a good position to overtake the Germans, for they had been partly stymied by resistance encountered in Casablanca and in Oran. On the other hand, the French army stationed in the regency definitely had the capability of repulsing the first German-Italian units hurriedly sent over by sea and air. But the French army, its leaders following Vichy's orders and Darlan's instructions, did not fight. Even while Darlan was working out the last clauses of the cease-fire with Clark in Algiers, he requested of Résident-Général Estéva, of General Barré, commander in chief of land forces, and of Admiral Derrien, commander of the naval base of Bizerte, that they observe strict neutrality toward the Axis forces. However, on November 12, General Juin, the commander in chief of French forces in North Africa, ordered officers in Tunisia to oppose the Germans; but instead of defending Tunis, General Barré moved his troops toward the western part of the country where after much hesitation he finally sided with the Allies on November 19.[1] As to Admiral Derrien, he retreated passively into his Bizerte base until December 12, on which date he submitted to the German ultimatum to abandon his fleet and his sailors, who were immediately disarmed.

In fact, up to the first week of December, the situation of the Axis forces was precarious. On November 30 there were no more than eight thousand Italians and three thousand Germans in the regency. General

Nehring, the commander of these troops, himself had not much faith in the success of this expedition — which caused him to be replaced on December 8 by General von Arnim.[2]

The Allies tried to take Tunis twice, and on November 24 and 25 they came so close to succeeding that Rudolph Rahn, who had arrived ten days earlier as plenipotentiary minister, thought it wise to remove his staff and transmission equipment to Naples (Hirszowicz 1966:273). On November 27 American tanks reached Mateur and Djédaïda, close to Bizerte and Tunis, while in the south the Allies were advancing toward Kasserine and Gafsa from where they planned to try to cut off the junction point of General von Arnim's "bridgehead" and Marshal Rommel's army, which was retreating in Tripolitania. The Germans counterattacked and on December 8 the front was temporarily stabilized along the line Djebel Abiod-Béja — Medjez el-Bab — Pont du Fahs — Enfidaville — Kairouan — Faïd — Gabès, with two Allied bulkheads toward Kasserine and Gafsa.

Thus, barely one-third of the Tunisian territory was under German and Italian control. Even though the Axis forces did succeed during the next two months in consolidating their positions and even in enlarging their perimeter, these successes did not significantly change the picture: the German army that awaited the Allies' confrontation, though undoubtedly still threatening, was but a shadow of the once glorious Afrika Korps of the desert sands. It was pounded without respite by the American air force, it had to cope with inextricable supply problems, and was moreover pulled apart by internal disputes among its generals and between the generals and their Italian colleagues. It was an army whose morale had been shattered by the Libyan collapse, an army doomed to engage in rearguard fighting before definitely passing to the other side of the Mediterranean to try to rescue from catastrophe a breathless, desperate, and warweary Italian ally.

The Axis situation was no less complicated on the political plane. As they had done in France in the former unoccupied zone, the Germans continued to recognize French sovereignty in Tunisia and allowed the *résidence-générale* (resident's office) to remain in existence the same way they had tolerated the Pétain-Laval government at Vichy. This policy was little appreciated by the Italians whose territorial ambitions regarding the regency were notorious. However, despite their protests and despite the promises the Germans made to their partners during the conference held in Rome on January 2, 1943,[3] Rahn persisted till the end in refusing Italian consular representatives in Tunis any sort of privilege outside their usual function. He used the difficulties of the military situation as argument for rejecting any Italian initiative apt to annoy the French too much. This did not mean that the Reich's repesentative had the least bit of confidence in Admiral Estéva[4] and his administration. This was evidenced by Rahn organizing a parallel French administration made up of militants from the P.P.F., the S.O.L., and the Chantiers de la Jeunesse. These militants were formed into a Comité d'Unité d'Action Révolutionnaire (C.U.A.R.) (united committee for revolutionary action), which, under the leadership of Jacques Guilbaud, sent from France by Laval and Marion,[5] was to provide the Germans with collaborators, few in number but fanatical. With the help of his assistant Jean Scherb, Peyrouton's former press secretary, Guilbaud took control of the paper *Tunis-Journal* and gave its editorship to P. Marty and Claude Martin. He proceeded to purge the *résidence-générale* of any civil servant suspected of sympathizing with the Allies by sending them back to France.[6] The maintenance of public order was ensured by the local police reinforced with S.O.L. militants, who themselves were supervised by S.S. officers, surprisingly few in number.

The Germans did not harbor any illusion about the efficacy of this support force. The report sent by Rahn to Berlin on December 24, 1942, clearly shows evidence of the feeling of powerlessness that was gradually taking over the Axis forces:

> Propaganda activity in Tunis is constrained by the fact that the Axis forces are confined to a very limited space, not unlike being in a fortress, and that they are hindered by a mixed urban population of more than 400,000 inhabitants subjected to constant bombing raids and difficult to control. Consequently, the threat of a breakdown in supply lines and the risks of epidemics and looting are that much greater. The German high command is forced to rely on the cooperation of the French administration, and, as a result of the rise in the number of assaults by Arabs on European settlers, it is forced to reinforce the authority of French bayonets. The fact that we have created our own units, among which an Axis police, to overcome the administration's passive resistance does not change the situation.[7]

In addition, "control commissions" composed of Italian civilians, Moslems, and pro-Vichy French were established to ensure the working of passive defense and the working of the municipal services disrupted by the war. Rahn notes in his report: "The fact that Arabs have equal rights and even sometimes leadership positions in these committees should have a great propaganda effect in the Moslem world."

Indeed, of all the categories of the Tunisian population, Arabs were to be treated with the greatest solicitude by the Germans and the Italians.

Under the benevolent gaze of the Axis forces, Moncef Bey took advantage of the new conjuncture to impart a nationalist imprint on his cabinet while Bourguiba and the leaders of the nationalist neo-Destour party were freed from their Marseilles prison and repatriated to Tunisia. Moreover, the Germans authorized the publication of the Destourian organs *Ifriqiya al-Fatat* and *al-Shabab* and gave permission for the holding of a Destourian youth conference and for the organization of a Tunisian Red Crescent[8] whose core was composed of nationalists. These also held control over the programming of Radio Patrie, which started to broadcast from Tunisia in January.[9] However, despite these shows of sympathy and despite the advice of the mufti of Jerusalem, the Reich's representatives refused to take any measure that in any way could be interpreted as favoring Tunisia's independence. Obviously concerned with avoiding irritating the French and the Italians who both opposed independence, Germany's Arab policy found itself mired in its own contradictions and was thus unable to induce the Moslem population's massive and active support. As a result, only a few dozen Tunisians signed up with the Arab units of the Wehrmacht (Deutscharabische Lehrabteilung D.A.L.) and in the units of the Phalange Africaine organized locally by French officers under the aegis of the Germans.

As we shall see, the military weaknesses and the contradictions within German policy in Tunisia were not without consequences for the situation of Tunisian Jews during the six months of Nazi occupation.

Jews and Germans in Tunis: First Contacts

Evidently, the treatment in store for Tunisian Jews had very little similarity to the deadly treatment that European Jews suffered at the time of the Final Solution. This difference in treatment did not stem from ideological reasons of the sort, for instance, that might have classified Tunisian Jews as not belonging to the Jewish "race" that Hitler doomed to extermination; and neither can it be attributed to some sudden pangs of conscience on the part of the Germans. Instead, it was simply a matter of circumstances: Tunisia was separated by the sea from the Hitlerian empire and thus could not be connected with the usual means to the deadly infrastructure established in central and eastern Europe. Thus, in contrast with distant Salonika in Greece whose Jewish victims had been transported by rail to Auschwitz, Tunis could be connected to the continent only by plane or by ship—means both expensive and unsafe and to boot within Allied shooting range. The Germans still had the possibility of setting up extermination camps locally, but, supposing such a project had been planned it would have required more space, time, and much secrecy.

These three factors were to elude the Germans in Tunisia where the number of Wehrmacht troops was barely enough to hold off Allied attacks.

According to a scenario used many times in Europe, the Germans had planned on instigating anti-Jewish pogroms right after stabilizing their presence in Tunis. But, as Rahn was to explain in his report, "instigating the looting of Jewish shops, protests, and pogroms, etc. . . . will not be feasible until our troops have reached the Algerian border, at the very least."[10]

The military difficulties encountered by the Germans also explain why they waited till November 23 to "make contact" with the Jewish community. On that day they arrested Moïse Borgel, the community's president; his predecessor, Felix Samama; and the Finnish consul, Jacques Cittanuova, as well as the son-in-law and brother-in-law of the first two.[11] The news of the incarceration of the Jewish notables was immediately brought to Admiral Estéva, who lodged a protest with Rahn demanding the immediate release of Borgel and Cittanuova on the grounds that the arrests were breaking the terms of his agreement with the Germans by which police power was to remain in French hands. Estéva wrote to Rahn:

> You must admit that despite the awkward circumstances in which the Axis troops have been brought to establish their basis in Tunisia, the public order has never been disturbed. This is because the whole population, regardless of race or nationality, has confidence in its government. The harmony achieved thanks to this offers the best guarantee of tranquility for the German troops. This harmony would be seriously endangered if German intervention caused worry, fear, and resentment. . . . Regardless of the number and the power of German troops stationed in Tunisia, I do not think that their commandant would remain indifferent to the prospect of these disturbances. Therefore he has every reason to avoid following this path.[12]

Against all odds, the resident-general's intervention to which Sheikh al-Madina[13] 'Aziz al-Jalluli joined himself was to bear fruits. Borgel was set free on November 26 with the stipulation that he would report twice a day to the *Kommandantur* to the S.S. chief, Col. Walter Rauff. Three days later while the Allies were approaching the gates of Tunis, the Germans freed the other Jewish prisoners except the Finnish consul.

Estéva's protest, as much in itself as by its content, stymied the German plans,[14] which like a precise clockwork were affected by the smallest "grain of sand." But the step taken on the same day by the Italian ambassador to Berlin with the German ministry of foreign affairs had much greater effect. Referring to an earlier note addressed on September 2 by Ambassador Alfieri to Ribbentrop,[15] the Italian government requested that the racial measures contemplated by the Germans not be applied to Tunisian Jews holding Italian citizenship.[16] The Germans, it seems, were impressed by the firmness of the tone of the Italian request. Already the next morning, Under Secretary of State E. Woermann suggested to the Wehrmacht Supreme Command (O.K.W.) that it order General Nehring to take no measures against Jews who were Italian nationals without first notifying the Italian consul general in Tunis: "In case of disagreement with the latter, the military command would have to postpone the execution of these measures."[17] On December 4 Woermann more specifically requested the O.K.W. to give satisfaction to the Italians "as long as this did not interfere with military requirements."[18]

Nonetheless, the German leaders were annoyed by their allies' attitude regarding this matter. On January 13, 1943, it was Ribbentrop's turn to address this topic in a cable sent to his ambassador in Rome. After deploring that the Italians could regard Jews as worthy of representing their interests abroad, he agreed to do the Italians a "special favor" by delaying till March 31, 1943, the application of racial laws to Italian nationals living in territories under German control. He wrote his ambassador:

> I am asking you to point out the great threat posed by Jews wherever they are. This threat is even worse in zones that are politically important as well as in those of every level of military concern. Among the most dangerous Jews are those having some sort of economic influence. You can relate to the Italians examples from our own experience by pointing out that the Jewry in its totality is our greatest enemy and the most steadfast adversary of our cause. This holds as much for Italy as for Germany. That is why we will not agree to any exception. We regard Italian Jews as being Jews, and as such they will fall under the purview of our legislation.[19]

As an integral part of "international Judaism," Tunisian Jews were also held "responsible for the Anglo-American attack against North Africa"[20] and for "the presence of Jewish political commissars in the Anglo-American army."[21] Consequently, besides other forms of persecution, the Tunisian Jewish community was to be forced to pay as a fine large sums of money to compensate civilian victims of Allied bombing raids. A French radio announcer of Radio Tunis commented on this:

> Taking into account that the present war is clearly of Jewish origin and that, in particular, the invasion of North Africa is the work of the inter-

national Jewry leading the destinies of the Anglo-American people just as, for our misfortune, it led for so long the destiny of our own people, we can but note that the decision is logical and realistic.[22]

A purpose lurked behind this reasoning: arousing local public opinion against the Jews. But, if we are to judge by the results, neither the appeals of Radio Tunis nor the information campaigns organized by the Comité de Secours Immediat (C.O.S.I.) (committee for immediate relief), which was entrusted with "distributing" the indemnities paid by the Jews, were to have a significant effect on the European and Islamic population of the regency. We believe that this "failure," as much as the protests of French, beylical, and Italian official milieus, caused at least the mix-up of German plans in Tunisia and perhaps even were obstacles to their implantation.

The evolution of the military situation, which was mostly unfavorable to the Axis forces, was to enter into play in a similar manner as the factors noted above. The Germans were waiting for the front to be stabilized before dealing the first blows to the Jews of Tunis. On Sunday, December 6, Moïse Borgel and Grand Rabbi H. Bellaïche were summoned to the *Kommandantur* by Rauff who read them an order from General Nehring ordering the dissolution of the Jewish community administrative committee and the mobilization of Jewish workers for the service of the Axis forces.

A committee of nine presided by the grand rabbi was to be established on that very day and its first task was to furnish, the following morning, a list of two thousand Jews from which would be picked workers to be assigned to earthworks and trench digging. Rauff specified to his astounded audience that he thought four to five thousand workers might be enough and that the future committee would be in charge of their equipment, transportation, and supplies. Moreover, the recruits would have to wear a large, highly visible yellow star on the chest and the back "so that they could be recognized even from afar and shot in case of attempted escape." Finally, to cut short the protestations of the two Jewish leaders, Rauff threatened them with nabbing ten thousand Jews from the streets of Tunis if the committee did not fill the order before the assigned deadline, an order that moreover had been approved by the bey and the *résident-général*.[23]

The committee was easily put together even though there were few volunteers for membership. Besides the grand rabbi and his secretary, the Germans had requested that it include a person in charge of finances, one in charge of administration, an interpreter, a person in charge of health

The Germans in Tunisia

matters, one in charge of food supplies, another one for equipment, and one in charge of aid for workers' families. Each of the members of the staff had requisition rights on all Jewish persons and property and each could hire helpers as he saw fit.

This task done, the next step was to compile the list of the two thousand workers required for the following morning. This proved impossible; the community lacked a registry of its population and the city's offices were closed on Sunday. The only solution was to ask for more time from the Germans, and again Admiral Estéva was asked to intervene to that end:

> M. Borgel[24] goes hurriedly to the Resident's Offices accompanied by Dr. Moatti. They are received by the admiral's cabinet chief and then by Admiral Estéva himself. The latter admits having had conversations with Minister Rahn regarding forced labor; he did not, however, know that the measures were to be implemented so brutally and would require an effort that was not humanly possible. He advises our delegates to be resigned and compliant. For his part, he will try to obtain an extension of the deadline for turning in the lists. (Borgel 1944:39)

The new step undertaken by the *résident-général* succeeded. Rauff agreed to postpone the required completion of the lists for twenty-four hours; on the other hand, he demanded that the number of workers be raised to three thousand.

On Tuesday, December 8, the committee compiled a list of twenty-five hundred persons composed mainly of laborers and the unemployed.[25] To everyone's astonishment, Rauff demanded that two thousand workers equipped with shovels and pickaxes be produced the next day, Wednesday, at 8:00 A.M. He warned that terrible sanctions would be ordered for lack of compliance and that, if needed, the S.S. would seize ten thousand workers.

The new demand was impossible to meet in such a short time and, moreover, was putting the committee in the odious position of having to hand over its own brethren to the Germans. The *résident-général* and the bey were again beseeched to intervene to prevent the execution of this order or, if this were impossible, to promulgate a requisition decree that would free the Jewish community of this painful task. The admiral refused, explaining that the Germans had notified local authorities that from then on the Germans alone would control their own relations with the Jews.

"We are now facing the monster alone," Paul Ghez was to write in his diary (Ghez 1943:19). From then on, Ghez was to play a crucial role in organizing the recruitment process.

A DIFFICULT LIBERATION

On the eve of the fateful day of Wednesday, December 9, calls were made for volunteers but at the time set for the workers' arrival, only 128 men showed up instead of the two thousand that the committee had been supposed to bring together at the Foch Barracks and the junction of the road to Moghran. Colonel Rauff flew into a rage at the sight of this meager gathering. He forced all the men to kneel and announced they were to be shot that day. He proceeded to the Great Synagogue, which he had soldiers surround. The Germans entered the temple and grabbed everyone there; a similar scene took place at the Alliance Israélite school, whose entire staff was arrested. At the same time, dozens of other Jews were arrested in adjacent neighborhoods. They were all marched by the German soldiers to the Cheylus camp about forty miles from Tunis. The group included a young cripple who fell from exhaustion during the march. A German soldier cold-bloodedly killed him with a shot of his rifle.[26]

Early in the morning, Moïse Borgel and Paul Ghez had gone to the *Kommandantur* where they were received by an enraged Rauff just back from the Foch Barracks: "Traitors! Cowards! Jew dogs! Pigs! Your obstructions, your schemings at the Resident's Office are acts of sabotage against the German army. I have taken care of Jews in Poland and Russia. I'm going to show you how it's done!" (Borgel 1944:49)

After announcing that they were to be shot along with the grand rabbi, Rauff nonetheless let them go, probably because of Paul Ghez's assurance that the requested workers would be assembled (Ghez 1943: 20). While this was going on, the S.S. came to the community's main offices and arrested everyone there. They demanded a list of 100 notables, who were immediately imprisoned as hostages. Among them were some Italian nationals who were soon freed thanks to their consulate's intervention (Borgel 1944:61). Before leaving the committee's offices, the Germans seized its typewriters and a rug collection belonging to President Borgel.

Left alone to deal with the Germans, the leaders of the Tunisian Jewry had no other alternative than to comply. At Paul Ghez's initiative, they had announcements posted calling on all Jewish males eighteen to twenty-seven years of age to present themselves immediately to the Alliance school:

> German authorities are in possession of civil status lists so that any targeted individual who will not present himself on Thursday, December 10, 1942, before noon will be declared eligible on the spot, will be sought by the authorities, and will be subject to punishment.[27]

Thus was to begin the Tunisian Jews' odyssey under the German occupation. A similar fate awaited the communities of Sousse, Sfax, Gabès, and even Djerba. On a single day, the ninth, seventeen hundred workers, which included a number of children, old men, and sick, were led to the front and assigned work that was as arduous as it was dangerous.

The Testing of the Community's Organization

The committee created on December 8 at Rauff's order was a paler version of the European Judenrät. It was to act as intermediary between the Jewish population and the German army. In accordance with the Machiavellian procedure for the delegation of power perfected by the S.S., the committee, generally referred to as Comité de Recrutement de la Main-d'oeuvre juive (committee for the recruitment of Jewish labor) had absolute power over the community. It was in charge of every aspect of the workers recruitment process and was also taking care of their transportation, equipment, food supplies, and their pay.

Isolated and cut off from the rest of the population, the community was thus given a genuine autonomous government complete with its own services and a bureaucratic infrastructure that had never before existed and touched upon almost every aspect of social life. Rauff, *deus otiosis*, abstained from practically all direct contact with Jewish leaders, delegating this task from December 10 onto the lower officers, Captain (Haupsturmsführer) Zaewecke and Sergeant-Major (Hauptscharfürer) Pohl. A similar role was filled in Sfax by Obersharführer Best, who was the brother of the governor of Denmark, and by Sturnscharführer Jensen. Best was also in charge of the Sousse community, which also received from time to time Zaewecke's visit.

At first conceived as directed by the grand rabbi, the committee was in fact presided over by Moïse Borgel whose taking over of this function did not cause any response by the Germans despite the fact they had appointed the spiritual leader to lead this organization. M. Borgel, assisted by his son and his nephew Elie Nataf, who himself had been president of the community for four years, was in charge of all "official" dealings with the German, French, and beylical authorities. He was the one who twice a day received Zaewecke's and Pohl's orders, which he relayed to all the offices through his secretary-general, Roger Temmam. The president's office concerned itself especially with the hostages problem whose liberation ended up proceeding in gradual steps. On January 17 there was only one hostage left in jail. Most of them were to be assigned to participation in the committee's activities.

Next to the president's office, an Interpretation service was hard at work under the direction of Maximilian Trenner, which included a Jew of Polish origin, Norytch; another of German origin, Rousseau, whose real name was Ruhlmann and who ended up deported to Europe; and a fourth one, Dr. Beretvas, of Hungarian origin. Trenner greatly intrigued Tunisian Jews, both because of his personality and the circumstances of his appointment by the Germans.[28]

> This man who does occasionally make a show of subtlety is really a dreamer. He always comes up with a plan for the solution of the most intractable problems. He has even come up with one to end the war and, in all seriousness, he proposes to have himself sent to Geneva to convince the belligerent parties of the necessity of a cease-fire. He goes to the *Kommandantur* to talk about it with Zaewecke but doesn't succeed in convincing him. He talks about having an underground city built for our workers in Bizerte where they would be sheltered from the bombing raids and where there would be games, orchestras, etc. . . . Finally, he has his plan for after the liberation of Tunis. He proposes to employ the workers in a huge radio and radio parts factory of which he would be in charge as he is an electricity specialist. There will no funding—never mind, he suggests the community create a corporation for that purpose. . . . (Borgel 1944:78)

Without underestimating the importance of the president's office and the role played by Moïse Borgel, it is without a shadow of a doubt Paul Ghez's "Recruitment Service" that formed the core of the Tunis committee. Ghez was a lawyer and a war veteran; he left the memory of being an impulsive man with boundless energy. Much shaken by his wife's illness and her death, which occurred amid the German occupation, he nonetheless expressed the principles that guided him as follows: "Complaining and moaning would only aggravate the situation. We might be beat but we must not be slaves. It is only by clenching our teeth, by enduring the ordeal with dignity, that we can hope to overcome the spite and loosen the grip that crushes us" (Ghez 1943:36).

Paul Ghez, seconded by Victor Bismut and Guy Boccara, respectively a lawyer and a war veteran like him, streamlined the work of his office by subdividing it into four sections: (1) the Secretariat for Recruitment and Records in charge of compiling lists of "mobilizable" workers and of summoning the various age classes; (2) the "Quartering Office," which recorded every departure and return of the workers; (3) the Camp Tally and Inspection Office; and (4) the Summons and Searches Office, whose role was to flush out labor dodgers and camp escapees. This job was performed by Paul Bonan with the help of his own "raiders." This particularly unrewarding job caused a lot of angry commotion within the community and fanned the workers' families hostility against Ghez:

The Germans in Tunisia

We have decided to stand our ground and to not grant any favor to anyone. This rule of action, the only honest one in these circumstances, has made us the butt of very unpleasant complaints and resentment. I am hounded, followed to the recruitment office by people who just won't give up and show a regrettable lack of discernment. I give in to no one. The slightest weakness would be an act of cowardice and would weigh heavily on my conscience. We are making exceptions only for notorious political militants who run the risk of terrible reprisals in case of denunciation. We are making their names disappear or we are giving them certificates of unfitness. but for everyone else there must be fairness, even in oppression. I know that I have made enemies, but that's unavoidable! (Ghez 1943:42)

The workers, once recruited, had to undergo a medical examination aimed not only at determining their fitness for labor but also at uncovering contagious diseases whose potential presence near German soldiers the S.S. was particularly wary of. The health services directed by R. Faldini and by Drs. Sfez, Moatti and Beretvas (the latter also a medical interpreter) was in charge of this job. The services were divided into several sections[29] and were entrusted with the care of the camps' wounded and sick who were treated on the spot by Jewish doctors. The health services had the power to grant exemptions for health reasons and were thus prey to workers' recriminations, who felt unfairly treated, and to the Germans' suspicion, who, from time to time, came to double check its work.[30] From December 15 to April 20, the health services exempted 1,765 workers, but the Germans excused only 623 of them; the others were assigned to lighter work or declared fit for regular labor.[31]

The supply office was in charge of delivering food to the camps and of supplying the workers with clothing and tools. It was put in the charge of René Solal and sent its own employees to the camps to insure the delivery and distribution of food, the portions of which had been carefully determined by a special commission. After February 10 the Germans took over the responsibility for food supply. A fee of twenty-five francs per man per day had to be paid to the Werhmacht, which, in exchange, promised provided the workers with the same rations as its soldiers. However, this promise was never kept and the committee was forced to keep on with the shipments of food to the camps.[32]

The committee had also organized its own transportation service. This system, which was made up of vehicles in poor condition and often did not receive adequate allocations of gas, had to provide a liaison with the camps and transportation for the workers.

A DIFFICULT LIBERATION

Finally, to stop German requisitions and looting of all kinds of objects from Jewish homes, the community thought it advisable to create its own "office of requisition and furnishings." This office took upon itself the task of "prospecting" and of requisitioning the contents of Jewish homes and shops.

> We tried to proceed equitably with this task, one as unpleasant as all the others imposed by the German yoke, by spreading the sacrifice around. We tried to do this with as much tactfulness as possible toward those forced to see go, sometimes with a great deal of sadness and resentment, familiar objects or pieces of furniture difficult to replace. Our prospectors' instructions were to avoid hurting feelings, to let our brethren know how sorry we were, to spare people of modest means, to avoid taking things that might be indispensable for some but superfluous for others. Nonetheless, there were hurt feelings, complaints. Some became angry at the organization. . . . Perhaps our representatives were not always tactful enough, but in all fairness they were very much pressured by the flood of requests to be satisfied. (Borgel 1944:95)

To support the workers, pay the fines imposed by the Germans, and administer its services, the committee set up a finance commission whose principal members were Victor Cohen-Hadria, who had been president of the local bar association, Henry Ghez, and Guy Boccara. The commission's first move was to levy a tax on every member of the community.

> We did not tax those resources according to a rigid ratio. We took into account a multitude of factors to be able to treat differently a retired person living on limited means from a capitalist whose enterprise was in full activity, a Jew with a household at his charge, or one whose progress had been shattered by racial laws. (Borgel 1944:98)

This commission's work was closely controlled by the *Kommandantur*, which had to be given the payment list. The Germans also had at their disposal the declarations of property and cash holdings made by Jews during the 1941 census. In Sousse, they specifically brought this up when imposing huge fines on the local Jewish population.[33]

Moreover, to keep tab on the funds used by the various offices, the Tunis committee set up a spending commission, which reviewed each office's requests for funds and was entrusted to Isaac Smadja. A controller general of spending, Albert Nataf, was put in charge of approving all proposed disbursements by the treasurer, and he also had the task of following up on the use of all disbursed sums (Borgel 1944:100-3).

One can only be puzzled by the Tunis committee's investment of so much painstaking effort, under unusual circumstances and in such a short time, to set up an administrative apparatus that was remarkably efficient and well organized. As if they were ignorant of the Germans' sinister plans for the Jews who fell under their yoke, the community's leaders seemed to have faith in the virtues of a well-organized bureaucracy, a bureaucracy that was to put much serious thought in ascertaining the number of calories required per worker and the means to fight infections picked up in the camps, or, as they put it, "in limiting the damage." The best elements of Jewish society took part in this undertaking and, never before or since, did so many members of the Jewish elite participate so fully in the life of their community. This mobilization of everyone's energies probably can be explained by a deep feeling of Jewish solidarity, wiping out all distinctions of class and national origins in the face of a common danger. But one cannot help noticing that this hotbed of lawyers, doctors, financiers, and wealthy notables that the "recruitment committee" had become also served as refuge for "well-born" youth and wealthy individuals wishing to avoid camp labor. The opportunity the committee leaders had of "requisitioning" whomever they wanted had a lot to do with this development. While President Borgel surrounded himself with his son and his nephew, Paul Ghez made much use of his colleagues and friends such as Victor Bismut, Georges Krief, André Nataf, Arthur Athias, Paul Bonan, and Edmond Smadja, who were put in charge of major services, jobs that at any rate they performed efficaciously.

This class division between "recruiters" and "recruitees" is implicit in most of the workers' eyewitness accounts collected after the war. The resulting tension, fitting so well with the wishes of the S.S. to inflame internal hostility within the community, had very harmful consequences for the committee's relations with the Jewish population. As a sequel to denunciations, the Germans demanded on several occasions the mobilization of the "bourgeois' sons" or that of the committee's employees who had been spared forced labor by the men in charge. Paul Ghez, who was the butt of the hostility harbored by a part of the Jewish population toward the committee, gives an account of the following events:

> March 8. The denunciations are continuing. The S.S. arrived this morning, triumphantly brandishing a list of 150 Jews. These are the bourgeois who are not at work! You must bring them to us within three days. At first reading it appears that many of the names have been exempted by the German authorities. Others do not belong to the age classes called. Some have left Tunis. There is even a woman. There are few left who can be used.

A DIFFICULT LIBERATION

Summon them anyway!
We begin by deleting the names of the soldiers who have rejoined the army and of those convicted for political offenses who run the risk of serious reprisals. We will find for each a plausible excuse. The others are summoned.

March 9. Today the Germans are double-checking all the community's services. Informants have accused us of hiding many bourgeois' sons here. Each individual case is examined with irritating picayune. Most of our associates are unfit or too old. The others are indispensable specialists. At the transportation service there are drivers and loading clerks who are fit but their work is hard.

Finally, the S.S. takes away from us seven men who will be sent to Bizerte. The informants are satisfied.

These accusations were only one aspect of the strained relations between the Jewish population and its elite, relations that on several occasions turned into regular riots. Paul Ghez and his recruitment office were the main targets, and the pages of his diary are filled with incidents where he is heatedly yelled at by angry protesters demanding the mobilization of the "labor dodgers." Unbending and managing his office with an iron hand, Ghez was not the kind of man who would allow himself to be influenced by "this sort of griping." At one point, "totally discouraged," he did hand in his resignation but when faced with Borgel's fit of temper, whom he had asked to come to his own office, he changed his mind and continued in his functions of "prime minister" and strongman of the Jewish community till the German's departure.

Camp Life

Some five thousand Jews experienced forced labor and camp life. In an attempt at fairness, the committee recruited workers by age classes. During December, the four age classes of 1912 through 1915 were called. At the beginning of February, the class of 1911 was mobilized; during the second half of March, the classes of 1910 and 1909, and on April 21 the nine classes of 1900 through 1908. The total of those called at first sight amounted to several thousand, but after the fear of the first few days eased off, many individuals failed to respond to the mobilization orders. From January 15 on, the new recruits were called mostly to replace sick workers, those who had been haphazardly nabbed by the Germans, those on permission, and escapees. The number of escapees reached large proportions starting in February when they were able to take advantage of the disorganization of the German lines retreating from the Allied advance.

Forced labor was extended to the other Tunisian towns occupied by the Germans but did not, however, reach the same scope as in the capital. In Sfax the S.S. demanded that 100 men be permanently available to work at unloading military vehicles and at building shelters. The mobilized men were paid by the community, which called upon the poorer elements of the population "who wished to earn 100 francs per day."[34] A few weeks after their arrival in this town, the Germans wanted to lock up every fit man of the community into a camp, but in the face of the risk of epidemics the community's president judiciously pointed out, they gave up on this project.

In Sousse, all Jews eighteen to fifty years old were assigned to forced labor. The workers gathered each morning in front of the Ardant du Picq barracks from where they were led to the harbor to repair damage caused by Allied bombings. As in Sfax, the Germans had wanted to gather every Jew of Sousse and neighboring areas into a large concentration camp. To accomplish this, they demanded that G. Binhas, the community leader, provide the Germans within four days with a plan for the relocation of the Jewish population. Binhas was to explain later: "By the deadline, no plans had been drafted or proposed; this puts him [Best, the S.S. head] into an indescribable fit of rage. I pointed out that the interpreter had not translated this demand, which was at any rate not feasible.[35]

In retaliation, the Germans ordered all Jews six years and older to wear the yellow star. This order likewise was to have no effect.

The laborers from Tunis and the Tunis area were assigned to about thirty camps, some of which were under Italian control. These camps were located right next to the front lines and operated as long as the situation on the battlefields allowed. The camps under Italian control were Zaghouan, Enfidaville, Sainte-Marie-du-Zit, Saouaf, la Goulette, Djouggar, Mohammadia, Sbikha, Kondas, and Djelloula; those in the German sector were Bizerte, Sidi Ahmad, Bir M'Cherga, Goubellat, Cheylus, Monarghia, Djefna, Saf-Saf, Ksar-Tyr, Bordj Fredj, Mateur, Massicault, Katach-Baya, Rossignol, Aïn Zammit, Ma-Abiod, and Drija. In addition, some of the workers were led each morning to locations in the Tunis area and returned home at the end of the day.[36] These locations were al-Aouina, la Marsa, l'Ariana, Mornaga, Gammarth, Bir Kassa, Kassar Saïd, Djebel Djelloud, Durosville, and M'rira. Usually the workers were used to assist the Wehrmacht with auxiliary nonmilitary tasks such as repairing paths, digging trenches, and carrying ammunition.

Most of the camps lacked adequate shelters and were in isolated farms or simply in open fields.[37] Bizerte was the only one of these work sites that resembled a regular camp.

Bizerte was the crucial point in the Axis defense system in Tunisia and it was the target of intensive air raids by the Allied air force. The first group of workers arrived there on December 11. The Jewish population of this camp was housed in the Philibert barracks. It started out with about five hundred internees and eventally grew to include about one-fourth of all the workers recruited by the committee. Living conditions there were very precarious:

> The workers, sleeping on straw that was never changed, had fleas, other assorted parasites, and scabies as daily companions. Their unsuitable civilian clothing soon was in tatters and left them exposed to the wet cold and sometimes shivering barefoot under the rain. They were put to work outside the city at carrying ammunition and burrying it under trees. Others had to unload coal and cement from ships.[38]

The internees were divided into work groups "managed" by a Jewish staff that included group leaders, intepreters, doctors or nurses, and commissary clerks—whose attitude and behavior were not always above reproach.[39] The members of the Jewish "cadres" were excused from labor and they were appointed by the Germans or by the committee. They were in charge of assigning jobs and in the case of doctors, could, at least in theory, recommend the freeing of the sick or at least their being assigned lighter work. The laborers who had to endure physical and psychological trauma were often suspicious of their "leader's" decisions. Moreover, just like their families and relative back in Tunis, they had the strong impression that the "children of the rich" were favored both in the kinds of jobs they were assigned and in the distribution of certificates of illness. Dr. Younès was to note at the close of an inspection tour at Bizerte:

> The camp morale goes up or down from day to day. Young men with education and from well-to-do families are picked on by workers who have been less kindly treated by fate. . . and by packages from their families. On the day of the departure of the sick, the animosity of the poorer class is triggered by the sight of the departure of the sick workers, sons of well-to-do families. We must note that the greater proportion of the sick is found among the sons of rich families.[40]

The situation usually became explosive when the replacements for the sick workers promised by the recruitment committee were slow to show up, for fewer and fewer of the members of targeted age groups responded to the recruitment office's summons. One of the internees of the Philibert barracks wrote bitterly to Paul Ghez:

Let the Bizerte workers go out and look for these young men and you will see that they'll find them. How can one be aware without shame that workers have suffered for more than fifty days only one and a half hours from Tunis while young healthy fellows, known jocks, labor dodgers, cowards, walk around without the slightest embarrassment in the streets of Tunis. . . . (Ghez 1943:79–80)

Even while deploring that the author believed it necessary to complain also to the German authorities,[41] Ghez did nonetheless agree with his point and concluded that "only brute force, a manhunt," was the sole means, a "painful and repulsive one," that could alleviate this situation. However, without Ghez being directly responsible for this, the "manhunt" was to be pursued mostly in lower-class milieus that were already overly represented in the camps.[42]

The Wehrmacht and the Italian army were alone in charge of the camps where apparently the S.S. never showed up, their authority being limited to Tunis and the other urban centers. The German guards comprised Alsacians who were former members of the foreign legion. This was so in Bizerte where the guards put the internees through a grueling regimen. They had to work fourteen hours a day without break, they were severely punished for the slightest infraction, and were summarily executed for any escape attempt.[43]

The workers were treated differently in the Italian camps, for their guards were no more convinced of their usefulness than of the reality of the anti-Semite beliefs that caused Tunisian Jews to be treated in such an unfortunate manner. However, even in some German camps German-Jewish relations ended up relaxing somewhat.[44] The bombing raids eventually demoralized the German jail keepers as much as they did the prisoners, and the keepers adhered less and less to the norms of "Hitlerian conduct" as the prospective defeat of the Tunisian units became more obvious. In Bizerte and elsewhere, more and more German guards "sold" decent treatment to the Jewish prisoners by extorting money and jewels from them.[45] Very much aware of the low morale of the occupation troops, the committee's "ants," in particular H. Sfez, A. Bonan, J. Taïeb, R. Chemla, and S. Baranès, took action to "very cleverly make escapes easier, enable the liberation of dozens of sich internees and of people who had been nabbed by the S.S., and improve work conditions," and even managed to have some camps relocated:

> Well provided with ammunition, in this case liqueurs, cologne, silk stockings, and other trinkets, they are the traveling salesmen who follow the

troops in the field. Like peddlers in whose wares one discovers rare, unheard-of objects, they are juggling, at times conjuring. . . . At each visit they leave behind a few bottles for the officers and the soldiers who accept them gracefully and they depart with many sick men to take home and . . . to replace. (Borgel 1944:112–13)

Sfez's and his comrades' activities, added to the slow disintegration of German and Italian defense lines, had the effect of emptying the camps of their Jewish internees several weeks before the Germans' definitive departure. On January 19 more than one-third of the workers were free; in that same month, the number of escapees from Bizerte was more than 200; toward mid-February this camp's population was reduced to 600 as a result of massive escapes while the total number of mobilized Jewish workers was down to 2,500 (Ghez 1943:97–98). At the end of March, the number of workers in the Italian sector went from 930 to 160 and by the end of April there were no more than 1,556 Jewish workers under German orders: only 1,198 assigned to the daily work sites of Tunis and its surroundings and only 358 in all the camps of the province including Bizerte (Ghez 1943:247).

On several occasions, German authorities tried to take the situation back in hand by sending patrols to Tunis to look for escapees. However, the feeling of powerlessness eventually affected even the S.S. officers Zaewecke and Pohl, whose threats did not succeed in stemming the tide of escapees nor in adding to the number of mobilized workers. The only thing they were able to do was to inflict in mid-February a fine of three million to the committee on the grounds of "faulty performance" in recruitment matters (Ghez 1943:99–100). Similar fines were also imposed on the Jews of Sousse, Sfax, Gabès, and Djerba.

The official purpose of the first sums extorted from the Jews had been the compensation of the civilian victims of the Allied bombing raids, but the new measures had as sole aim the satisfying of the looting impulses of an army in disintegration and prey to insurmountable supply problems. Both in Tunis and Sousse, German soldiers daily demanded a variety of objects: furniture, blankets, towels, watches, linen, suitcases, radios, typewriters. Binhas was to recall later: "At the time their retreat from Sousse was announced, the Gestapo officers . . . were still making urgent demands, backed by the usual threats, for jewelry for themselves and their families. They refused a first delivery as unsuitable but they kept it to ensure the second delivery; when the latter was made, they kept everything."[46]

On February 13 it was the turn of the Jews of Djerba to be forced to pay a fine of ten million francs. Foreseeing that their grip on the island was to be short-lived, the Germans gave the community's leaders only two hours to pay this sum, but because the Djerbian Jews had no cash the Germans condescended to accept 100 pounds of gold as substitute:

> Even though it was Saturday, a holy day of rest for such a pious community as that of Djerba, the grand rabbi and the Jewish leaders made a car tour of the towns [Hara Kbira and Hara Sghira] to collect this gold. Short of time, they were forced to address themselves to poor families, the only ones who had remained in these towns, the better-off families having been able to spread out in the small properties they owned in the countryside. And thus, modest objects, laden with family memories and sentimental value, were turned over to the Germans. Their weight that day came to eighty-six pounds.[47]

Temporarily satisfied, the Germans gave the Jews till the next day to deliver the balance, but they were never to return to Djerba to collect.

On March 27, on the eve of their departure from Gabès, the Germans had the banks open their safes and Jewish deposits turned over to them. Their loot came to 400,000 francs.[48]

Besides these official acts of extortion, there was much individual looting some of which was harshly punished by the German chief of staff,[49] who evidenced the great slackening of discipline within the German army a few weeks before the Allied arrival in Tunis. Consequently, the committee had no trouble getting the S.S. to forbid access of the *Hara* (Jewish ghetto) to German soldiers, who, led by Arab and European hoodlums, went there to extort money and food from the Jewish inhabitants. The Hara was declared an epidemic zone and, from mid-January on, military police patrols were positioned in it to arrest the drunken soldiers who wandered around the neighborhood (Trenner n.d.:69–70).

The committee's interpreters, who had daily contact with the occupation forces, soon noticed the extent of the distress spreading among the German troops. While S.S. officers were requesting their recall to Berlin, as for instance Pohl did to get medical treatment for a sudden stomach ailment, the rank-and-file soldiers without a qualm tuned into B.B.C. broadcasts. They were informed of these broadcasts by the interpreter Norytch; he had to hand over to them the radios from the stock taken from the Jews. Maximilien Trenner, who did not shun exaggeration, was to report:

> In this manner, Jewish radios brought their anti-Hitlerian "poison" into the most inaccessible Nazi ranks and have considerably contributed to

the Allied victory in the Tunisian region. . . . Those Germans with non-combat jobs . . . such as those in charge of supply depots and ammunition transport, . . . were the first to abandon their positions on the front line thus creating an incredible chaos. . . . This was in great part the work of the radios stolen from the Jews and of a little Pole who had accounts to settle with the Germans. (Trenner n.d.:69-70)

Tunisian Public Opinion and the Fate of the Jews
The attitude of the Tunisian population toward the Jews during the six months of German-Italian occupation was basically one of indifference with occasional gestures of friendship or, inversely, acts of hostility.

The administration, expressing neither surprise nor indignation, matter of factly accepted that a part of its subjects became "German property" after it itself had isolated them from the rest of the population by locking them into the web of Vichy's racial legislation. It is true that Admiral Estéva and Moncef Bey did intervene on various occasions to save one or another Jewish personality from the German's grip or to obtain the delay of one German measure or another. However, these interventions were inconsistent and of a limited scope; they were more motivated by the desire to maintain public order and the prerogative of sovereignty than by a consious will to protect the Jewish community from the treatment meted out by the Germans.

The *résident-général* relinquished the firmness of tone that had characterized his first stance favorable toward the Jews and locked himself into an attitude of icy neutrality. On December 14 he reproached M. Borgel and P. Ghez, who had come to ask him to try to have the recruiting of Jewish workers delayed for their lack of docility and submissiveness toward the Germans. He accepted his own powerlessness as a dictate of fate and believed that the "heavy burden" he carried was the proof that God had elected him to "expiate the sins" of others. Thus the best advice he felt he could give his Jewish interlocutors was to fulfill their mission "to the end" and to thank the Almighty (Ghez 1943:33-34).

Nonetheless, thanks to Admiral Estéva's help, the Jewish communities of Tunis, Sfax, and Sousse were able to pay the huge fines imposed by the Germans. In view of the very little time allowed for these payments to be made, it was impossible for the Tunisian Jews to get hold of the required funds without the help of the administration. Thus in Tunis, the *résident-général* requested of the Caisse Foncière (state-controlled savings and loans bank) to lend the community a mortgage loan of twenty million to be disbursed before the deadline set by Colonel Rauff. The Resident's Office gave the following instructions to the Caisse Foncière: "As soon as

The Germans in Tunisia

the agreement is signed by the borrowers, a check will have to be delivered immediately without waiting for the signatures to be notarized or for the act to be registered or for it to be inscribed in the property register" (cited in Borgel 1944:140).

More or less similar types of banking operations were undertaken in Sfax, whose Jewish community was imposed a fine of fifteen million on March 26 and another one of twenty million at the beginning of April.[50] Somewhat less unlucky, the Sousse community was at mid-March hit with a fine of fifteen million to be paid within the "unusual" deadline of eight days. Binhas was to testify that "[this fine] had been imposed on us under the threat of bloody reprisals. It appeared that the threats were serious because when I went to the Résidence Générale to explain our situation, we were advised to defer to German demands both for the tranquility and safety of the Jewish community and for the general interest of Tunisia."[51]

On March 17 Colonel Rauff requested the police *préfet* of Tunisia to force the Jews of the country to wear the yellow star. This request caused much turmoil at the Resident's Office, which, among other considerations, did not appreciate the fact that only the Jews who were French or Tunisian nationals, rather than Italian nationals, had to wear the distinctive sign.[52] The legal adviser to the Tunisian government came to the conclusion that the bey "would look upon this as a measure taken against his subjects' nationality rather than their race."[53]

In addition, French official milieus worried that such a measure would cause unrest that could be made use of by Moslem nationalist elements. Those "who already have the tendency to sow discord within the country would find in the proposed measure one more pretext to worsen the state of confusion."[54]

At any rate, a juridical text ended up by being written. It used as legal basis the beylical decree of March 12, 1942, which had defined the Jewish status:

> On all territory of the regency, every person of either gender who is defined as a Jew according to the terms of article 2 of the decree of March 12, 1942, shall, from the age of eighteen on, be required to wear a yellow emblem in the shape of a six-pointed star. This emblem shall be made of lemon-yellow cloth and shall have a width of five centimeters. All its points shall be solidly sewn, the way insignia are on clothing, on the left side of the chest and be perfectly visible.[55]

Only two weeks were allowed for the making of the insignias. But by that date the Germans had more pressing concerns than the enforcement of the wearing of the yellow star: the "Mareth line" had just been broken by the Allies, who from March 20 to April 14 repulsed the Axis forces out of Sfax, Sousse, and Enfidaville.[56]

French and beylical authorities intervened from time to time to have certain Jewish individuals excused from forced labor. Generally, their requests were addressed to the recruitment committee rather than to the Germans and, more often than not, they were on behalf of personalities connected with the bey's entourage or the Resident's Office through business or friendship. However, on two occasions, public authorities became concerned with the fate of two well-defined social groups, war veteran civil servants and pharmacists.

The first group was the object of the concern of the secretary general of the Tunisian government, who in a letter to President Borgel expressed the wish that these civil servants would be "the last ones" called because "the question arises" whether they are actually Jews according to the terms of the March 12, 1942, decree.[57] As for the pharmacists, their mobilization would have caused the closing of all the pharmacies of Tunis, for almost all the pharmacists were Italian or Jewish.[58]

Despite all this, when, on January 4, the Germans requested the Resident's Office provide them with a group of eight thousand Tunisian workers, it found it normal to "hand down" the German request to the Jewish committee, which thus found itself faced with the order to recruit three thousand additional workers besides those it had already mobilized under direct German orders. The attitude of the French authorities provoked the indignation of the Jewish leaders who, through one of fate's ironies, had to call upon Commandant Zaewecke's help. "He himself seemed surprised and a bit shocked," wrote Robert Borgel. 'The Jews are his and no one else's.' thus we did not hear any more of this request" (Borgel 1944:152).

Besides the "official" administration that basically collaborated with the Germans more out of inertia and powerlessness than out of conviction, there was the C.U.A.R. and the militants of the P.P.F. and the S.O.L. whose anti-Jewish zeal almost outdid that of the S.S. Alone, or along with German soldiers, they "raided" Jewish streets. Under the threat of their guns, they cleaned out the stocks of stores, extorted money, and expulsed dozens of Jewish families from their homes.[59]

But their most odious act was the arrest and the denunciation to the Germans of about twenty militant Socialists and Jewish and non-Jewish members of the Resistance. They were sent to the camps of Sachsenhausen, Dachau, Auschwitz, and Orienenburg and some of them, namely, Gilbert Chemla, Joseph Chemla, Victor Cohen-Hadria, Edouard Dana, and Edouard Nataf, were never to come back.[60]

The Germans in Tunisia

As to the attitude of the Moslem population, the more or less avowed Germanophilia of its politically active class almost never, it seems, turned into active anti-Semitism. The outcome was similarly negative when it came to the results of the incitement by French extremist movements to anti-Semitic hatred, the Arab language broadcasts on the German radio, and the rabidly anti-Jewish articles in the Paris paper *El-Rachid*.

El-Rachid was started in January 1943 by the Comité Musulman de l'Afrique du Nord (C.M.A.N.), which was itself a German-sponsored organization. The paper's moving force was the Algerian Mohammad el-Maadi,[61] and in every issue it lambasted "Giraldistes" and "Gaullards" [62] as well as the "Judeo-Anglo-American" hegemony against which it advocated the alliance of the Arabo-Berbers with the "New Europe." *El-Rachid*, steeped in Nazi ideology, maintained that North Africa had a "Moslem-Jewish problem" of the same nature as the "Aryan-Jewish problem" in Europe and that the solution of one problem would bring about that of the other:

> There as elsewhere, in one way or another . . . the Jews tend to ensure their supremacy by imposing a liberal-democratic system that weakens the feeling of nationality and race in the people and allows the Jews to become the undisputed masters over persons and wealth thanks to their undeniable abilities for plunder, theft, and scheming. The Moslems, following the example of Europe, which has thrown the Jews overboard, must, as they have done in the past, relegate the Jews to their *mellah*. There is no other solution for the welfare of the Arabo-Berber people. . . . The Moslems of North Africa are faced with a long-term project requiring systematic preparations. If they really want it, they will be capable of great things. It is desirable that they work in concert with European [German] troops to succeed in this project. (*El-Rachid*, March 20, 1943)

If we are to judge this propaganda by its local effect, the results in the urban areas where almost all Tunisian Jews lived were meager. The hazings, the insults, and the attacks reported by witnesses[63] usually took place in the countryside and were the work of "hoodlums," of peasants who evidently were not able to grasp the implications of the propaganda themes expounded by *El-Rachid* and its Paris and Berlin confederates, nor to understand the posters and the radio broadcasts of the C.O.S.I.

When on April 10 the obligation to do forced labor was extended to the whole population, there were very few Tunisians who still believed in the idyllic picture of the country's situation and of German-Tunisian relations that the pro-Nazis tried to paint.[64] Tunisian press organs, aware of this measure's negative effect on the population's frame of mind, tried to explain how it was different from the forced labor imposed on the Jews. In the May 4 issue of *Tunis-Journal*, it was pointed out:

> The call to the young men of Tunisia to do obligatory work service has been enacted by the admiral *Résident-Général*. It is a measure that is already in existence in France and for which Tunisia at war has an urgent need. . . . It is the only opportunity that circumstances have given us to satisfy our desire to serve—in the noblest meaning of this term. . . . In contrast, what are Jewish labor camps? Well, they are nothing but heaps of individuals, members of a sorry race, human material retrieved by the Occupation authorities. This material is good for any unloading and carrying chore, for scraping and raking barracks and stables. Jews are dirty-job peons in the use of the expeditionary forces. (*Tunis-Journal* May 4, 1943)

This was one week before the Allied troops' arrival and much more convincing arguments would have been needed to give new life and confidence to the last holdouts of collaboration.

As for the Axis soldiers, they were forced during the following days to free the last Jewish workers whom they had forcibly taken along in their desperate run to the shoreline.

Their time having run out, the Germans were not able to carry out their plans to deport the president of the Jewish Committee as well as other community notables. A few days earlier, Moïse Borgel had been warned of his impending arrest by a highly placed Moslem personality who offered him shelter in a secluded house in the city's Arab neighborhood.

On May 7, early in the afternoon, the Allies liberated Tunis and Bizerte. Six days later, the campaign of Tunisia came to a close.

8

The Jews of North Africa from Darlan to Giraud

The Jews of Algeria and Morocco after the Allied Landing

The Jewish Affairs Office (Service des Questions Juives) was maintained in Algiers till the beginning of March 1943. This, more than anything else, evidenced the disquieting continuity of Vichy legislation in the Maghreb. The circumstances in which the Jewish Affairs Office was eliminated are in themselves pregnant with meaning. Giraud's decision was not motivated by the wish to break from the past but was a result of the turmoil caused in Anglo-American milieus by the Jewish Affairs Office publishing the texts of two laws promulgated by Vichy three weeks before the landing; the authorities had so far neglected to make the two laws applicable to Algeria.[1]

The higher-ups in the Algerian administration sensed that the wind was turning and took pains to contact the Jewish community's leaders as early as November 9. From Yves Châtel, the governor-general, to R. Franceschini, the director of the Office of Economic Aryanization, they did their best to convince their interlocutors that they had taken in the past two years "certain measures that have painfully affected the Jews" because "it was not really possible to do otherwise." Châtel, who felt the most insecure, even claimed to be ready "to show some of his files" to Grand Rabbi Eisenbeth to prove his own good intentions. "If I had followed Darquier de Pellepoix's instructions, who secretly came to Algiers, you Jews would not be around anymore," he told him (Eisenbeth 1945:64).

As to Franceschini, he worried that dispossessed Jews would take advantage of the unsettled situation and try to take back their property by force.[2]

The atmosphere of the meetings between the leaders of the Algerian

Jewry and the authorities completely turned about during the days after the Darlan regime managed to consolidate itself. The Jews were advised "to express their joy less noisily" and to show less "insolence" (Eisenbeth 1945:64). In the meanwhile, the first arrests were made from among the resistants of the Geo-Gras sport center (Aboulker 1952:224), and in the towns of the interior, officers of the Légion and S.O.L. militants were intensifying their anti-Jewish provocations.

In the wake of Roosevelt's declaration, Algerian authorities did, however, show some intent to soften the effect of racial laws, but only on an individual basis. For instance, using as a pretext the mobilization of a few temporary trustees of confiscated Jewish property, public authorities consented to return the properties they had been administering to their former owners. A similar process was at play in the civil service where some former Jewish civil servants were rehired but only as assistants and temporarily. In the face of the grand rabbi's protests, who ceaselessly demanded the straightforward repeal of all the anti-Jewish measures imposed by "foreigners," Yves Châtel explained that "neither the Americans nor the Moslems would look kindly upon the immediate abolition of the Jewish Statute, the first because they do not want to be thought of as meddling in internal French affairs, the second because they do not wish Algerian Jews to become French citizens again" (Eisenbeth 1945:65). This second argument was to become the core of the antiabolitionist discourse of the last Algerian Vichyst holdouts.

It was then that general mobilization was proclaimed. In conformity with Vichy legislation Darlan and Giraud refused to mobilize the Jews. Instead, they conceived of assigning them to pioneer companies "that were in nature halfway between disciplinary regiments and concentration camps minus ill treatments" (Aboulker 1952:221). As several "internal memos" were to make clear, this measure was taken to prevent Jews from acquiring the status of war veterans, which would have made it easier for them to acquire French citizenship. However, Jews who were members of the reserve were allowed to volunteer but only "under the status of natives" in some fighting units such as the Corps Francs and other colonial outfits where "their use would not cause any harm." Jewish officers and noncommissioned officers could only be reintegrated with the armed forces if they fulfilled the following two conditions: either wounded or cited during combat and favorably reported on by their immediate superiors.[3]

Recruitment centers for Jewish pioneers were set up in each department: Cheraga in the Algiers department, Bedeau in that of Oran, and El-Guerra in that of Constantine. More often than not, the men in charge were former legionnaires of German origin or former S.O.L. section leaders who openly vented their anti-Semitism and made the pioneers endure the same treatment the guards had previously inflicted upon the Jewish workers interned at Bedeau. And thus thousands of Jewish reservists found themselves breaking stones or felling trees rather than engaged in military or military-related activities. They officially did have the opportunity to volunteer in fighting units, but the conditions for volunteering were so vague and the military authorities so reluctant to encourage the integration of the Jews in the regular armed forces that the choice for a long time remained theoretical for all intents and purposes.[4]

With this set-up, Algerian authorities were aiming at the realization of a dual purpose: on the one hand, to perpetuate within the armed forces the racial segregation established by Vichy and, on the other, to represent the Jews as incapable of fighting arms in hand—which fitted in perfectly with the image of the Jewish soldier as a perpetual dodger, an image the anti-Semites had always held.

In these circumstances, the abolition of pioneers corps was to become one of the main themes of the Algerian Jewry's campaign aimed at reinstating the rights of the community. This campaign had been launched by the grand rabbi immediately after the Allied landing and was taken over by the Comité juif Algérien d'Etudes Sociales (social studies committee), which had been inactive since the 1940 armistice and became the sole representative organ of the Algerian Jewry on the basis of an agreement entered into by the Jewish leaders of the three departments. On November 27 its presidency was entrusted to Dr. Henri Aboulker who had played an important role in the preparations of the November 8 "putsch" and whose home, located at 26 Michelet Street, had been used as headquarters by the Algerian Resistance. Adding a distinguished military record to this "pedigree," Dr. Aboulker had been one of the few Jewish doctors to be allowed to continue practicing during the Vichy regime. Consequently, he allowed himself to take a very firm tone in his dealings with public authorities. This is certainly evidenced in the following excerpts from two letters addressed in December respectively to Admiral Darlan and to General Giraud. To the high commissioner he wrote:

> What we were hoping from you was a few lines wiping out the texts of the laws of deprivation and hatred decreed against French citizens of the Jewish religion. What we were hoping from you was an appeal that would ease burdened French consciences. But nothing has been forthcoming except, first, the new provocations to anti-Semitic hatred evidenced in the appeals "to Christians and Moslems" from Governor Châtel

and yourself. And then has come the military law of direct Hitlerian inspiration, and this is the most grievous offense.[5]

The letter he sent to General Giraud on December 24 was no less vehement:

> Today, in a French North Africa that is free again, when Frenchmen are called to battle against Germany, those of Jewish origin are penned into laboring groups . . . just like in Hitlerian lands. You have taken responsibility for a shocking gesture harmful to national defense because it eliminates soldiers who have magnificently served on the field of battle. (Ansky 1950:235-36)

However, Dr. Aboulker was soon to pay dearly for these comments. On December 28, four days after Darlan's assassination, he was arrested along with his son José and most of the other Jewish and non-Jewish leaders of the November 8 movement; among those arrested were Raphaël Aboulker, Armand and Pierre Alexandre, René and Emile Moatti, Fernand Morali, André Temime, and police *commissaire* Achiary. The gendarmes who came to arrest them had been instructed to shoot at the slightest show of resistance (Gosset 1944:272-73) but luckily none of them decided to make any trouble. They were then led to the Maison-Carrée prison and from there they were sent to Laghouat in the south. The plan was to take them from Laghouat to Attar on the edge of the Moroccan desert: "There, there are so many stray bullets, so many wandering scorpions, so many nomads going around raiding and killing haphazardly that it would have been easy to have to deplore soon a few premature deaths"(Aboulker 1952:255).

In the meanwhile, Bernard Karsenty who had barely escaped the gendarmes, and Dr. Aboulker's daughter, who had witnessed her father's arrest, informed the American delegation of these happenings. Despite Murphy's equivocal attitude, the officers of the Psychological Warfare Division immediately intervened and had the police car carrying Pierre Alexandre and René Moatti stopped at Blida. The news soon broke out and it became the object of sharp criticism in the Allied press. This forced Rigault, Châtel, and Bergeret[6] to reconsider their original plan and to keep the prisoners in Laghouat.[7] Finally, Dr. Aboulker remained in prison five weeks, during which time he was replaced by Prof. Robert Brunschvig at the helm of the Social Studies Committee.

Following General Giraud's appointment to the position of high commissioner, the Jewish population was faced with one disappointment after another. The Vichyst administration, which had been maintained by Darlan, was kept in place almost in its entirety by Giraud with the notable exception of Châtel who lost the governorship but only to be replaced by Marcel Peyrouton, the very man who had signed the first anti-Jewish texts of October 1940. Moreover, Giraud granted amnesties on the occasion of his coming into power that favored several Fascist militants who had been arrested after the Allied landing.

For instance, in Blida, the president of the local Action Française, who was also a leader in the Légion des Combattants, was released, while in Oran, the warships that had fought against the Allies during the landing were given a citation. In contrast, there was no official ceremony for the two resistants, Captain Pillafort and Lieutenant Dreyfus, killed during the "taking" of Algiers.

In Morocco, the Americans had entered Casablanca on November 11, 1942, after three days of intense fighting against General Noguès's troops. the Jews had all the more reasons to rejoice because the local section of the P.P.F. had openly been making preparations for a pogrom against the *mellah*. They had set November 15, the day of the swearing-in of the S.O.L., as the date for this attack. Anti-Jewish posters covered the walls of major cities and on November 8, the *Vigie Marocaine* published the first of a series of rabidly anti-Semitic articles that were to prepare public opinion for the projected November 15 events.[8]

We can thus well understand the great relief experienced by the Jewish population upon reading copies of President Roosevelt's message dropped by the thousands over Casablanca by Allied planes during the first few hours of the landing: "We have come to free you from the conquerors, who only want to deprive you forever of your right to independence, your right to freedom of religion, your right to pursue your own life-style without interference."

But in Casablanca, as in Algiers, the time for disappointment came all too soon. Noguès, who was located at a relatively safe distance from the perusal of Allied journalists and who enjoyed General Patton's full support (Murphy 1964:151–53), continued to rule over his Moroccan "fief" just as he had done under Vichy and, for a long time after November 11, kept in close contact with Laval through the intermediary of Spanish intelligence services (Gosset 1944:335–37).

Thus there were no changes within the ranks of the administration and in the staff of the press organs that continued to attack Jews, Gaullists, and supporters of the Allies as if the Americans were a thousand miles from the country. Encouraged by the public authorities' attitude, the S.O.L. and the Légion des Combattants undertook a "punitive action" against the Jews of Casablanca only a few moments after the first parade of American troops in the city. The *mellah* was invaded, an synagogue desecrated, and several people were physically assaulted and robbed.[9] Similar types of troubles took place during the following days in several other cities of the kingdom with the active participation of agents of the state, policemen, European soldiers, Moslem *goumiers*, as well as native elements. German propaganda broadcasts aimed at Morocco, which had been intensified after November 8, and the incitements to hatred of the slogans generated by extremist European groupings[10] were not the only factors at play in the new attitude of the Moslem population, which, up to then, had showed much restraint in their behavior toward the Jews. Without meaning to underestimate the aggravating effect of these factors on Jewish-Moslem relations, it is clear that these relations were directly connected to the atmosphere of confusion that settled over Morocco on November 12. Just as had taken place after the 1940 armistice, this new encounter with the unknown brought long buried ethnic tensions to the fore. The Jew, whether seen as a French or as an American "agent," remained the catalyst for all the frustrations of a hated past and the designated target for the disappointment of the present whose nature was both unwanted and unclear.

As well, the official character of the anti-Jewish riots and acts was striking. More than one Jew was arrested and thrown in jail for having invited an American soldier into his home or simply for having struck a conversation with him in the street. In Rabat, the Jewish neighborhood was cordoned off by police on November 12 and the siege lasted several weeks. During that time, dozens of people were nabbed right in the streets and condemned on the spot to forced labor, while the *goumiers* forced the terrorized inhabitants to lodge and feed them for the duration: "One wondered if it was the Americans or the Germans who had landed in Morocco."[11]

The same treatment was meted out to the *mellahs* of Meknès and Fez. The locking in of the Jewish neighborhoods was explained as a preventive security measure, but their inhabitants perceived it as punishment and with good cause: only those persons in possession of special passes could get out of the *mellah* and, as Jews were constantly the subjects of searches, persons who had forgotten to get a pass were thrown in prison without further formality.[12]

Small inland communities were not spared any more than those of major cities. In Beni-Mellal, the *contrôleur civil* (official in charge of civilian control) set up a regime of terror of rare cruelty. He allowed any European wishing to settle in the town to choose from among the houses inhabited by Jews the one he wanted. The inhabitants were forced to leave their homes within three to forty-eight hours under threat of forced labor. The controller extended the same favor to the Moslems who could choose among Jewish shops the ones they fancied. The unfortunate owners were given twenty-four hours to hand over their businesses. The Jewish community of Beni-Mellal, some three thousand strong, was worked and taxed at will like medieval serfs and was the constant butt of requisition and plunder.[13]

In Irfoud, in the Tafilelt area, Jews were dispossessed of the palm groves they had bought in 1918,[14] while in Azilal the entire Jewish population was forced to do corvée labor,[15] and in Tinerhir, in the Ouarzazat region, the director of the Office for Native Affairs forced Jews to wear only black clothes.[16] These excesses continued long after the abolition of the racial laws in March 1943.

Thus, on July 30, 1944, *goumiers* stationed at Sefrou organized a punitive expedition against the Jewish neighborhood of this town after a trivial argument between a Moslem soldier and a young Jew. Taking advantage of the inaction and perhaps even the complicity of their French officers, the *goumiers* perpetrated the worst acts of violence on the Jewish population, which was, on that day, commemorating the destruction of the Temple (Tish'a Be'Av). At the close of the attack, local officials arrested two hundred Jews and cordoned off the *mellah* for four days. The aggressors were assigned the task of guarding the *mellah* and, not satisfied with the damage they had already wrought, they forbade the inhabitants to leave their neighborhoods and prevented food supplies from reaching them.

Besides these acts of violence more or less condoned by a French administration hardly purged of its extremist elements, the Jewish population of Morocco had to endure the hardships of a food-rationing system that, up to 1945, continued being administered along racial criteria established by Vichy.[17]

The Problem of the Political Prisoners and of the Refugees

"I have requested the liberation of all persons in Northern Africa who had been imprisoned because they approved the efforts of the Nazis to dominate the world." These words, spoken by Roosevelt on November 17, were for a long time to have no effect on almost all prisoners in North Africa. Except for American and British citizens who were to be freed shortly after the landing,[18] very few "foreign workers," internees of "guarded centers," and political prisoners got a taste of freedom after November 8. The sustained joint action by the Allied press and Allied spokesmen in Algiers was to be required for the first "mass" liberation to take place in February 1943 and another two months had to elapse before the closing of the camps was ordered.

A DIFFICULT LIBERATION

In the meanwhile, the internees of several camps were to suffer reprisals from their guards who had been annoyed by the prisoners' displays of rejoicing and of a lack of discipline that followed the news of the American troops' arrival. During the following weeks, French officials tried mostly to calm the prisoners' misgivings by trying to convince them either of the importance of the trans-Saharan railroad to the Allied war effort or of the threat the freeing of thousands of individuals lacking work and shelter would pose to the public order.

For instance, the Kenadsa internees were told that their departure could not be authorized before replacements were found. Yet since the landing, the camp population of the area had swelled with many Italian prisoners who, to the internees' chagrin, enjoyed a favoring treatment from their keepers who had no intention of making them work the mines.[19]

In March 1943 the political prisoners of Berrouaghia who had still not received an answer to their request for freedom were advised by the camp chief to have patience and "not to let themselves be swayed by false reasoning. Daily," he explained to them, "our leaders are absorbed in new events of the highest import, which to an extent stops the flow of administrative processes."[20]

For that matter, French officials' attitude was not the sole factor preventing an early solution of the internee problem. In January, Eisenhower had set up a tripartite commission (American – French – British) to deal with the question of political prisoners and refugees (Szajkowski 1975:183-84). French officials agreed to free in priority those citizens of countries at war against the Axis powers and those that had consular representatives in Algiers. Poles and Czechoslovaks belonged to the category, but their respective consuls were not always willing to intervene in favor of internees of Jewish origin, or of Communist persuasion, or who were veterans of the international brigades.

The following account of the Algiers Polish Consul's visit to Djelfa clearly illustrates this state of affairs:

> Count Czapski, the Polish consul, has also paid a visit to the camp to take with him Poles for the Polish army. But he was asking each Pole three questions: (1) Are you Jewish or Polish? (2) Have you been authorized by the Polish government to serve in the international brigades during the Spanish civil war? (3) Would you fight against the Soviet Union if the need arose? To the first, he said the Polish army did not need Jews; to the second, that they had lost their Polish citizenship because they had fought in Spain. To the third he stated that a Polish soldier must fight

against anyone whom the Polish government found it necessary to fight. Thus about thirty Poles were not recognized by him as Poles.[21]

Soviet internees, as citizens of a country at war with the Axis powers, were told of their liberation on February 15 but because the Soviet government had no representative in Algiers they had to wait for the arrival of a Soviet delegation, which finally arrived April 25, to be handed over to it. Between these two dates, the Soviet prisoners were separated from their comrades and gathered in the Fort Caffarelli prison, where they spent the two months waiting in very unpleasant circumstances.

> The Russians were piled up at Caffarelli in two large rooms that had all their windowpanes broken. They had to sleep on straw deposited directly on a cement floor. . . . They had a space of one foot and half per man. . . . Outings were forbidden. One hundred twenty people had to wash with only one faucet in the courtyard. The Russians were not even allowed to go near the walls or the door of the fort. The windows in the rooms were barred.[22]

Even harder to fathom is the treatment meted out to internees of German and Austrian origins. Even though they were almost all Jewish, they were looked upon as suspicious and dangerous for the simple reason they were nationals of Axis countries, even though everyone knew the reasons that had led them to North Africa. After many entreaties, the French finally did agree to free those among them who were willing to enlist in the Corps Francs or the foreign legion. But most of them, as former auxiliaries or enlisted volunteers, harbored unpleasant memories of their service under the French flag. Thus, with a few exceptions, they all turned down this solution. As two Zionist leaders were to explain to the American officers of the Psychological Warfare Division:

> The solutions offered within the French framework (foreign legion, Corps Francs) raise considerable difficulties. The foreign legion is not suitable because of unfortunate precedents and the recent unhappy experience they had with it. The anti-Semitism and the moral climate prevailing in the legion are not conducive to easing their legitimate apprehensions. . . . As for the Corps Francs, they will always be foreigners within it, stateless men totally lacking the protection of the laws of war, having to obey the orders of a hierarchy whose lower ranks would probably manifest the same hostility toward them as in the legion. To serve as free men under

A DIFFICULT LIBERATION

the American or British flag in a Jewish corps — this seems to us the solution most likely to satisfy everyone.[23]

Thus internees responded with great enthusiasm to the enlistment opportunities offered them by the Regiments of Foreign Pioneers of the British armed forces. Col. F. M. Brister, who engineered this project, rescued from internment camps some eleven hundred people. Two-thirds of the first company he organized (the 337th) was made up of Austrian and German Jews most of whom had previously served in the foreign legion. In March, as the closing of the camps appeared more and more real, five other pioneers companies were formed (338th, 361st, 362d, 363d, 364th) that included volunteers of every nationality: Germans, Austrians, Hungarians, Poles, Romanians, and Russians.[24]

The internees were thus freed on an individual basis and their liberation was tied to their incorporation into fighting units. Assuredly, no prisoner objected to this "deal" that nonetheless and all things considered required former enlisted volunteers, badly affected by the deprivations and ill treatments of a long detention, to earn the freedom that the powers-that-be had condescended giving them by proving themselves again on the battlefield.

Besides these able-bodied men, the population of the camps also included many unfit and older men who, lacking adequate military potential, had to remain in the camps longer than the others. Rejecting the authorities' offers to sign "civilian" contracts with the Mediterranean-Niger Company for which many of them had previously worked in the camps of Colomb-Béchar, Bou-Arfa, and Kenadsa, they addressed themselves to the relief committees of Casablanca and of Algiers, which, with the help of the J.D.C. and the American Friends Service Committee, found them work in the American and British military bases in Morocco and Algeria. In July 1943, 4,653 former prisoners thus found work (Szajkowski 1975:180–81, 190). The camps were officially closed by order of General Giraud on April 28, 1943. Four months later there were no less than 700 people left in Moroccan camps alone. They were distributed as follows: Fqih b. Salah: 10; Settat: 100; In-Fout: 230; Sidi al-Ayashi: 30; Oued Akreuch: 100; Djerada: 50; Berguent: 150; Bou-Arfa: 25; Foum-el-Flah: about 50; Missour: 5 or 6; Oued-Zem: 10 to 20.[25]

Few refugees were able to leave North Africa for countries of immigration after November 8. Exit visas were granted very sparingly by the high commissioner's office,[26] and the means of sea transport were practically forbidden to civilians. Because of these difficulties and the drastic reduction in immigration quotas to the United States, only Palestine could have provided a satisfactory alternative, but the possibility was thwarted by well-known political obstacles, and it was only after much effort that the British agreed to issue about 100 travel certificates to refugees in North Africa.[27]

Under these circumstances, North Africa was to play only a secondary role in the evacuation of Jewish refugees blocked in Spain whose numbers had swelled after the Nazi occupation of France's Free Zone.[28] A few hundred French Jews did succeed in getting to North Africa, but up to the day after the Bermuda Conference (April 19, 1943) not one "expatriate" had been admitted to North Africa. During the conference the Americans as well as the French objected to proposals to transfer the refugees from Spain to Morocco by arguing that their arrival would create turmoil within the Moslem population (Friedman 1973:197–202).

However, thanks to Churchill's intervention and after long discussions between the Americans, the French, and the British, a camp that could shelter a part of the refugees was established in Fedala. The operation started only in May 1944 and accomplished the evacuation of only 630 refugees.[29]

9

Toward the Abolition of Racial Laws

The Effect of Allied Public Opinion and of American Jewish Organizations

The North African Jewry could not make itself heard in Algiers and thus it turned to Allied public opinion and Jewish organizations in the United States. Disappointed by the attitude of Murphy and of Eisenhower, who had let themselves be convinced by Darlan's and Giraud's arguments against abolishing racial laws, the spokesmen of the Algerian Jewry did, however, find a sympathetic ear with the journalists who were reservists assigned to the Psychological Warfare Division. Their initiatives in the field and leaks to the American press were to hinder the policies of the Algiers regime.

American Jewish organizations, on the other hand, showed great restraint during the first weeks of the landing, torn as they were between their loyalty to their government's policies and their solidarity with their North African brethren. Despite the fact that it was probably thanks to the urgings of the American Jewish Congress (A.J.C.) that President Roosevelt asked for the abolition of Nazi laws in his November 17 address (Cohen 1972:267), the American Jewry was concerned with its vulnerability to the insinuations emanating from isolationist milieus that it was pressure from them that caused the United States to enter the war. As a result, the American Jewry intervened directly only after the major New York papers had expressed their deep discontent in the face of the worsening of the internal situation in North Africa. Up to then, the American Jewish organizations had accepted at their face value all the statements and promises pertaining to the abrogation of anti-Jewish legislation.

President Roosevelt's November 17 speech triggered a great wave of rejoicing among American Jewish organizations that believed the president's wish had been immediately realized. As a result, the press organ of the American Jewish Congress announced three days later that the "Allied occupation of French territories in North Africa had put an end to the Nazi-inspired legislation enacted by Vichy."[1] Philip S. Berstein of the J.D.C. explained in *The Nation* that "Jews were again admitted to the French army and the *numerus clausus* had been abolished at the university and schools" (*The Nation*, January 3, 1943). It is not very likely that the leaders of the American Jewry were not aware of North African reality when locally Jewish American soldiers were protesting to Murphy the maintenance of Vichy's anti-Jewish legislation (Murphy 1964:147). In the United States itself, doubts began to take hold of the B'nai B'rith organization, which, on November 27, noted with regret that "the American troops have not yet entered the camps in the desert where the Jews are incarcerated" (*B'nai B'rith Messenger*, November 27, 1942). However, American Jews having full confidence in their government's policies, generally accepted with little reticence the explanations given by their country's official spokespersons, notably those given by Murphy. Fearing repercussions of German propaganda in the Maghreb, Murphy worried that the repeal of racial laws would cause violent turmoil in North Africa, an outcome that would harm the Allied cause. His adviser, Paul Warburg, who belonged to a well-known family of Jewish bankers, entirely shared this viewpoint. Murphy later related, with a touch of irony, how, against Warburg's opinion, he advised Henry Morgenthau to meet with the leaders of the Algerian Jewish community.

If we are to believe Murphy, Roosevelt's Jewish cabinet member was somewhat amused upon hearing the "benign" and probably futile complaints of the Algiers Jews (Murphy 1964:147-48).

Darlan's unkept promise (he had on December 15 announced that the victims of all racial laws were being given back all their rights),[2] the sequels of the assassination of the high commissioner and the arrests of the leaders of the Algerian Resistance, the hope born out of the Anfa Conference that immediately vanished upon Marcel Peyrouton's appointment— all these developments led the American Jewry to the realization that its November optimism had been premature, to say the least. They had been wrong to assume that the abolition of racial laws "would follow the Allied occupation of North Africa as the day follows the night" (*Congress Weekly*, December 18, 1942). The cricitism and the protests voiced by the Jewish press showed, however, great restraint and they never adopted the sharpness of the editorials in the *Christian Science Monitor*, the *New York Herald Tribune*, *The Nation*, the *New York Times*, and the *New Republic*.

The latter, for instance, on January 25 and February 1, 1943, demanded Murphy's recall, the abrogation of racial laws, and the setting up, with General de Gaulle's participation, of a temporary French government in North Africa.[3]

This press campaign did affect the Algiers authorities, who agreed to alleviate anti-Jewish laws but only to an extent. Until mid-March, Giraud obstinately refused to change any principle of Vichy legislation. On January 28, 1943, Governor Peyrouton summoned seven Jewish notables, among them Grand Rabbi Eisenbeth, to announce that some anti-Jewish measures (the Aryanization of property, the *numerus clausus* in primary and secondary schools, and the firing of civil servants) were to be gradually done away with. Pétain's former minister began by expounding the following points to his audience:

> (1) The Jews and the members of parliament have been declared responsible for the defeat. This defeat has caused a general outburst of anti-Semitism in every class of the country. Anti-Semitic laws have been enacted in France as a reaction to foreign Jews who were becoming newly naturalized ever since the coming into power of Premier Blum; (2) one of the main conditions of the armistice was that racial legislation be introduced in France; (3) the abrogation of racial laws would at present cause discontent; (4) Algeria is still a part of France and cannot consider itself separately and enact legislation on this matter; (5) Jews are talking too much with American and British officials. . . . (Eisenbeth 1945:78–79)

Thus the only thing Peyrouton could offer the Jews of Algeria was the restitution "in stages" of confiscated Jewish property, the abolition of the *numerus clausus* in the liberal professions, and the gradual rehiring of low-level civil servants in the institutions that had let them go. As to the Crémieux decree and the political rights of Algerian Jews, there was absolutely no possibility of considering them until after the war and the liberation of metropolitan France.

The Jewish delegation rejected outright all Peyrouton's propositions. Peyrouton, who was a more astute politician than Giraud, was not personally opposed to granting more of the Jewish population's demands (Eisenbeth 1945:78–79). His stance stemmed from the growing pressure put by the Allied papers and the equally growing popularity of General de Gaulle, who had distanced himself from Giraud during his press conference of February 9. This made the commander in chief's position precarious and threatened to sweep away the last pieces of the Vichyst construction upon which he had chosen to build his power.

Toward the Abolition of Racial Laws

On their part, Jewish organizations were voicing their protests in stronger and stronger tones. On February 8, Dr. Joseph Schwartz of the J.D.C. directly attacked Murphy by expressing serious doubts about the truthfulness of some of his allegations. The president's representative stated that not all Jewish leaders in Algeria favored a straightforward return to republican legislation and that many of them understood the impossibility of reinstating the Crémieux decree (*Contemporary Jewish Record*, February 1943).

Two days later, the World Jewish Congress and the American Jewish Congress strongly deplored that three months after the landing, 330,000 North African Jews still lived under the yoke of Nazi laws, while in Syria and Libya these same laws had been abolished immediately after the occupation of these territories by Free France and British forces.

> We have remained silent during these months because we have appreciated to the full the difficulties, military and otherwise, of the situation, and because we wished to avoid saying anything which might embarrass those who bear the burden of responsibility. But it has become clear that the principles of human rights and democracy have been suspended, if not waived, in North Africa. It is impossible for us by our silence to appear to acquiesce in this policy, a policy which by implication denies the principles upon which these United States were founded, and in defense of which we have accepted the Nazi challenge. . . . Liberty is indivisible. To tolerate denial or abridgement of human rights anywhere is to challenge them everywhere. We ask for the complete restoration of human rights to those who have been robbed of them in North Africa as a contribution to the defeat of the purposes of the enemy and to the establishment of the democratic world order which our country is pledged to create. (*Congress Weekly*, February 19, 1943)

In reponse to this protest, which was summarized in the *New York Times*, the head of the French military mission in the United States, General Bethouart, tried to convince American public opinion that real progress had been achieved in North Africa, for instance, the restitution of Jewish property confiscated under Vichy and the return of Jewish children to public schools. General Bethouart's statements on Giraud's policies were reproduced without much conviction in the Jewish press and on February 25 triggered a heated response from the committee of French representatives to the World Jewish Congress. This response condemned the delays of the Algiers authorities and their refusal to perform an act of basic justice "when the North African situation did not present any obstacles to the return to France's national traditions." Eminent French Jewish personalities were associated with this committee; they included Baron Edouard de Rothschild, the jurists Paul Jacob and Henry Torrès, Prof. Jacques Hadamard, Marc Chagall, André Spire, Pierre Dreyfus, and others.

However, it took Jean Monnet's arrival in Algiers for Giraud to change his policies. Giraud had appointed Monnet as his adviser at the behest of the Americans.[4] As Giraud explained:

> From the start, he brought my attention to my personal image in the United States. Thanks to Gaullist propaganda, I was seen as a reactionary, without feeling for democracy, and basically anti-Semitic. According to him, this propaganda was bearing fruits and would hinder the rearmament of the French armed forces in the manner I had conceived and planned it. There was only one means open to counter this propaganda: publicly affirm my loyalty to democratic principles and give back to the Jews of North Africa some of the basic prerogatives essential to any citizen of a civilized society. (Giraud 1949:119)

Jean Monnet skillfully explained to him that, without these concessions, the Americans would refuse to deliver him the war material required by the troops:

> It took six weeks to convince me and it wasn't easy. I have always abhorred politics. I am still more convinced than ever of its ill effects particularly in time of war, particularly with the French, particularly in North Africa, in the colonies where natives live side by side with us, watch us, and keep scores. But we needed the armament. It was of vital necessity for France. Thus I deliberately decided to take the path toward which Monnet and Linarès were dragging me.[5] And on March 14, 1943, at the general reunion of the refugees of Alsace-Lorraine I pronounced the first democratic speech of my life. (Giraud 1949:121)

And as if to ward off any misunderstanding on the nature of these new "convictions," he himself added; "If Paris was well worth a mass,[6] this armament was well worth a speech" (Giraud 1949:124). This speech was given in Algiers on the occasion of a demonstration by refugees from Alsace-Lorraine who had gathered to protest the annexation of their provinces to Germany. Every civilian, military, and religious personality of Algeria was present alongside the Allied repesentatives as well as many British and American journalists.

Giraud formally repudiated the Vichy regime, restored republican institutions, and announced the abolition of laws of racial discrimination "imposed on France by the Nazis." But at the same time and "with the same intention of eliminating every form of racial discrimination," he abrogated the Crémieux decree, "which had, in 1870, established a difference between Moslem and Jewish natives."[7]

Thus it came to pass that in the space of three years the decree granting French citizenship to the Jews of Algeria was abolished twice: under Vichy and under Giraud who took pains to present this repeal not as a simple juridical decision taken by the French state but as the expression of a particular political outlook, an outlook that moreover was definitely racist: "As for the relations between Moslems and Jews, they must be those of men called upon to complement each other economically—one in the workshop the other in the field—without either one having superiority over the other, while France ensures security and tranquility to each."[8]

As a part of public opinion became quickly aware, Giraud, by maintaining the abrogation of the Crémieux decree, enmeshed himself in an untenable web of contradictions. In his speech he had called on the republican principle by which "only the people's will can be the basis of law" and "without it, legal texts are invalid." Accordingly, he nullified legislation enacted after June 22, 1940, which had been conceived and promulgated "without the French people and against it."[9] However, the abrogation of the Crémieux decree had been one of these laws and had, no more than the Jewish Statute, emanated from "the people's will." Moreover, the decree itself had been enacted on October 24, 1870, by a legitimately elected government legitimately making laws. The decree had been maintained in the French civil code for seventy years by legislative assemblies that alone had the right to make laws. Consequently, by abolishing it, Giraud went against the very principle upon which he had based his own annulment of the texts after June 22, 1940.

Michel Ansky was to note that Giraud's speech caused some confusion. His audience, taken aback to hear him condemn racial persecutions, did not fully comprehend "the passage pertaining to the abolition of the Crémieux decree. Most of the listeners were persuaded that Giraud was giving back to the Jews the totality of the rights they had enjoyed before the armistice" (Ansky 1950:285). The real meaning of Giraud's words was only understood with the publication on March 18 in the *Journal Officiel* of the various ordinances translating Giraud's ideas into juridical terms.

In the interval before the organization of the fight for the restoration of the Crémieux decree, Algerian-Jewish public opinion focused on the application of the concrete measures dictated by the new texts. The *numerus clausus* was suppressed almost immediately in the liberal and teaching

A DIFFICULT LIBERATION

professions. The reintegration of the fired civil servants with public service and concessionary enterprises was slower, and up to June 1943 there were many civil servants whose situation had not been normalized. The same situation occurred with the restitution of property. The procedures and the delays for the claiming of confiscated real property were complex. Moreover, the ordinances published by the adminstration in April forced the evicted owners to pay the salaries of the trustees they had neither wanted nor chosen. In the military domain, the Pioneers Companies were officially abolished on March 15, but for several more months Jews coming from these companies were purposely assigned to noncombat units or to special units segregated from the non-Jews.[10]

The abolition of the racial laws in Tunisia occurred two months after the March 15 speech. It was pronounced by General Mast immediately after the liberation and he simultaneously dissolved the Jewish Recruitment Committee.[11] Although the laid-off civil servants gradually recovered their former jobs, the community's notables were faced with the urgent task of dealing with the debts contracted during the German occupation, particularly those assumed to pay the fines exacted by the Germans. French officials agreed to regard as war damages the Tunisian Jews' losses caused by the German presence and even to suspend payments on the debts owed the banks. But this solution, even though it postponed the juridical settling of the problem till the end of the war, maintained the mortgages on a portion of the properties of the country's Jewish middle and upper classes whose members had had to guarantee the solvency of the Jewish community.

The questions of principles raised by this problem were believed important enough by the United States to warrant the personal intervention of President Roosevelt.[12] He looked upon the situation in which the Tunisian Jews had been put as an "additional proof" of the atrocities committed by the Axis powers "upon the innocent populations of occupied territories." Thus on June 29, 1943, the American president requested his secretary of state to remind French authorities that, according to the terms of the resolution adopted in December by the United Nations, transfers of wealth performed during the German occupation were invalid. Consequently, the protectorate's administration should forbid any attempt at collecting interests on the mortgages taken to pay the fines imposed by the Axis forces.

A series of negotiations among American, British, French, and Jewish Tunisian representatives took place the following months.[13] Early in September, the French authorities proposed a temporary solution till the problem could be permanently solved: the mortgages on Jewish property would be canceled and the interest on the various loans would be paid by the government. The Jewish community would not be freed of its debts to the banks, but the government would put at its disposal the money raised by specially issued public bonds so that it could pay back its creditors.

Besides this matter, the Tunisian Jewish community had to face a much more sensitive human problem. On the day after the liberation, Jews of Italian nationality were the object of special measures because they were citizens of an enemy country. Their properties were sealed, their bank accounts frozen, and two hundred of their lawyers, doctors, and other notables were led to a camp near Sousse.[14]

And thus, several months after the arrival of the Allies, the Jews of Tunisia found themselves coerced into forced labor and were subjected to conditions that strangely resembled those they had had to endure a short time earlier during the German occupation.

The Struggle for the Reestablishment of the Crémieux Decree

Besides the juridical and moral considerations that gave impetus to the campaign against the exclusion of Algerian Jews from French citizenship, the abolition of the Crémieux decree was regarded by Jewish organizations as a direct blow to one of the cornerstones of Jewish emancipation. This was because this abolition again put in question Jews' rights to political assimilation, a right regarded as theirs by every European nation from the eighteenth century on. The World Jewish Congress, and American Jewish Committee, the J.D.C., and B'nai B'rith were moreover horrified at the thought that the status of the Algerian Jews could become a precedent and that the future survivors of the territories to be liberated from Nazi occupation would not be automatically returned to their prewar status. Finally, while information was piling up more and more each day on the scope of the genocide perpetrated by the Germans, the hesitant attitude of American officials toward the problems facing Algerian Jews added, to say the least, a cynical dimension to the evasive answers of the state and war departments to Jewish leaders inquiring about the means to stem the Final Solution.

For these and other reasons, the campaign for the reestablishment of the Crémieux decree reached dimensions unmatched since November 1942. Taking off at a decisive point in the Giraud–de Gaulle conflict, the outcome of the campaign was to be closely linked to the generals' showdown. One was for or against the Crémieux decree according to whether one was a Gaullist or a Giraudist. Thus, in contrast with the first campaign against racial laws, which had been almost exclusively undertaken by the Algerian Jewry and American Jewish organizations, the last phase of the struggle against the juridical sequels of Vichy's legislation was to involve a substantial portion of French public opinion in North Africa, the United States, and Great Britain.

The people in charge of juridical affairs in the French Committee for National Liberation formulated in London as early as March 15 their first criticisms of Giraud's decision to nullify the Crémieux decree. In a memo written to René Cassin, the National Commissariat of Justice made the following points, which ended up serving as models for all subsequent arguments:[15]

1. In his speech, General Giraud brought up the same arguments for the abrogation of the Crémieux decree as those propounded earlier by the Vichy government and press.
2. How could General Giraud reconcile his solemn pledge to leave the settling of all political questions to the French people and government with his decision to maintain some of the texts promulgated by Vichy, texts that pertain to political questions of primary import?
3. Besides the fact that this abrogation legitimized the violation of acquired rights, it was surprising that the lining up on the same plane of Moslem and Jewish Algerians was done through the loss of one of the group's French citizenship — this in view of the fact that the law of 1919 allowed Algerian Moslems to acquire these political rights almost without formalities. Yet it was a well-known fact that only a few Moslems had availed themselves of this opportunity.

In the United States, the World Jewish Congress and the American Jewish Congress waited till the publication of the ordinances of March 18 to protest against the abrogation of the "Gambetta-Crémieux" decree, abrogation that was putting Algerian Jews back into the status they held under Napoleon III (*Congress Weekly*, March 19, 1943). At the same time, Baron Edouard de Rothschild denounced Giraud's decision as one that relegated Algerian Jews to a position inferior to that of the Arabs and the blacks in the French empire (*New York Times*, March 18, 1943).

These stances were discussed at length in the English-language press, which had first warmly greeted Giraud's March 14 speech. This press finally began to wonder about the real implications of his actions. The following comments by Ewin L. James appeared in the *New York Times*:

> The General said that the purpose of his ruling was to wipe out the inequality between the Jews and the Arabs of Algeria. It is possible to understand that he would wish to make a gesture towards the Arabs, who form an important part of the forces fighting under his command. . . . Now, to become French citizens they must, as before, agree to accept the French

Civil Code.... It is thus very difficult to see that General Giraud did anything for the Arabs....

It seems doubly unfortunate that at a time when Washington and London are trying to work towards French unity, General Giraud has taken a step which, with all fairness, does not appear to be above suspicion. (*New York Times*, March 21, 1943)

In the face of these mounting criticisms, much of which was also directed at the state department,[16] Sumner Welles, the under secretary of state, was forced to take a stand and publicly defend Giraud's policy. He did this in a letter addressed to Baron de Rothschild on March 28 in which he labeled the picture painted by Rothschild as "completely erroneous" because, among other reasons, the abolition of the Crémieux decree did not affect Jews of Algeria who had been born in France or were the descendants of parents born in France.[17] This small concession did not assuage the apprehensions of the committee of French representatives to the World Jewish Congress nor those of the American Jewish Committee, which, on May 17, sent Sumner Welles a long report on the effects of the abrogation of the Crémieux decree.

This report, probably written with the collaboration of Henry Torrès and Paul Jacob, took up and developed most of the arguments formulated so far against the measure taken by Giraud.[18] Its authors pointed out, among other things, that by excluding from French citizenship the descendants of the beneficiaries of the Crémieux decree, Giraud had broken the French law of August 10, 1927, stipulating that any individual born on French soil from French parents is French. Logically, only a few sexagenarians could be said to be naturalized directly as a result of the Crémieux decree and thus only they were liable to lose their citizenship because of the March 18 ordinance. However, by retroactively including their descendants, Giraud went against a basic principle of the French civil code whereby "the law makes provisions only for the future; it has no retroactive effect." This report included a wealth of documentation comprising excerpts from legislative texts that pertained to the history of the Crémieux decree, to the juridical status of the Moslem population, and to various documents on the relations between Jews and Arabs. On this latter topic, a large place was allocated to refutations of the belief, widespread in Algiers, that the adoption of the Crémieux decree had been the root cause of the Kabyle revolt of 1871. The last part of the report was made up of various statements in favor of reestablishing the Crémieux decree, expressed by personalities close to French pro-Gaullist milieus. Among those cited were R. P. Maynard of the French church of the Holy Spirit in New York,

A DIFFICULT LIBERATION

Prof. Francis Perrin in exile at Columbia University, the journalist Emile Buré, and Jacques Maritain, president of the executive committee of the New School for Social Research in New York. The famous French theologian pointed out in his statement:

> The natural way to remediate the unequal treatment of which Algerian Arabs might complain is to gradually guide toward the status of French citizenship those among them who show their sincere desire to become a part of the French community. In the face of the dangerous incitations of German propaganda, stripping Jews of their rights is not the right way to protect the Moslem population from this propaganda. Instead, this will be achieved by assuring Algerian Arabs that on the day the French people will be able to express its will, their legitimate demands will be strongly defended on the condition that they cooperate loyally in the efforts undertaken for victory over the enemy.[19]

Regardless of it being myth or reality, the scarecrow of Arab revolt was waved in front of the Americans by Darlan and Giraud just as, in the recent past, it had been waved in front of the Germans and Italians by Vichy officials hoping to discourage them away from North Africa.

Assuredly, the relations between Jews and Moslems were not idyllic but nothing seems to confirm, not even the Moroccan incidents that had occurred in the wake of the Allied landing, that German propaganda was solely responsible for the worsening of the relations between the two communities. Even though this propaganda did help stimulate Maghrebian national feelings, few Moslem nationalists, in contrast with their prewar outlook, considered French citizenship a genuine sign of political emancipation or an ideal worth striving for. In fact, few were concerned one way or another with the fate of the Crémieux decree.

In a letter addressed on November 29, 1942, to Jewish personalities of Algiers, the lawyer Boumendjel, who along with Ferhat Abbas was one of the leaders of the Parti du Manifeste Algérien, was to express the opinion prevailing in Moslem political milieus as follows:

> I can assure you that Moslems have generally understood that it would not be in their interests to rejoice at the discriminatory measures of which the Jews of Algeria are the victims. Moslems cannot rationally take the side of those who practice a racial policy while they themselves are daily the butt of racism. Our adversaries have not comprehended that by making Jews inferior they could only bring them closer to Moslems. . . .

Toward the Abolition of Racial Laws

Most of them believed that the Moslems would rejoice at the abrogation of the Crémieux decree but in fact the Moslems were made to realize that a citizenship that could be withdrawn after seventy years had been turned into a privilege of dubious value, and this by the very people who had granted it. This country's ruling classes must come to admit that discriminatory measures, regardless of where they have been generated and which communities they affect, are greeted with sadness in the hearts of the Moslems of Algeria. They refuse to be treated as "big children," as pawns or as exchange currency.[20]

In fact, the Moslem scarecrow was to become less and less convincing as time went on. Besides the fact that the Germans' departure from North Africa made the possibility of an Arab uprising nonexistent, American diplomats could not remain unreceptive to another argument bandied about frequently in the American press: the abrogation of the Crémieux decree, transposed into the American experience, amounted to abolishing Lincoln's Emancipation act on the pretext of satisfying the demands of extremist Southerners and with the aim of promoting equality between American blacks and Indians.

Consequently, in his reply to the American Jewish Committee, Sumner Welles used another argument in rejecting the demands put upon the state department: "North Africa is not under the military occupation of the United States and all decisions [regarding the Crémieux decree] have been taken by French authorities."[21]

The under secretary of state was perhaps right from a strictly formal viewpoint, but he was strangely underestimating the immense influence wielded by the United States over North African internal politics, an influence that began to lessen only with General de Gaulle's arrival in Algiers. Paradoxically, the state department openly took a stance in favor of the reestablishment of the Crémieux decree only after Giraud's gradual withdrawal and de Gaulle's gradual taking over. But by that time the United States had turned its efforts toward Europe and the Americans were to have less and less influence on the evolution of the Algiers situation where de Gaulle was able, despite Roosevelt's and Murphy's threats and remonstrances, to push aside Peyrouton, Boisson, and other former Vichyst elements who had been able to gain the Americans' confidence.

Jewish organizations had not waited till May 30, the date of de Gaulle's return to Algeria, to set up relations with Free France. These relations were begun shortly after the June 18 appeal through the intermediary of the British section of the World Jewish Congress and then through the writer Albert Cohen, who became the liaison between the World Jewish Congress and the London headquarters of the Gaullist movement (Kubowitzki 1948:210–11).

On August 5, 1941, Free France had made a point of informing the main seat of the World Jewish Congress, located in New York, of the abolition of racial laws in Syria and in Lebanon. Two months later, on the occasion of the 150th anniversary of the emancipation of the Jews of France, General de Gaulle, in a letter to Dr. Stephen Wise, stated that the changes made to the French constitution and laws by the Vichy government were invalid (Kubowitzki 1948:212).

At the start of the campaign for the reestablishment of the Crémieux decree, various Gaullist spokesmen condemned Giraud's anti-Jewish policy. On March 24, 1943, in response to a cable from Dr. Wise to de Gaulle, René Massigli, Free France's representative in Washington, unambiguously expressed support for the reestablishment of the Crémieux decree. However, he expressed the following qualification for the benefit of Jewish organizations: "You will ask your correspondents not to publicize our stance at present. You will point out to them that the rebuilding of French unity is the surest way for our views to prevail in this domain as in others" (Ansky 1950:298).

The Jewish organizations did not much appreciate the Gaullist representative's prudence. In fact it foreshadowed the pussyfooting attitude to be adopted by the French National Liberation Committee for several months after its arrival in Algiers.

On July 16, 1943, Albert Cohen explained to the Political Bureau of the Jewish Agency the reasons for this attitude, which was quite unexpected, to say the least. According to the information given to him by André Philip, who filled the functions of Commissaire de l'Intérieur (commissioner for internal affairs), of the fifteen members of the committee, twelve were in favor of the reestablishment of the Crémieux decree, a thirteenth, General Catroux, was indecisive, and the last two, Generals Giraud and Georges, were adamantly opposed to it. When, still according to André Philip, General de Gaulle arrived in Algiers, the first topic that Giraud spoke to him about was the abrogation of the Crémieux decree. Subsequently he threatened to resign if the committee decided to reestablish the decree. And because the Americans had put the maintaining of Giraud in power as condition for reequipping the French army, the Liberation Council had been unable to make any decision on the Algerian Jews' citizenship status. The only advice André Philip could give Jewish organizations was to intensify their pressure on the state department![22]

It took till October 20 for the Crémieux decree to be reinstated. But

Toward the Abolition of Racial Laws

this "act of justice" produced no official text solemnly repealing Giraud's ordinance. The official communiqué published that day by the French National Liberation Committee did reestablish the decree but only because the March 18 ordinance had not been followed up, as it itself required, by the publication of its terms of application and consequently it had become obsolete. Moreover, the declaration by the National Liberation Committee borrowed a sentence from Giraud's March 14 speech that added an ominous reservation to it: "This declaration does not infringe upon the future decision-making prerogatives of the French government, which must definitely determine the status not only of Algerian Jews but also of the other categories of the Algerian population" (Eisenbeth 1945:84).

As Grand Rabbi Eisenbeth was to put in his letter of thanks to General de Gaulle, Algerian Jews had to wait almost a full year for the reestablishment of their political rights, after they already had had to wait almost five months for the abolition of the racist legislation enacted by Vichy (Eisenbeth 1945:98).

The Germans, in invading France and in smoothing the way for the coming into power of the Vichy regime, were the origin of racial laws in metropolitan France and North Africa. But three years later it was Frenchmen, free from any external constraint, who were solely responsible for preventing the abolition of these laws.

Conclusion

Following "Operation Torch" and the subsequent liberation of Tunisia six months later, the first bits of information on genocide of the European Jewry began to reach the Jews of North Africa. In comparison with the horrors of the Final Solution, whose true extent was yet to be fathomed, the persecutions that they themselves had suffered seemed only a brief nightmare, one among the many that overburdened their long history. And so, while their rabbis called upon the multitude to join in ceremonies of remembrance and days of collective fasting in memory of their sister communities of Europe, their traditionalists were seeking in the Book of Esther and in the history of ancient Persia antecedents relating to the present situation. Thus Roosevelt appeared to them as an Assureus who had acted under divine inspiration when he intervened on "that fateful night" of November 8 to stem the diabolical plans conceived by Hitler-Haman.[1]

Few — and for good reasons — were those who dared to propound any kind of factual or analytical link between the fates of North African Jews in 1940–43 and that of their European brethren. The anti-Jewish policies in the Maghreb had included neither mass destruction nor plans of extermination. Consequently, any analogical connection with the odious carnage perpetrated in Europe could, on the surface, only appear false and even ridiculous.

Nonetheless, what is known as the Holocaust cannot be reduced to the grim count of the Jewish victims of Nazi terror. The traits that differentiate the genocide of the Jews from the other war crimes perpetrated by the Germans pertain not only to the magnitude of the disaster and the "liquidation techniques" used but also to the series of steps preliminary

Conclusion

to the final collective killing. Defined "scientifically," objectified juridically, the Jews had been systematically expelled from society, and branded, penned, starved, and diabolized before the massacre.

Luckily for the Jewish inhabitants of North Africa, this final phase never materialized there. However, it is not possible to ignore the proximity in time of events connected with the assuredly much more violent ones that occurred in Europe during the same period. Besides this chronological contiguity, the treatment of the Jews on both sides of the Mediterranean was inspired by the same principles, the same language, and the same methods. Presumably, one could indulge in endless debates on the differences between the anti-Semitism of the Vichy regime as it was applied in unoccupied France and in North Africa and the racial anti-Semitism practiced by the Germans in the occupied zone before the summer of 1942. But from the viewpoint of the Jewish victim, could there have been any difference between being banned from society, dispossessed, and Aryanized in the name of the "state anti-Semitism" of Alibert and Vallat and having suffered the same treatment in the name of Nuremberg laws?

Until November 8, 1942, North Africa was a colonial appendage of the French state, and the anti-Jewish laws in effect there were of the same nature as those in unoccupied France. Far away from the real or imaginary scrutiny and interferences of Abetz, Oberg, and Dannecker, the anti-Semitic policy aimed at Moroccan, Algerian, and Tunisian Jews was totally and exclusively French. It was orchestrated by the Commissariat-General for the Jewish Question of the Vichy government but was implemented by the regular administrative apparatus of the three countries, an apparatus that moreover was composed of upstanding civil servants. There were far more republicans and at-heart anti-Germans among their ranks than avowed collaborators and corrupt or unprincipled opportunists. However, leaving nothing to chance and to emotions, this administration was primarily concerned with work well done and well organized. It looked with as much perplexity and disdain upon those whose humanitarian leanings made them want to soften the blows of racial laws as upon those who, substituting themselves for the state, wanted to engage in "spontaneous" actions against the Jews.

The anti-Jewish legislation of the Pétain government was part of the dynamics of the "Pétain mystique," which spread like wildfire across North Africa. This legislation drew the sympathy of the European population of the Maghreb, which on various occasions asked for the "correction" and adjustment of some clauses that were thought to be too soft or not rigorous enough. Letting the Jews alone believe that this legislation was imposed on France by the "enemy," the *pieds-noirs* saw in it, on the

CONCLUSION

contrary, a golden opportunity to settle their accounts with a Jewish population who for three-quarters of a century had troubled the privileged sleep of their dominant colonial caste. Yet there were a few isolated and anonymous voices objecting to the imposition of the anti-Semitic scourge, but one looks in vain among them for the protests of personalities as influential as Cardinals Saliège and Gerlier and Pastor Boegner, who spoke up in France during the same period. Today we know for certain that the consequences of "the war against the Jews" would have been less catastrophic if the Nazis and their followers had not benefited from the implicit or active support of civilian populations. And thus the events of North Africa confirm in their own way and in a minor register this sad lesson from the history of the genocide.

As paradoxical as it might seem, North African Jews owed their survival in part to interventions of their behalf by fascists and openly pro-German countries: Franco's Spain and Mussolini's Italy. The Italian intervention was certainly the most spectacular and effective, particularly regarding a portion of Tunisian Jews. The Italians showed consistency in their behavior by adopting the same attitude toward the Jews of Provence and those of Croatia despite the fact that, in their own country, and even in Lybia, they did introduce very harsh racial laws. Setting aside these contradictions and inconsistencies of Italian policy, what could have been more discouraging for a Jew subject or citizen of France than to see Darlan complain to the Germans about Italy's attitude because it hindered the progress of the anti-Jewish legislation promulgated by Vichy in North Africa?

The situation of Tunisian Jews under their brief German occupation brings forth much insight backing the conclusions brought to light by Holocaust research. Thus even though we are almost certain that the fate the Germans planned for the Jews of the regency was like the one they had meted out to Jews elsewhere, it is nonetheless clear that the Nazi "death machine" did not encounter in North Africa conditions favorable to its functioning. This then proves that, when submitted to Allied attacks and unable to obtain the collaboration and secrecy necessary for the execution of their plans, the Germans acted like vultures with broken wings, falling haphazardly on their prey.

The Axis forces had entered Tunisia after the Allied landing in Morocco and Algeria. The American and British arrival awakened a tremendous hope in the Jews, who, logically enough, expected that the first act of the Anglo-Saxon democrats would be to nullify Vichy's anti-Jewish legislation. They were quickly disappointed as the Americans, in the face of Giraud's and his associates' opposition, an opposition that definitely

Conclusion

confirms the purely endogenous nature of this legislation, showed little interest in the fate of the Jews. The Americans showed no compunction in brandishing the flag of freedom and of the rights of man while, a few steps away from their barracks, hundreds of people were still detained in labor camps and thousands more languished under the burden of anti-Semitic laws.

It might be hasty and even unfair to judge Allied attitude toward the Jewish question in general on the basis of the North African case. However, the responses of the State Department and the Foreign Office toward North African Jews shed an unsparing light on the "incredulity" of high Allied officials upon receiving the first information on the massacre of European Jews, or when being asked to undertake military measures to slow down deportations toward the death camps, or when requested to enlarge immigration quotas for Jewish refugees.

We focus now on the responses of the Jewish population of the Maghreb during these three years. Their shock at Vichy's measures was matched only by the tenacity with which they organized their community life despite the threats that piled up from day to day. The Algerian Jewish population, out of all three the most lacking in community institutions, distinguished itself, among other things, by the creation out of thin air or almost thin air of a high-quality educational system. Jewish schools worked so well that when, in 1943, students and teachers returned to the public institutions from which they had been expelled, they did so with a touch of regret.

North African Jews submitted themselves to every law, and their leaders undertook every task assigned them by the French and German authorities. This was so with even the most thankless of those tasks, the setting up in Tunis of the "Committee for the Recruitment of Jewish Labor," whose actions and distress gave birth to reactions and controversies of the same nature as those even more emotional stemming from the behavior of certain European *Judenrät*.

This Judaism, submissive on the surface, nonetheless produced resistants in disproportionate numbers in relation to the Jewish ratio in the population. The most outstanding example was that of the Algiers November 8 movement, which was mainly composed of Jewish resistants. Most of them came from the community's most distinguished families and they avoided giving their undertaking a "confessional" character. Their fight had as sole aim the liberation of France from the German yoke, and to accomplish this they were willing to associate with the most antirepublican and anti-Semitic right-wing milieus.

Also, we need mention here the immense psychological trauma felt

CONCLUSION

by the younger Jewish generations of the Maghreb for whom the French ideal had been in itself a political and cultural dogma. Without meaning to exaggerate its import, we note that there was a genuine birth of Jewish consciousness within a substantial portion of Jewish youth, which, up to the fall of 1940, had put all its hope into European civilization and the universal message of contemporary ideologies. Zionist envoys who renewed contact with the North African Jewry in the summer of 1943 were thus to find a large audience ready to attempt the *Halutzik* experience in the Promised Land. Similarly, thanks to the connections developed during the war with American Jewish organizations, the North African Jewry henceforth found it important to let its existence be known on the Jewish international scene. In November 1944 a large North African delegation made up of the three countries' representatives participated in the work of the extraordinary session of the World Jewish Congress in Atlantic City, New Jersey. But this "awakening" of Jewish awareness was far from being universal in Jewish milieus. In Oran, for instance, the members of the association Entraide Israélite, presided over by the lawyer Karsenty, strongly opposed sending Algerian delegates to the World Jewish Congress. In a letter of protest addressed to de Gaulle, they argued: "The undersigned oppose the concept of a Jewish race or Jewish people, which anyway is contrary to the findings of anthropology and to historical evolution, and which would, willy-nilly, give reality to Nazi racial theories even after Nazi defeat."

In fact, even while stating their solidarity with the tragedy undergone by all the Jewish people and even while giving their assent to the motion advocating the creation of a Jewish state, the North African delegates made it a point to emphasize their loyalty and attachment to France, "to the France of the Revolution, of Clémenceau, of de Gaulle." In every one of their speeches they carefully avoided dwelling on the painful experiences of the years 1940–43, wishing to perceive them only as the consequences of the "betrayal" of one man — Pétain — and a result of the pressure exerted on the "Vichy-Berlin regime" by the German occupant.

Swallowed up soon after by events that were to put back in question their very presence, as well as the presence of France, in Maghrebian lands, the Jews of North Africa obstinately chose to blot out of their memories this brief span of their history.

Abbreviations

A.A.N.	Archives André Narboni (Tel Aviv)
A.E.P.	Archives du Ministère des Affaires étrangères (Paris)
A.F.O.M.	Archives de France d'Outre-Mer (Aix-en-Provence)
B.F.S.J.A.	Bulletin de la Fédération des Sociétés Juives d'Algérie (Algiers)
B.O.M.	Bulletin Officiel du Maroc
C.A.H.J.P.	Central Archives for the History of the Jewish People (Jerusalem)
C.D.J.C.	Centre de Documentation Juive Contemporaine (Paris)
C.G.Q.J.	Commissariat Général aux Questions Juives
C.Z.A.	Central Zionist Archives (Jerusalem)
D.G.F.P.	Documents on German Foreign Relations
F.R.U.S.	Foreign Relations of the United States
H.I.A.S.	Hebrew Sheltering and Immigrant Aid Society
I.J.C.	Institut du Judaïsme Contemporain (Jerusalem)
J.D.C.	American Jewish Joint Distribution Committee
J.O.A.	Journal Officiel de l'Algérie
J.O.T.	Journal Officiel de Tunisie
YVSH	Yad Vashem Archives (Jerusalem)
R.H.D.G.M.	Revue d'histoire de la Deuxieme Guerre Mondiale

Notes

Introduction

1. [Bône: the present city of Annaba, Algeria.—*Trans.*]
2. [The Consistory was the official organization of the Jewish congregations established in France by the Napoleonic administration in 1808. It designates a centralized system of committees of rabbis and laymen responsible for the adminstration of the Jewish congregations at the regional and national levels. This system lasted officially till the separation of church and state in 1905 but was retained voluntarily by many Jewish communities after that date.—*Trans.*]
3. [*Dhimmi*: Arabic term for "protected." It was traditionally applied in Moslem states to define legally the status of the "People of the Book," i.e., Jews and Christians, but in the sense used by the author it obviously refers only to the status of Jews under the French regime.—*Trans.*]
4. [Resident-General: highest French executive and administrative official in a French protectorate—*Trans.*]
5. One of history's ironies: this measure adopted in 1920 was sponsored by Emile Morinaud, who a few years before had been one of the staunchest opponents to sustaining the Crémieux decree in Algeria.
6. See Cohen-Hadria's (1980) intelligent and lively comments on the Tunisian Jewish press and its leanings. On North African Zionism, see, for instance, Bensimon-Donath (1970:45–78) and Abitbol (1980b:197–210).
7. On these nuances and their meanings, see the editorial of June 30, 1936, in *L'Avenir Illustré*.
8. [*Pied-Noir* ("Black-feet"): generic, nonpejorative term designating French settlers in Algeria and including settlers of other European origins (mostly Spanish and Italian) who became French after moving to North Africa.—*Trans.*]

Chapter 1. A Colonial Phenomenon: Algerian Anti-Semitism

1. See Sivan 1980 for a study of the main themes of Algerian anti-Semitism.
2. The official count lists 26 dead of whom 23 Jews and 3 Moslems, and 81

Notes

wounded of whom 38 Jews, 35 Moslems, and 8 members of the police forces. See Ageron 1973 for a synthesis on the riots.

3. Besides the protestations of loyalty expressed by Moslem notables of every political tendency immediately after the riot, mention must be made of the account by R. Dournon of the *Presse Libre*; "A large red, white, and blue banner was displayed at the entrance of the Sidi-Rached bridge and beneath it another banner bore in French and in Arabic the inscription "Long live France!" (*Bulletin du Comité de l'Afrique Française*, September 1934, p. 521). Moreover, none of the reports at our disposal mentions any voicing of anti-French slogans by the rioters.

4. Among the many rumors that made the rounds a few hours before the grave events of August 5, the worst one was that Dr. Bendjelloul, a member of the city council and co-leader with F. Abbas of the *Mouvement libéral nationaliste*, had been murdered by the Jews (ibid., p. 520).

5. French Socialist party.

6. In fact many Jews had participated in Father Lambert's electoral campaign.

7. A.F.O.M. 16g. *Rapport du Commissaire divisionnaire, chef de la Police Spéciale Départementale à Monsieur le Préfet d'Oran*: February 1938.

8. The newspapers *Petit Oranais*, *Oran-Matin*, and *Echo d'Oran* made plenty of space available to G. Lambert and his friends.

9. *Le Républicain* (Constantine), July 8, 1938.

10. Emile Morinaud was mayor of Djidjelli. He had his sights on the post of mayor of Constantine he had lost a few years earlier.

11. A.F.O.M. 16g. *Rapport du Préfet de Constantine au Gouverneur Géneral de l'Algérie*: July 6, 1938.

12. Ibid., December 8, 1938.

13. Ibid., December 13, 1938.

14. The new decree stipulated that individuals would not have to fulfill the requirements of the Lambrech law if "their father or one of their paternal ascendants had been registed in an electoral list of French citizens previous to the current year." Lucien Bellat had, as a late imitator, Rozis, the mayor of Algiers, who two months after the promulgation of the Sarrault decree, tried to delete from the voting lists about 150 Jews whose ascendants presumably had never participated in an election. The mayor of Algiers sent them each a registered letter forty-eight hours before the local elections of March 1939.

15. The social composition of the Committee of the Amitiés Françaises is given here as example: President: Morinaud; "neighborhood leaders": Redarès (lawyer, member of the city council), Guignon (medical doctor), Giuly (mayor of Mila), Duplan (member of municipal council), Sancede (assistant to the mayor of Constantine); Treasurer General: Dessen (director of the chain of stores, Magasins du Globe). (A.F.O.M., Constantine: July 6, 1938).

16. Claude Martin has written a Ph.D. thesis on the Jews of Algeria. Its quality is dubious because of the anti-Semitic convictions of its author who collaborated with the Germans in Tunisia in 1943.

17. This project aimed at granting the rights of citizenship to specific categories of Algerian Moslems who would no longer be forced to give up their special personal status to make use of these rights (Julien 1972:113–14).

NOTES

18. A.F.O.M., Constantine: May 13, 1938.

19. Ibid., October 24, 1938.

20. During the organizational meeting of Amitiés Françaises, one of the assistants expressed his surprise that Morinaud continued to have his newspaper, the *Républicain*, printed by Attali, a Jewish printer. Morinaud promised to change the printer "within three weeks at the latest" (A.F.O.M., Constantine: July 5, 1938).

21. A.F.O.M., Oran: June 19, 1937.

22. A.F.O.M., *Rapport du Chef de la Police Spéciale Départementale*, Constantine: December 21, 1938.

23. A.F.O.M., Constantine: December 14, 1938.

24. A.F.O.M., *Rapport du Préfet de Constantine au Gouverneur Général de l'Algérie:* July 6, 1938.

25. A.F.O.M., *Rapport du Préfet d'Oran au Gouverneur Général de l'Algérie*, Oran: June 25, 1938. It must be noted that two months earlier, Louis Boujard had advocated sanctions against Lucien Bellat for his role in the electoral lists affair (April 25, 1938).

26. A.F.O.M., *Rapport du Centre d'Informations et d'Etudes de la Prefecture d'Oran*: October 27, 1939.

27. A.F.O.M., *Rapport du Chef de la Police Spéciale Départementale*, Constantine: November 23, 1939.

28. A.F.O.M., *Centre d'Information et d'Etudes*, Oran: September 14, 1939.

29. A.F.O.M., Constantine: February 1, 1940. Other accusations of the same type implicating Jewish notables were reported in various Algerian cities: Algiers, Tlemcen, Mascara, Mostaganem, Médéa, Blida, Sétif, and even in Laghouat.

30. A.F.O.M., *Centre d'Information et d'Etudes*, Algiers: July 12, 1938.

31. A.F.O.M., Oran: June 27, 1938. H. Zaoui, who was beheaded in front of ten thousand spectators, denied till the very end having committed this crime. In the emotionally charged atmosphere of Algeria at the time, people were for or against his sentence according to whether they were on the political right or left and whether they were anti-Semitic.

32. A.F.O.M., *Le Commissaire Central de la ville d'Oran au Préfet du Département*, Oran: June 15, 1938.

33. A.F.O.M., *Discours de M. Olivier devant la Section musulmane des Amitiés Latines*, Oran: June 15, 1938.

34. *La Lutte Sociale*, June 18, 1938.

35. Kaddour Belkaïm, *La Lutte Sociale*, October 15, 1938.

36. M. S. Zahiri, *"La propagande anti-juive dans les pays arabes,"* Oran Républicain, June 19, 1938.

37. On June 23, 1938, they were concerned with the visit of a local representative of the L.I.C.A. to the Great Mufti of Oran.

38. A.F.O.M., *Centre d'Informations et d'Etudes de la Prefecture d'Oran*: October 17, 1939.

39. See, for example, the "Message of Alarm" published by Elie Gozlan in the newspaper *Libération* of April 29, 1938.

40. Organization of young militants of the revisionist Zionist movement whose paper was significantly titled *Hacoakh* (strength).

Notes

The revisionist movement had already for many years advocated a policy of activism. In 1931 the newspaper *la Réveil juif* of Tunis heatedly attacked the leaders of the Jewish community of Oran who were fighting Dr. Molle's views solely by preaching civism: "It is with fighting that one must respond to Judeophobia. One must respond to a blow by a blow and to outrage by a good lesson. Generally speaking, the anti-Semite is a coward; if he dares attack it is because he has learned from his masters and from daily experience that the Jew is even more cowardly" (F. Allouche, "Au coup par le coup," *Le Réveil juif*, May 1, 1931, p.1). See also in the same newspaper, issue of June 26, 1931, the answer by Alfred Djian, the president of Oran's Club Civique who was "proud to state" that, thanks to the campaign conducted by his organization, "we have succeeded in shutting up the source of Oranian anti-Semitism, or at least to make it so benign that today it is reduced to being but a mere literary anti-Semitism."

41. A.R.O.M., *Rapport du Chef de la Police spéciale départementale au Préfet*, Oran: May 9, 1938.

42. Ibid.

43. Ibid.

44. These were Dr. Lévi-Valensi, president of the committee; E. Gozlan, journalist and secretary-general of the committee; Ghanassia, lawyer with the appelate court of Algiers; and M. Ghighi, councillor-general of Oran.

45. Authorities on Islamic law and theology.

46. For instance, Dr. Bendjelloul suggested in 1938, during the Financial Delegations session, that the census of the Algerian population should make a distinction between "citizens of European origin" and "citizens of Jewish origin." This led to a vehement protest by Ghighi, councillor-general of Oran, who also reproached the government's commissaire for having agreed to consider Dr. Bendjelloul's proposition: "It is Dr. Bendjelloul's own business if to satisfy the dictates of his politics he should ask for the moon or the Colonne Vendôme. But I cannot understand that you, Monsieur le Commissaire du Gouvernement, should declare that the administration will study the Bendjelloul project of discrimination against French citizens within the French Family. . . . " (Conseil général d'Oran: July 1, 1938).

Chapter 2. Moroccan and Tunisian Jews in the Face of the French Extreme Right and German and Italian Agitation

1. As example, here are some of the titles of these newspapers: *La Voix Française*, which was the organ of the Moroccan section of the P.P.F.; *Libre Parole Nord Africaine* of Algiers; *La France enchaînée* and *Réveil du Peuple*, both of Paris; *Halte-là* of Palikao (Algeria); *Bougie* of Fez.

2. Elie Cohen-Hadria tells of the circumstances surrounding this protest as follows: "Resident-General Peyrouton had Bourguiba and the neo-Destour leaders deported for reasons of internal Tunisian politics. Incidents analogous to those of Constantine would probably justify his decision. Agents, provocateurs cleverly set to work. But the Destourian leaders still in liberty caught wind of the scheme and caused it to fail by having the protesters adopt the rallying cry "El Yohoud Khouatna" (Cohen-Hadria 1980:63).

3. Incidents of a similar type occurred in 1932 in Sfax and in the Tunis region.

4. They were claiming that ever since Léon Blum had been in power the Jews

NOTES

had the tendency to forget that they were subjects of the Sultan. Some went so far as to demand the reestablishment of the laws used in the past against Jews in Islamic lands.

5. *La Voix Nationale*, November 1, 1938. On March 12, 1938, Radio-Roma broadcast the following declaration made by Makki al-Nasiri in Tétouan: "We hate France, the enemy of Islam and of religion because it is ruled by atheists and Jews, and particularly by such as Mr. Léon Blum."

6. This term is the equivalent of prime minister.

7. Equivalent to governor of a province or smaller area.

8. For an overall view of German and Italian propaganda see: Ageron 1977, 1979; Rainero 1977; Bessis 1981.

9. Ageron 1979:4–5. See also the information on this matter in the *Bulletin du Comité de l'Afrique Française*, November 1934, pp. 699–707.

10. For instance, *La Dépêche algérienne* of May 27, 1933, reports the following: "An Algiers industrialist had for the last thirty years a large body of customers drawn from the Moslem population of the three departments. . . . These last few days the rumor spread in the markets, in the *fondoks* [Arabic term referring to the places in a market area that serve as storage areas as well as inns—*Trans.*], and even into the encampments that this industrialist had fired his native workers to replace them with German refugees that had been expelled from their country by Hitler. The rumor was false. . . . The natives, not knowing that they had been duped, refused to purchase the familiar product and some were even seen trampling underfoot merchandises they had already bought, spitting on them, and forbidding their brethren to use them under threat of force. . . ." Following a similar mode of thinking, the makers of a well-known brand of Algerian cigarettes, wishing to promote sales among the Moslem population, had the idea of printing a swastika on its cigarette papers.

As to the actual possibility of immigration of Jewish refugees of Germany and central Europe to French overseas territories, it was unanimously opposed in the French colonial circles. (See, for instance, the position taken by A. Lahague in the article "Colonisation juive et colonies francaise" in *l'Afrique Française*, January 1938, pp. 6–10.)

11. The anti-Jewish policies manifested in fact the assimilationistic orientation of Italian colonialism. They are more reminiscent of the policy practiced by the Roman Empire in Judea and elsewhere than of contemporary anti-Semitic persecutions. On the origin of Mussolinean anti-Semitism, see Bernardini 1977: 431–53 and Bessis 1981: 189–92.

12. Police departments in Morocco recorded some examples of this direct propaganda: "One Cavazutti Guiseppe while passing through Meknès had asked for some oil for his car. . . . He refused to buy the Shell brand offered him and told the gas station operator: 'I do not want this brand because its Tangiers sales rep is a Jew.' Upon being told that the Meknès representative is French, he replied: 'French or Jew, it's the same thing.' Another Italian tourist traveling in Marrakech inquired on several occasions about relations between Moslems and Jews. He asked several Arabs: 'Do you like Jews? What kind of contacts do you have with them?' He explained to the guide who was taking him to various stores that he did not want to buy anything from the Jews. Upon giving alms to beggars he would ask if they were Jews or Moslems, adding that

he did not want to help Jews because Italy was anti-Semitic"(A.F.O.M. 27 x 21, *Direction de la Sécurité publique — La politique italienne en zone française du Maroc*: October 1938).

13. In fact, many Jews — particularly Tunisian — had not waited for these events nor for the anti-Jewish evolution of Italian fascism to renounce their Italian citizenship or to give up their activity in the service of Italy. Thus most of the Jewish members of the Unione quit the management of the newspaper in March 1926 (*Bulletin de l'Afrique Française*, April 1926, pp. 127-28; Bessis 1981).

14. After massive withdrawals by Jewish customers from the Italian Banque Commerciale of Casablanca, this establishment solicited the Moslem businessmen of the city by pointing out it was in their interest to deposit their money in the now "Aryanized" bank (A.F.O.M. 15 x 21).

15. On this topic, see *Le Réveil Juif*, issues of March 31, April 14 and 21, May 12, and June 2, 1933.

16. C.D.J.C: CDL-47, *Ambassade d'Italie à Madrid*: cable dated May 17, 1933; CDL-10, *Consulat général d'Italie à Rabat*: cables dated April 20 and May 17, 1933.

17. J. Ohayon, "Equilibre et sécurité," *l'Avenir Illustré*, June 30, 1936.

18. *L'Avenir Illustré*, May 31, 1936, related that an incident occurred in Fez between a group of young Jews and a European bookstore owner who was exhibiting in his store's window an anti-Semitic work. The newspaper concluded that "this act [by the Jews], far from helping the Jewish cause, endangered the reputation of our youth"; see also in the same vein the editorial "Neither Agitators, Nor Agitated" (ibid., June 30, 1936).

19. In Tunis, *Réveil Juif* (till 1934), *Semaine Juive*, and *Nouvelle Aurore* were the main organs for this tendency.

20. An anonymous report from Morocco addressed to the Jewish Agency advocated the publication of a major Jewish paper "written in Arabic, distributed free in specific Arab milieus, and which could offer with illustrations and supporting details an exact account of the Palestinian events as well as any event that, in all Arabic-speaking countries (North Africa, Middle East, etc.), would bring out the commonality of Judeo-Arab interests" (C.D.J.C.; 386-9).

21. In an article published in the Jewish paper the *Union Marocaine*, the president of the Casablanca section of the L.I.C.A. gave the following advice to the Jewish youth of Morocco: "Never abuse any of the power or any of the authority that fortuitous circumstances might put in your hands. . . . Make yourself respected, make yourself liked, and you will hold the key to the Judeo-Moslem rapprochement" (Dr. Bienvenue, "Le rapprochement judéo-marocain," *Union Marocaine*, April 30, 1937).

22. See Coidan 1946 on the circumstances of its organization.

23. "In defending France we will uphold our rational conviction that we are defending our religion and our customs, our freedom, and our culture that liberal and generous France has always respected," declared the president of the Jewish community of Mazagan (Morocco) during a formal meeting, and he invited the young Jewish men of the town to "voluntary enlist, to take up arms and to go fight at the side of the French soldiers" (*L'Union Marocaine*, September 8, 1939).

24. In Tunisia, Paul Ghez was the force behind this movement.

NOTES

Chapter 3. Toward Pétain's "National Revolution"

1. A.F.O.M., 26H20, *Résidence Générale de France à Tunis: Service d'information – Bulletin quotidien*, no.155 (March 16, 1940), *Allocution du Grand Rabbin de Tunisie, Haïm Bellaïche*.
2. Ibid.
3. Ibid.
4. A.F.O.M., 26H21, *Bulletin Quotidien*, no. 202 (May 21, 1940) and no. 205 (May 24, 1940).
5. A.F.O.M., 26H21, *Bulletin quotidien* no. 207 (May 26–27, 1940).
6. A.F.O.M., 32H6, *Résidence Générale de la République Française au Maroc: Direction des Affaires Politiques – Bulletin de reseignements Politiques et Economiques*, September 17–23, 1939.
7. Ibid., *Bulletin hebdomadaires* (May 5–11 and 19–25, 1940)
8. *Bulletin hebdomadaire* (May 26–June 1, 1940).
9. *Bulletin hebdomadaire* (August 4–10, 1940).
10. *Bulletin hebdomadaire* (July 21–27, 1940)
11. *Bulletin hebdomadaire* (September 8–14, 1940).
12. *Bulletin hebdomadaire* (September 15–20, 1940).
13. A.F.O.M., 26H21, *Résidence Generale de France à Tunis: Service d'Information – Bulletin quotidien*, no. 235 (June 28, 1940); no. 260 (July 27, 1940), nos. 267–69 (August 4–7, 1940); no. 274 (August 13, 1940); no. 275 (August 14, 1940); no. 277 (August 17, 1940); no. 278 (August 18–19, 1940); no. 281 (August 22, 1940); no. 298 (September 11, 1940).
14. Ibid., nos. 267–69 (August 4–7, 1940).
15. A.F.O.M., 16g, *Centre d'Information et d'Etudes*, Oran: July 15, 1940.
16. Ibid.
17. Ibid., Algiers: August 4, 1940.
18. In the Constantinois region, Dr. Benjelloul is thought to have had circulated at the beginning of September an appeal to stay calm directed at the Moslem population, which in Bône and in Constantine was delivered by town criers inviting it to ignore the anti-Jewish agitation of the P.P.F. (A.F.O.M., 16c, *Rapport du Commissaire de la Police Spéciale départementale*, Bône: September 10, 1940).
19. This decree, passed on March 21, 1939, by the Daladier administration, forbade all acts of incitement to social or religious hatred. Its repeal by the Pétain regime on August 27, 1940, is considered the first anti-Jewish action taken by Vichy.
20. A.F.O.M., 16g, *Centre Départemental d'Information d'Oran*, Nemours: August 19, 1940.
21. Ibid., *Centre d'information et d'Etudes*, Algiers: September 4, 1940.
22. Ibid., *Police Spéciale du Département d'Oran*, August 31, 1940.
23. Ibid., *Préfecture de Constantine–Centre Départemental d'Information*, Constantine: October 1, 1940. In Constantine and in the other Algerian cities, the police came by this information from agents, for the most part Moslems, who had more or less "infiltrated" Jewish milieus. More provocators than informants, they were producing reports filled with improbable facts, such as this dialogue between Jews overheard by a "good informant" of the C.I.E. during the visit of Admiral Abrial, governor-general of Algeria, in Constantine:

Notes

"We must absolutely get rid of Pétain."
"Don't worry; we have enough money for this. Haven't we bought the Crémieux decree from France in 1870? We will always be able to take care of things with our money." (*Centre d'Information et d'Etudes*, Constantine: August 8, 1940)

24. "Let's kick them out as they did in Europe. We will have to kiss our freedom good-bye if others do the kicking out for us." This was printed on a leaflet distributed in Constantine on September 12, 1940.

Chapter 4. The Maghreb after the Armistice: Attempts at Resistance and Militant Pétainism

1. On this question and on the discussions within the French government on the eve of the armistice, see, for instance, Aron 1954:25-73; Noguères 1955:77-114; Truchet 1955; Goutard 1961; Paxton 1966:25-33.

2. Résident-général of Morocco since 1937 and commander-in-chief of the North African war theater.

3. Governor-general of Algeria since 1936.

4. D.G.F.P., series D, vol. 10, Madrid (July 3, 1940), p. 99; Tétouan (July 8, 1940), p. 160. See the reports of the American ambassador to Madrid on the prevailing opinion in Spain regarding a possible attack against French Morocco, F.R.U.S., vol. 2, 1940: Madrid (July 26, 1940), pp. 575-76.

5. On this topic, see the "confiding" of Auer, the German consul in Casablanca, to R. Murphy, in Murphy 1964:78-79.

6. F.R.U.S., 1940, Vol. 2: Casablanca (November 3, 1940), p. 620.

7. This was the name given in Algiers to the legion's insignia.

8. In fact, the marshal seriously considered removing Noguès from office. He changed his mind after the interventions of Weygand and of General Georges, who felt that "it might be dangerous . . . to do without the services of a resident-general whose authority was recognized and acknowledged by every Moroccan leader" (Weygand 1950:339-40).

9. His opposition to the American plans had been known for a long time. On this, see Murphy 1964: 112.

10. In his *Memoirs*, Weygand praises himself for having prevented Doriot's stay in Algeria and for having limited the P.P.F.'s activities in North Africa (p. 496). One cannot say as much for Yves Châtel, his successor, whose right-hand man was Canavaggio, one of the better known leaders of the P.P.F.

11. F.R.U.S., 1942, vol. 2: Casablanca (September 29, 1942), pp. 382-83.

12. To these sources of information, one might add radio, films, and newspapers published under German sponsorship in Paris such as *Gringoire, l'Illustration, Je suis partout, L'Action française*.

13. Aboulker 1952: 80-83; Cohen-Hadria 1976: 156-57. See also the complaint filed by the resistance groupings of France Combattante against the *Echo d'Oran* on May 26, 1945 (C.D.J.C.: 385-22, p. 10).

14. In his message pledging his allegiance to the new regime, the Moroccan sultan made a point of mentioning the role played by Marshal Pétain in the squashing of the Rif rebellion (*New York Times*, July 22, 1940).

NOTES

15. One can read in an official report on the political atmosphere in Guelma (Algeria) in October 1940: "One gets the feeling of a marked change in the natives' feelings toward us. The excitement has gradually subsided these past few weeks; the attitude of insubordination, the arrogance, and devious hostility that for a while seemed to dominate their attitude toward our authority have completely disappeared" (A.F.O.M., 11H 51, *Bulletin d'Information*, no. 347, October 23, 1940).

16. *F.R.U.S.*, 1940, 2: Washington (October 30, 1940), pp. 606-7.

17. Ibid., 1941, 2: Lisbon (January 14, 1941) (Murphy report), pp. 206-12.

18. On German propaganda and its influence on the political evolution of Moslem milieus during the war, see Ageron 1973, 75, 77, 79; Kaddache 1979. See also the archival documents reproduced in Driss 1979.

19. Ageron 1979:24; the *Bulletin d'Information* of the resident's office notes that, in Casablanca's Moslem neighborhoods, "the Germans are often referred to as *Haj* and the term *m'allem* (master) is used to designate the führer" (A.F.O.M., 32 H 6, *Rapport hebdomadaire*, May 16, 1941).

20. A.F.O.M., 11H51, *Bulletin d'Information*, no. 338,Algiers (October 11, 1940).

21. According to some sources, the sultan himself might have been in contact with the abwehr to which, through the intermediary of the mufti of Jerusalem, he is supposed to have conveyed the news of the November 1942 Allied landing as well as the detail of the Anfa meeting (on this topic, see Paillole and Ageron 1979: 25–26 and notes 46-47). In Casablanca Noguès had access to the German consulate forbidden to Moslems. While in Algiers, the president of the Moslem scouting organization was arrested and eventually shot for having contacts with members of the Armistice Commission. Moreover, French authorities tried to reduce the number of voluntary North African workers sent to the Occupied Zone of France (Ageron 1979: 27; Kaddache 1979: 112–14).

22. Notable's son and former master sergeant, al-Maadi Lakhdar had been a member of the Cagoule [*Cagoule* means "hood." It refers to an extreme right-wing organization that operated in France during the last years of the Third Republic— Trans.] in 1937. He had also organized an association called Algérie Française, which was violently anti-Communist and anti-Jewish. In 1943 he took over the directorship of the pro-Nazi paper *El-Rachid*.

23. *F.R.U.S.*, 1942, 2: Algiers (November 6, 1942), pp. 427-29.

Chapter 5. Vichy and the Jews of North Africa

1. See, for instance, François Charles-Roux's answer to the comment of the American chargé d'affaires who saw in the Jewish Statute another proof of the influence of Nazi ideas on the French government (*F.R.U.S.*, 1940, 2: Vichy [October 18, 1940], pp. 567–68). See also in the same vein Darlan's answer to Admiral Leahy's critical comments (ibid., 1941, 2, p. 511).

2. We do not intend, in the few general comments that follow, to give a full account of the situation of France's Jews under Vichy. On this topic, see, for instance, Billig 1955–60; Aron 1956; Hilberg 1973; Paxton 1973; Marrus and Paxton 1981.

3. And thus while Laval, Darlan, and Vallat liked to give the Germans the impression that Marshal Pétain was indecisive and hesitant (N.G. 24323, 4, 1941; N.G. 2442, March 6, 1941), P. Baudoin, on the contrary, refers to him as a man of resolve and "severity" toward Jews (Aron 1956:167).

4. For the comparison of the German and French texts, see Billig 1955-60: pp. 149-195; on the problem of the Karaites and other "legally ambiguous" minorities, see Green 1979.

5. Yad Vashem Archives, N.G. 2432 (YVSH-N 11/634/E): cable from Otto Abetz to Berlin, Paris, April 3, 1941.

6. X. Vallat's statement, dated March 5, 1941, to General von Stulpnagel, the German military commander of France (C.D.J.C., 75-145).

7. L'Echo d'Alger, August 29, 1941 (after Vallat's trip in North Africa). Even though they were included under the heading "France" in the sinister statistics of the Wannsee conference where on January 20, 1942, it was decided to set the Final Solution in motion, and even though German authorities in Paris occasionally mentioned them in their correspondence, it does not appear that North African Jews were the object of any particular "attention" on the part of the Nazis before the occupation of Tunisia in November 1942.

8. La Rocque, "La question juive," *Le Petit Journal de Paris*, October 5, 1940.

9. Statement by J. Barthelemy, justice minister, to the periodical *Patrie* in August 1941, cited in the *Bulletin de la Fédération des Sociétés juives d'Algérie*, no. 71 (August 1941), p. 3.

10. Under Charles Maurras's pen, this idea of French "hospitality" was expressed in the following manner: "We are the masters of the house that our fathers have built and for which they have given of their sweat and their blood. We have the absolute right to impose our conditions on the nomads we allow in. . . . " (*L'Action Française*, October 19, 1940).

11. *L'Echo d'Oran*, January 14, 1941. Statement by General Paquin, president of the Algerian Légion des Combattants.

12. According to the conditions set up by this law, any Algerian could on demand obtain French citizenship if he was 25 years or older and if he was monogamous or single. In addtion, he must have served in the armed forces or be the recipient of a French decoration. There is no doubt that many Algerian Jews could without too much difficulty meet the conditions required by this law. The definitive status of Algerian Jews was set by the law of February 18, 1942.

13. *L'Action Française*, October 9, 1940; see also, in the same vein, the response of Stanislas Devaud, the leader of the Algerian P.S.F., in *Le Petit Journal*, October 9, 1940.

14. *La Croix* (Paris), October 9, 1940.

15. A.F.O.M., 11H51: *Bulletin d'Information*, no. 345 (October 20, 1940).

16. Ibid., no. 342 (October 17, 1940).

17. Ibid., no. 357 (November 6, 1940).

18. Ibid., no. 344 (October 19, 1940).

19. Ibid., no. 348 (October 24, 1940).

20. Ibid., no. 349 (October 25, 1940).

21. A.F.O.M., 16C. *Centre d'Informations et d'Etude*, Algiers: October 19, 1940. A similar response was noted in Morocco where "the marshal's popularity is still very large thanks to the repeal of the Crémieux decree" (A.F.O.M., 32H6, *Bulletin Hebdomadaire*, October 13, 1940).

22. A.F.O.M., 11H51, *Bulletin d'Information*, no. 354 (November 2, 1940).

23. A.R.O.M., 16g, *Centre d'Information et d'Etudes*, Algiers: October 24, 1940.

24. Ibid., Oran: October 18, 1940; October 22, 1940.
25. Ibid., Algiers: January 16, 1941.
26. Published in the *Bulletin de la Fédération des Sociétés Juives d'Algérie*, no. 65 (1940); it is also reprinted in Eisenbeth 1945:15.
27. J.O.E.F., October 18, 1940; J.O.A., October 29, 1940. See Lubetzki 1945, 28–39, for a detailed analysis of the racial motivations of this law as well as of its "loopholes" and the juridical problems raised by it.
28. However, we must note that, unlike the German law, the French one was meant to be a "police law" and not a law for the protection of racial purity. It did not forbid intimate relations between Jews and non-Jews and it did not adopt the German notion of *Mishlinge* (half-Jew) with all its different variants.
29. The Moroccan *dahir* was promulgated on October 31, 1940 (B.O.M., November 9, 1940), while the Beylical decree was promulgated only a month later on November 30, 1940 (J.O.T., December 3, 1940).
30. France's Conseil d'Etat [highest body of civil servants in France—*Trans.*] had decided that only the administrators, directors, and secretaries-general of these concessionary or subsidized entreprises (such as public transports) would be affected by this interdiction. In Algeria, Admiral Abrial extended the interdiction to cover all employees dealing with the public. He refused to give them back their jobs following the decision of the Conseil d'Etat "because of the repercussions such a step would have in European and native milieus." He advocated that the situation as it stood should be legitimized with the promulgation of an appropriate decree. He explained to Admiral Darlan that "such a decision is entirely justified in Algeria because of the proportionally higher Jewish population there than in metropolitan France, or the relatively large number of Jewish employees in all the various adminstrations, public services, and enterprises, and of the keen attention Algerian milieus, and more particularly native ones, pay to every measure aimed at diminishing Jewish influence" (C.D.J.C.: 371-39: Algiers, April 14, 1941). Admiral Abrial's suggestion was submitted to the Commissariat-General for the Jewish Question, which found it important enough to make it a part of the new Jewish Statute of June 2, 1941 (C.D.J.C.; 371-39, Vichy, May 3, 1941: Xavier Vallat to Admiral Darlan).
31. The Moroccan text sets another date, that of October 24, 1919. We have not uncovered the reasons for these differences.
32. These provisions, which created a privileged situation for Jews of Tunisian origin who had been naturalized French, were all the more surprising in that in metropolitan France, according to the law of July 17, 1940, only native French or individuals born of a "French father" had the possibility for similar exemptions.
33. It was *le Petit Matin*, whose editor-in-chief was Max Zetlaoui; despite its official subtitle, this newspaper does not seem to have played the role of organ for the defense of the "legitimate interests" of Tunisian Jews.
34. In Morocco, the new law was promulgated on August 5, 1941 (B.O.M., August 8, 1941), while in Tunisia only a Beylical decree was promulgated on June 26, 1941, pertaining to "modifications of the decree of November 30, 1940 (J.O.T., June 28, 1941).
35. See Lubetski 1945:31–39 for some of the cases brought to the rabat and the Algiers courts.

Notes

36. This provision, which in Morocco applied "to Jews other than Moroccan Jews," (articles 1, 4, and 6) is not mentioned in the Tunisian decree.

37. *Dépêche Algérienne*, November 30, 1941. The broadening in Algeria of the meaning of the term *public function* (civil service) used in the law was such that assistants, concierges, masons, and locksmiths were fired under the pretext that they were paid by a public body or by a concessionary service. Later, when the law setting compensations to be paid to civil servants affected by the Jewish Statute was enacted, many of them were told they had no right to these compensations because they were not. . . civil servants. Thus these words had a different meaning when Jewish employees were fired and when they were to be compensated.

38. As in metropolitan France, the corresponding texts were published in North Africa on the same date as the June 2 statute.

39. In Tunisia, this deadline was extended by a month by a decree of August 13, 1941 (J.O.T., August 26, 1941).

40. The census in Algeria furnished many useful details on the Algerian Jewry; there had been no official statistical data since the end of the nineteenth century. It turned out there were 116,800 Jews in Algeria in 1941; this amounted to 1.63 percent of the total population and 14.09 percent of the European population of the colony. These figures were below the estimates of the commissariat-general, and so Xavier Vallat requested the governor-general "to complete this first census with a series of measures aimed at bringing out Jews who had tried to evade the provisions of the law" (C.D.J.C.: 81–30a, Vichy, November 28, 1941).

41. J.O.A., November 10, 1941. In Morocco, the *numerus clausus* was applied with uncommon stringency. In Oujda the bar had excluded Jewish lawyers from its ranks well before the publication of the decree's order of application (*le Petit Marocain*, June 27, 1941). In Casablanca, out of a total of thirty Jewish lawyers, only four were kept (among whom a war prisoner and a *pupille de la nation*). The public authorities there went so far as to disbar J. Bonan, one of the country's most eminent lawyers, despite the decision in his favor by the appelate court of Rabat (C.D.J.C.: 54–19: *Dossier Bonan*, January 1941-May 1942; 54–24: *Extrait du Registre des Délibérations de la Cour d'Appel de Rabat*, August 18, 1941).

42. B.O.M., March 6, 1942. On the other hand, General Noguès denied the community's request to allow the expelled Jewish doctors (seventeen out of a total of thirty-four) to continue to provide care for their patients.

43. Another exception was the decree of June 6, 1942, which forbade Jews the professions of actors in plays, movies, and operas and was not applicable to Algeria.

44. This decree, promulgated in Algeria on November 19, 1941 (J.O.A., November 19, 1941), preceded by about a month the corresponding decree promulgated in metropolitan France (decree of December 26, 1941).

45. Decree of February 3, 1942 (J.O.A., February 27, 1942).

46. Decree of February 8, 1942 (J.O.A., March 3, 1942).

47. Decree of September 9, 1942 (J.O.A., October 20, 1942).

48. *Echo d'Alger*, August 16, 1941. The residents-general of Morocco and of Tunisia argued that the special organization of the two protectorates as well as budgetary difficulties made it impossible for them to agree to the commissariat-general's request that they proceed similarly as in Algeria, or at least that they accept delegates from

NOTES

the commissariat. On October 12, 1941, Admiral Darlan declared to Xavier Vallat that "the resident-general of France at Tunis feels that the sending of a delegate from the commissariat does not meet a need because his administration is already provided, thanks to you, with all the material pertaining to the Jewish problems." As to Admiral Noguès, "he feels that your representative's mission in Morocco should be limited to the study in the field during a relatively short time of some doubtful cases" (C.D.J.C.: 86-16: Vichy, October 11, 1941). In his answer, Xavier Vallat expressed his "great surprise" in the face of the two residents' responses: "The sending of a *chargé de mission* . . . could not be seriously interpreted as an attempt to take over any of the prerogatives stemming from their responsibilities. . . . As I see it, on the contrary, the aim is to put at the disposal of Monsieur le General Noguès and of Monsieur l'Amiral Estéva an agent able to help them benefit from metropolitan France's experience, particularly in economic Aryanization" (C.D.J.C.: 239-43: Vichy, October 18, 1943).

49. In the absence of universities attended by Jews, this law was not relevant in Morocco and Tunisia.

50. R. Brunschvig, "Les mesures anti-juives dans l'enseignement en Algérie sous le regime de Vichy," *Revue d'Alger* 1 (1944), pp. 57-79.

51. It took up to October 19, 1942, for a law to be passed that formally set "the conditions for the admission of Jewish students in institutions of higher learning" (J.O.A. November 6, 1942). In addition, this lack of legal basis did not prevent the authorities of the Moroccan protectorate from extending to the high schools and elementary schools of the Shereefian kingdom the provisions enacted in Algeria by instituting a *numerus clausus* of 10 percent (*Circulaire no. 887 de l'Instruction Publique de 1941*). In Tunisia as well, Jewish students were excluded from the secondary cycle under the same conditions as in Algeria.

52. *Circulaire no. 7738/a du Recteur de l'Académie d'Alger* (October 17, 1941), cited by Ansky 1950: 124-25.

53. *Bulletin de la Fédération des Sociétés Juives d'Algérie*, no. 83, October 1942, p. 3.

54. It can been seen that the number of students maintained in the system was well beneath the official *numerus clausus*. This stems from the fact that the *numerus clausus* was applied in each class rather than in each institution. We must note also the stringent instructions given by the Algerian Academy, which forced school principals to discount fractions beyond the highest unit in calculating admission percentage (Brunschvig 1944: 65).

55. C.D.J.C., 371-46: letter from General de la Porte du Theil to Xavier Vallat, Châtel Guyon, February 7, 1942.

56. According to the figures provided by the general, there were four hundred Jewish members in 1941 to which were to be added five hundred to six hundred new recruits for 1942.

57. C.D.J.C., 371-46: Xavier Vallat to General de la Porte de Theil, Vichy, February 23, 1942.

58. J.O.A., November 7, 1941. This text was simply an Algerian version of the French decree of July 28, 1941, which, however, in its initial version had been declared nonapplicable to Algeria, to the colonies, and to the protectorates.

59. *Arrêté* of October 30, 1941 (J.O.A. November 7, 1941).

Notes

60. J.O.A., December 12, 1941. This text was replaced later by the law of November 17, 1941, which was applied to Algeria through the decree of April 13, 1942 (J.O.A., May 12, 1942).

61. The law was not taken lightly at the comissariat-general. Having noticed that it was applied leniently in the cases noted above, Jarnieu, the head of Office for Economic Aryanization, asked the governor-general "to make very careful use" of his right to grant exceptions because "of the importance of the economic Aryanization of Jewish enterprises in Algeria" (C.D.J.C., 381–47: Vichy, May 6, 1942).

62. *Arrêtés* of December 16, 1941 (J.O.A., December 23, 1941), March 25, 1942 (J.O.A., March 27, 1942), and July 20, 1942 (J.O.A., July 24, 1942).

63. *Arrêté* of March 29, 1942 (J.O.A., March 24, 1942) and the law of June 30, applicable directly to Algeria, pertaining to the deadline for the bidding on Jewish property (J.O.E.F., June 24, 1942).

64. Law of November 2, 1941, applied to Algeria through the decree of March 3, 1942 (J.O.A., April 14, 1942) and through the *arrêté* of April 13, 1942 (J.O.A., April 14, 1942).

65. Applied to Algeria through the decree of March 15, 1942 (J.O.A., March 31, 1942).

66. Law of July 2, 1942 (J.O.A., July 28, 1942).

67. *Arrêté* of September 7, 1942 (J.O.A., September 11, 1942).

68. Decree of April 30, 1942 (J.O.T., May 2, 1942).

69. Decree of April 30, 1942 (J.O.T., May 2, 1942).

70. Vallat was to contrast with Admiral Estéva's attitude not only that of General Noguès but also that of the bey's prime minister who was supposed to have notified the commissariat-general "of his master's impatience to sign the decrees applying the French legislation to the French protectorate" (C.D.J.C.: 239–43: Vichy, October 18, 1941).

71. *Arrêté* of May 12, 1942 (J.O.T., May 19, 1942).

72. *Arrêté* of May 18, 1942 (J.O.T., May 19, 1942).

73. *Arrêté* of May 18, 1942 (J.O.T., May 21, 1942).

74. *Arrêté* of May 30, 1942 (J.O.T., June 6, 1942).

75. *Arrêté* of June 2, 1942 (J.O.T., June 11, 1942).

76. *Arrêté* of June 19, 1942 (J.O.T., June 27, 1942).

77. B.O.M., August 22, 1941, According to the clauses of this *dahir*, Jews who could not prove that they lived at their present address before September 1, 1939, were to vacate their housing before September 22, 1941, a day that coincided with the Jewish new year.

78. C.D.J.C. 82-12: "*l'application du statut des Juifs et des dispositions raciales à la population juive du Maroc,*" February 1943).

79. The largest "catch" was that of the Algiers police, which arrested twenty Jewish wholesalers who were to be brought to trial at the end of 1941 before the state tribunal (*L'Echo d'Oran*, November 30, 1941).

80. Cited in the newspaper *Dernières Nouvelles* (Algiers), November 19, 1941.

81. There were, however, some silences pregnant with meaning, such as the North African church and its top dignitaries among whom, to our knowledge, not a single one had the courage or the will to criticize openly Vichy's racist policy—this in contrast with church dignitaries in metropolitan France.

NOTES

82. The only official document we know of that mentions the unpopularity of anti-Jewish measures in North Africa comes from the Inspection Générale des Renseignements Généraux (main office overseeing the gathering of general information) in Vichy and not from police departments in North Africa. The document points out that these measures were mainly unpopular in Morocco "where Spanish envoys were cleverly using them against our country." This document, the original of which is at the C.D.J.C. (80-11a: Vichy, August 29, 1941), is published in Ansky 1950:151.

83. After the war, Moïse Borgel, the president of the Jewish community of Tunisia, publicly praised Admiral Estéva. "I am doing justice to the truth in acknowledging that Admiral Estéva, whose deeply religious feelings we were well aware of, seemed to make an effort to lessen the inhumaneness of the implementation of racial laws. I have kept the impression that he had slowed down this process or that he had in some way tried to limit its impact" (C.D.J.C.: 388-35: *Lettre de M.Borgel á Maître Chresteil*, Tunis, February 28, 1946).

84. This letter is published in Sabille 1954:166.

85. Deceased on June 19, 1942, Ahmad Pasha Bey, who had ruled since February 1929, was succeeded by Moncef Bey, who, after the Liberation, was deposed and exiled to France by General Juin.

86. These were an opthalmologist, Dr. Nataf, and a lawyer, Paul Ghez who was to play a crucial role in the Jewish community during the German occupation.

87. The place allocated in the *Petit Matin* (June 25, 1942) to this statement uttered by the sovereign in front of Admiral Estéva, leads one to surmise that as far as the "Jewish newspaper" was concerned, the bey's statements were aimed primarily at the Jews, because neither the Europeans nor the Islamic Tunisians needed this well-meaning but ambiguous reassurance.

88. *Petit Matin*, September 12 and October 12, 1942. Through this implicit disavowal of the anti-Jewish policy of the government, Moncef Bey, who was said to be close to the nationalist position, thus distanced himself from the residency and France.

89. NG-054 (YVSH.N-11/553/E): State Secretary Document no. 507: Berlin, September 2, 1942.

90. Ibid., Weizsacker to Under Secretary of State Luther, September 3, 1942.

91. NG-5094 (C.D.J.C., 127-39): Under Secretary Luther, notes for a report (*Report on the Jews of France*).

92. NG-4960 (YVSH.N-11/553/E): Italy and the Jewish Question (November 1942).

93. Of course, there were among the French personnel of the residency and of the protectorate's offices some high-ranking civil servants who did find opportunity to express their sympathy to the Jews, but their actions and influence were usually as futile as they were limited. (See, for instance, the report by Gould, the American general consul, on the friendly attitude of Cointard, the contrôleur civil [civilians' controller] of Casablanca, toward the Jews of his city.) (*F.R.U.S.*, 1940, 3: Casablanca, August 12, 1940, p. 577.)

94. This rumor, which over the years and up to the present was to paint the Moroccan sultan as defender and even as savior of his country's Jews, made its way to the Jewish milieus of the Free Zone. According to a report from the office of Renseignements Généraux (dated May 29, 1941), ". . . they are claiming [in those milieus], on

Notes

the basis on British-originated information, that the Moroccan sultan has refused to apply French anti-Jewish laws on the grounds that he could not detect any difference in the loyalty of his subjects. They praise the good sense of the soverign and they openly state that the French government could use some lessons in tolerance from him" (C.D.J.C., 31-47). To our knowledge, no anti-Jewish measure was ever supressed or slowed down as a result of the Sultan's intervention.

95. C.D.J.C., 82-12, L'application du Statut des Juifs. According to this eyewitness account, the sovereign had stated to the Jewish notables that he regarded them as Moroccan as the Moslems, and equal to other Moroccans, and that they were not to be affected "in their persons or their property."

96. El-Mundo (Madrid), June 20, 1941. For a study of Spain's attitude toward the Jews during the Holocaust, see Avni 1975.

97. Letter from M. Battani to Xavier Vallat: Algiers, July 20, 1941 (C.D.J.C.: 371-6).

98. Letter of M. Bullier to Darquier de Pellepoix: Oran, July 13, 1942 (C.D.J.C.: 35-59).

99. A. Roncoeur to Xavier Vallat: Algiers, December 5, 1941 (C.D.J.C.: 114-77a).

100. L. Bonzon to Xavier Vallat: Paris, May 16, 1941 (C.D.J.C.: 371-2).

101. C.D.J.C. 35-54: Chinchant (Oranie), May 24, 1942. Removed from the office of mayor by Admiral Abrial, Lambert described his new circumstances to Darquier de Pellepoix as follows: "[After being removed from my position] I went to the countryside in search of peace. I am now a settler in a tiny village; I am raising hundreds of hogs, cows, and am growing thousands of quintals of vegetables. My wife, a settler's daughter, is a perfect mate and we are awaiting your visit; there is plenty of room and no restrictions. We'll choose a fat little lamb from the flock and prepare a succulent mechoui [word of Arabic origin meaning the roasting of a whole animal on a stick over an outdoor fire—Trans.] and then you can choose from among the chicken, geese, guinea fowl, ducks, etc., whatever you feel like eating. And you will thus gain strength for the big job that awaits you in France and Algeria—particularly in Algeria."

102. It appears from the severity of his decisions that there were few requests receiving a favorable answer. Dr. Costa was particularly vehement regarding Dr. Levy, a former mayor of Algiers and a Catholic with only two Jewish grandparents. He wrote to Gazagne: "Let us not confuse race and religion. A baptized nigger is still a nigger" (C.D.J.C.; 87-27: Algiers, January 27, 1942).

103. Lucien Costa to René Gazagne, October 17, 1941 (C.D.J.C. 84-14).

104. M. Ansky estimates the number of requests to be temporary trustees of Jewish properties reached six thousand (1950:168).

105. Letter from the president of the Ordre des Avocats de Sétif, H. de Bourges to Xavier Vallat, May 16, 1941.

106. Report of the Cooperative des Blés d'Oran to the Commissariat-General for the Jewish Question of September 22, 1942 (C.D.J.C., 117-114). In January 1941, however, the president of the Algerian Business Union had warned the governor of Algeria about the dangers inherent in any attempt to destroy the wholesale grain industry, controlled almost totally by Jews. According to him, the Jews had specialized in this field because they were natives of the colony "and consequently more apt to understand the needs of the natives." He made similar comments regarding the leather and the cloth industries, where Jewish participation also predominated (C.D.J.C., 54-12: Algiers, January 6, 1941).

NOTES

107. Ever since the abrogation of the Marchandeau law, the authorities did not have to forbid the expression of anti-Jewish propaganda. But this did not mean that they should support it! The anti-Semitic pamphlet *Les Droits de la Race supérieure* by Isaac Blumchen (pseudonym for Urbain Gohier) was mimeographed into 600 copies at the quarters of the forty-first Corps of Engineers at Rabat by order of Commandant Pelissier of the Camp of the Tourarga (C.D.J.C., 82-1).

108. A.F.O.M. (Aix), 16g, various police reports: Algiers, October 15, 1940; Orléan ville, December 2, 1940; Constantine, December 18, 1940; Bône, December 23, 1940; Algiers, January 8, 1941; February 11, 1941.

109. Ibid., Constantine, March 14, 1941.

110. Ibid., Aumale, November 10, 1941.

111. C.D.J.C., 386-18: *Lettre des Présidents des Communautés juives du Maroc au Général Noguès*, Casablanca, June 27, 1941.

112. Ibid., 80-11b: *Rapport de l'audience accordée par Xavier Vallat aux anciens combattants juifs d'Algérie*, Algiers, August 25, 1941.

113. A.F.O.M., 32H6: Résidence Générale du Maroc, *Bulletin d'Information Hebdomadaire*, December 8, 1940.

114. This attitude is implied in the cited texts and notes 1 and 3, p. 143. To this we can add the following statement by Grand Rabbi Eisenbeth to Xavier Vallat: "We Jews we do not understand the opposition between Marshal Pétain's evangile and the actions of his government. Racial theories come from the other side of the Rhine. Why not tell us that the rebuilding of France requires this sacrifice by the Jews? Faced with such a frankness, we would be able to accept every sacrifice required of us for the greatness of France" (Eisenbeth 1945: 30).

115. B.F.S.J.A., no. 69, May 1941: *Un acte de foi* by J. Shapira.

116. See, for instance, B.F.S.J.A., no. 66 (March 1941); no. 75 (December 1941), and no. 82 (August-September 1942).

117. See, for instance, J. Ginvert, *la tâche capitale du judaïsme moderne*, B.F.S.J.A., no. 74, November 1941; A Syngalowski, "O.R.T.," ibid., no. 77, February 1942; J. Kalstein, *Souvenirs d'un voyage en Palestine*, ibid., no. 82 August-September 1942.

118. Eyewitness accounts of S. Barad (summer 1978), M. Cohen (summer 1978), and A. Scemama (summer 1979). Among these *shlihim*, the most active was Nahum Yerushalmi, who was in Tunis since 1938.

119. North African Jewish communities also were concerned with the fate of Jewish prisoners incarcerated in camps in southern Morocco and southern Algeria. This impulse of solidarity was not looked upon kindly by the administration nor by a part of European public opinion that accused Jewish communities of engaging in black market activities to be able to help their refugees. (See on this topic the cable sent to Darquier de Pellepoix by the leader of the S.O.L. of Relizane after the arrival in the Oran department of some Jewish families, refugees from Libya.) (C.D.J.C., 111: 48, September 9, 1942.)

120. We know that the A.I.U. schools were not much affected by racial legislation. In September 1941 Admiral Darlan intervened with Xavier Vallat to have the freeze of A.I.U.'s funds lifted: "In case the German authorities should raise some objections, we must point out to them that the Alliance Israélite constitutes an important means of exerting influence, and the British government would inherit

this means should we hinder its functioning" (C.D.J.C., 31-13: Vichy, September 10, 1941).

121. The Algiers committee was presided over by Dr. A. Levi-Valensi and had as principal leaders Rabbi Eisenbeth and Elie Gozlan. The Oran committee was led by A. Smadja, the president of the consistory of this town, and by Rabbi Askenazi. The Constantine committee was organized by André Bakouche, president of the local consistory, and by Rabbi M. Jais (Eisenbeth 1945:20-22).

122. In Oran, the local section the Jewish Boy Scouts of France organized in 1942 a preapprenticeship center where about twenty teenagers were enrolled. Besides general "cultural, ethical, and physical" instruction, they also received vocational training in carpentry, welding, or industrial drafting (C.D.J.C., 420-21: Oran, July 29, 1942).

123. E. Gozlan, *Pour nos enfants*, B.F.S.J.A., no. 75, December 1941.

124. C.D.J.C., 385-18: *La condition des Israélites français d'origine algérienne.*

125. J.O.A., January 30, 1942. The initiative for the promulgation of this text came from the Service Algérien des Questions Juives, which formulated its provisions before submitting them for the approval of the Commissariat-General for the Jewish Question. (On this topic, see the correspondence between Franceschini and Jarnieu, C.D.J.C. 81-29a: Algiers, October 30, 1941; 371-44: Vichy, November 11, 1941, and February 17, 1941.)

126. J.O.A., August 12, 1942. This order was followed on August 21, 1942, by a second one (J.O.A., August 28, 1942), which made the provisions of the December 31 law applicable to the southern territories.

127. This is the decree of February 14, 1942, making applicable to Algeria the law of November 29, 1941, instituting a Union Générale des Israélites de France. We note that, since the armistice, Grand Rabbi Eisenbeth was considered by authorities the qualified representative of Algerian Jewry, a role his official functions would not have qualified him for under ordinary circumstances. This "promotion" of Rabbi Eisenbeth, who, it must be emphasized, did enjoy his brethren's full support, translated the public authorities' intent to regard the Jewish element as a religious minority that, like the Moslem population, could be represented only by its spiritual leaders.

128. This was William Oualid, a professor of law, who had performed important functions in the Central Consistory at Paris during the 1930s. Himself of Algerian origins, Professor Oualid felt that the situation in Algeria was different from the one in France. In the metropolitan territory, he explained, "the Union Générale had been the first measure making the totality of the Jews of France outlaws," while in Algeria it was the law of abrogation of the Crémieux decree that had set them aside from the body of French citizens. Algerian Jews, moreover, had more reasons than their French brethren to accept the creation of the *union* because in contrast to the U.G.I.F. whose members were designated solely by the commissariat-general, the U.G.I.A. was to be formed through mutual agreement with the communities or the religious authorities of the Algerian Jewry (Eisenbeth 1945:57-58). The professor was probably right from a strictly juridical perspective. But purposedly or not, he made no mention that the same ideological motives were at the basis of the creation by Vichy of both *unions*.

129. Letter from André Bakouche to Yves Châtel (September 29, 1942), cited in Eisenbeth 1945:60.

130. The committee was headed by Moïse Borgel but it was Albert Bessis who

NOTES

as a delegate from the committee provided the liaison with the public authorities. During the German occupation, this role was to be played by Paul Ghez, himself a member of the 1941 committee.

On the activity of the Temporary Committee and the Administrative Committee, see the report submitted by M. Borgel to the resident-general on the day after the German occupation (C.D.J.C., 388-34: Tunis, May 15, 1943).

131. In October 1940 the Nazis deported there in a single convoy seventy-five hundred Jews, the totality of the Jewish element in the population of Baden, the Palatinate, and a part of the Würtemberg. (On this topic see Weill 1946:22-24.)

132. See Avni 1975:83-101 on the role of Spain and Portugal between 1940 and 1942.

133. See Bauer 1981 for a view of the efforts of the American Jewry during World War II.

134. L. J. Borstein, "Agenda for North Africa," *J.D.C. Digest*, vol. 1, no. 6 (December 1942), p. 2.

135. This figure is much lower than the 60,000 refugees mentioned by Cazès-Benathar several years later. We think that there were no more than 5,000 civilian refugees "settled" in Morocco, 300 to 1,000 in Tangiers, as many in Algeria, and from 3,000 to 4,000 "foreign workers" in the camps of Morocco and Algeria.

136. The information on the Casablanca committee comes from the archives donated by Hélène Cazès-Benathar to the Central Archives for the History of the Jewish People (C.A.H.J.P.) in Jerusalem. Because the classification of these documents has not yet been completed, we are referring to them by their temporary call numbers.

137. C.A.H.J.P., Fond Bénathar, p. 229: Casablanca, May 30, 1942.

138. Ibid., notice on the transit through Casablanca, n.d.

139. Ibid., 3824/7: Casablanca, June 23, 1941.

140. C.D.J.C., R.F.-1204 11-113a: March 25, 1942; R.F.-1205 11-113a: June 8, 1942. On July 10, 1942, Dannecker, in charge of Jewish affairs in France and in Belgium, was ordered to put an end to the emigration of Jews from Casablanca (RF-1206, 11-113a: Berlin, July 10, 1942).

141. On these convoys see: C.D.J.C., R.F.-1204 11-113a: March 25, 1942 and June 8, 1942, as well as C.A.H.J.P., Fond Bénathar, P. 229: April 1, 1942; April 11, 1942; April 22, 1942; Wischmitzer 1956:169. Thus in the space of three months, nearly twenty-five hundred refugees reached Casablanca. Even though this figure is incomplete it does give a precise indicator of the role played by the Moroccan port in the rescue of the European Jewry.

142. YVSH, Shwartzbart collection, M2/387: Casablanca, September 17, 1940.

143. F.R.U.S., 1940, vol. 2: Casablanca, August 12, 1940.

144. C.A.H.J.P., P. 229: Casablanca, May 30 1942; 3824/7: *Note sur le Comité d'Assistance aux Refugiés de Tanger*, n.d.

145. C.D.J.C., 385-15: *Activité du Comité d'aide aux refugiés*, n.d. Appeals to the public's generosity were regularly published in the *Bulletin de la Fédération des Sociétés Juives d'Algérie*. Here is one example: "We all know by now that a great many of the refugees interned at present in North African camps and enduring the rigors of winter are suffering from lack of clothing and blankets. Most of them live in tents, and we are receiving moving letters from our distressed brothers who beg us to send them

Notes

something to protect the against the cold of the high altitudes. Unfortunately, we can find in the retail outlets neither new nor used clothing, the sale of clothing being forbidden by the authorities. But do we have the right to remain indifferent to the painful situation brought to our attention? We don't think so. Thus it is our duty to urgently appeal to all Jewish families to find in their closets some used clothing or underwear and to send it to us as soon as possible" (B.F.S.J.A., no. 74, November 1941, p.1).

146. C.A.H.J.P., P. 229: Casablanca, May 30, 1942.

147. C.A.H.J.P., P129/263: Mogador, March 17, 1942.

148. It must be noted that these camps also contained North African Jews who had been arrested for various political infractions (communism, Gaullism, etc.) and for various common law breaches, notably black market activities.

149. On the planning and discussions among high French government officials, see the information furnished by General Weygand who, however, avoids mentioning the "human" aspects of this entreprise (Weygand 1950: 508–17).

150. *New York Times*, June 25 and August 6, 1941; *The Nation*, May 3, 1940; *Life*, November 17, 1941. See also the diplomatic reports cited in Sjaskowski 1975: 87–93. On Nazi Germany's colonial ambitions in Africa, see in particular Kuma's N'Dumbe 3, 1980: 135–49.

151. C.D.J.C., 375-16: L'histoire des prestataires en Algérie. Several similar eye-witness accounts can be found in various archives; see, for instance, C.D.J.C., 301-29, account of Hermann Nahman; YVSH, E693, 101: *A l'ombre du Tricolore: récit vécu d'un refugié, 1939–1945*, by Dr. G. Bergman; C.A.H.J.P., Fonds Bénathar, P. 129/263, account of Karl Stossler; C.Z.A., 525/5217, account of Kurt Willy Stern.

152. [In the French colonial empire a *goumier* was a fighter provided by Arab tribes to police a territory.—*Trans.*]

153. C.D.J.C., 386-15: *Engagés volontaires concentrés dans les camps de travailleurs étrangers au Maroc* (August 1943).

154. Ibid., 385-13: letter from E. Birenbaum, Colomb-Béchar, December 6, 1942; see also A. D. Printer, "Spanish Soldiers of France," *The Nation*, April 3, 1943. According to some eyewitness accounts, several "volunteers" from Hadjerat M'Guil were sent to do forced labor in Germany (Moine 1972: 193).

155. C.D.J.C., 385-5: *Le traitement infligé aux soldats français d'origine juive: le camp de Bedeau*.

156. C.D.J.C., 385-3: *Quelques renseignements sur le camp d'interneés politiques étrangers de Djelfa* by Dr. A. Roubakine (end of April 1943); other eyewitness accounts of this camp have been published in Moine 1972: 195–96.

157. C.D.J.C., 101-29, account of Hermann Nahman.

158. *Aufbau*, November 15, 1942. At that same time, official French sources gave the figure of 3,357 as the total number of internees of Moroccan camps and 2,185 for the Algerian camps. Other larger estimates are given in Szjkowski 1975: 87, 97–98.

Chapter 6. Operation Torch and Its Consequences

1. F.R.U.S., 1942, 2: Washington, September 22, 1942, pp. 380–82.

2. Ibid., Algiers, October 19, 1942, p. 398; October 20, 1942, pp. 398–400.

3. Ibid., Vichy, October 2, 1942, p. 387; Algiers, October 2, 1943, pp. 387–88.

4. See, for instance, YVSH, JM 3171, *Télégrammes de la Commission d'Armi-*

NOTES

stice au Ministère des Affaires étrangères à Berlin: Algiers, August 1942; September 2, 1942; December 21, 1942; Gosset 1944: 137-46; Adès 1979.
   5. "La part de la Résistance française dans les événements de l'Afrique du Nord," Les Cahiers français, no. 47 (August 1943), pp. 13-14.
   6. Another leader of the Algerian Resistance.
   7. Les Cahiers français, no. 47 (August 1943), p. 18.
   8. Eyewitness account of Bernard Karsenty, Les Nouveaux Cahiers, no. 3, 1972-73, p. 6.
   9. See Danan 1963: 97-125, for the details of the happenings of that day and the following two days.
   10. On these dealings, see Murphy 1964: 124-34; Crawford 1943: 69-79.
   11. "France's ordeal: Americans attempt a landing in North Africa" was the headline in La Dépêche Marocaine of November 8-9, 1942.
   12. [Poor neighborhood of Algiers.—Trans.]
   13. [Pejorative term for "German" in widespread use during the war in France.—Trans.]
   14. See Michel 1959; Kaspi 1971: 45-47.
   15. The former prisoner of Koenigstein seemed to have been a poor historian as he apparently ignored that Algerian Jews had already renounced their personal status one century previously.
   16. On the Darlan-Noguès race, see Danan 1963: 130-36.
   17. See, for instance, his proclamation of November 15, 1942, published in the Dépêche Algérienne: "Légionnaires, civil servants of every rank, officers, noncommissioned officers, and soldiers of land, sea, and air forces who have sworn allegiance to the marshal must realize that they are loyal to the marshal when they obey my orders."
   18. C.D.J.C., 53-54a: Note d'Orientation à Messieurs les Sous-Préfets, Maires, et Administrateurs de communes mixtes, Oran, November 26, 1942.

Chapter 7. The Germans in Tunisia (November 1942 to May 1943)
   1. Serigny 1972, vol. 1: 137-38.
   2. See Jars 1957:192-247 on the evolution of the military situation.
   3. Hirszowicz 1966: 283-84.
   4. On November 14, 1942, when the German soldiers were beginning to settle in Tunis, Estéva had all political prisoners, Gaullists, and Communists freed from prison thereby saving them from certain death.
   5. Vichy's propaganda minister.
   6. Cohen-Hadria 1976:161.
   7. NG-4882 (YVSH N11/465/E): December 24, 1943.
   8. [Equivalent to the Red Cross in Islamic lands.—Trans.]
   9. Report by Rahn, Gli Annali dell'Africana Italiana, 6 (March 1, 1943), pp. 254-56; Hirszowicz 1966:286-99; Kraiem 1975: 286-87; Bessis 1981:317-52.
   10. NG 4882, (YVSH N 11/465/E).
   11. On the circumstances surrounding these arrests, see Borgel 1944:21-29.
   12. C.D.J.C., 388-35: "Note pour Monsieur le Ministre Rahn," November 24 and 25, 1942.
   13. Governor of Tunis.

Notes

14. According to Borgel, the plan was to rapidly execute Jewish notables "to create the intimidation and terror that always accompanies their taking over a country" (Borgel 1944:24).

15. See above, p. 77.

16. NG-2346 (YVSH-N11/465/E): *Mémorandum addressé par le Conseiller d'Ambassade le Comte Gassato à E. Woerman*, November 24, 1942. Gassato, among other things, points out that "at the present time," the protection of "non-Aryan Italian subjects" is a crucial political concern to the Italians. The recall of the September 2 note is very revealing in itself. What had been presented at the time as a step taken to foil French underhanded dealings against Italy's interests in the regency has in the meanwhile become a tenet of Italian foreign policy, a policy that had nothing more to fear from the French because the Italians were occupying the country.

17. Ibid., November 25, 1942.

18. Ibid., *Note à l'intention de Schnurre*, December 4, 1942.

19. NG-4961 (YVSH,-N11/465/E), January 13, 1943.

20. NG-4882, report of Rahn.

21. Statement made by Colonel Rauff to Moïse Borgel, cited in Borgel 1944: 34, and by the interpreter Trenner, in Trenner n.d.:13.

22. C.D.J.C., 388-25: February 3, 1943.

23. On this meeting, see, for instance, Borgel 1944:34–36; Ghez 1943:15–16; Sabille 1954:38–40. According to Trenner and confirmed by Sabille, the resident-general's opinion had not been sought; he had simply been "informed" of a decision taken without consulting him. However, the report sent that very day by Rahn to Berlin indicates that the German order had first received the admiral's approval (NG-2099 [YVSH-NII/1013/E], December 6, 1942).

24. Even though he was not officially a member of the committee, Borgel assumed its de facto presidency.

25. C.D.J.C., 388-4, according to the information provided by Moïse Borgel in May 1943, on the day after the liberation.

26. On this murder and other events of that day, see Sabille 1954:45–54.

27. See Sabille 1954:47 for the complete text of this notice.

28. Trenner had arrived in Tunis a few days before the German landing. He was put in jail from which the Germans pulled him out and "introduced" him to Borgel when the latter was arrested on November 23.

29. See Sabille 1954:72–73 for the specific assignments of these sections.

30. M. Trenner recounts in unsparing terms how he fooled Pohl, whose "fear of bacteria" he was well aware of, by describing diagnoses of benign illnesses in terrifying terms such as tuberculosis, syphilis, tracheitis, and pleurisy. (Trenner n.d.:38).

31. C.D.J.C., 388-30: *Rapport sur l'activité du service médical de la main d'oeuvre juive*, Tunis, May 3, 1943.

32. C.D.J.C., 388-30: *Note au sujet du ravitaillement des travailleurs juifs*; see also Borgel 1944:82–85; Sabille 1954:76–78.

33. C.D.J.C., 388-23: *Rapport G. Binhas*, July 13, 1944.

34. C.D.J.C., 387-20: *Rapport I. Sperber*; IJC, *Temoignage de P. Ghez* (1966). In Tunis, the workers' pay was forty to sixty francs. It was paid in part to the workers and in part to their families.

NOTES

35. C.D.J.C., 388-23: *Rapport G. Binhas,* July 13, 1944.
36. C.D.J.C., 388-5: *Extrait du Procès Verbal d'Audition de Paul Ghez,* February 6, 1945.
37. See, for instance: IJC,-*Témoignage de A. Zitun* (1966), on Mateur and Saf-Saf; Y. Doueb (1964), on Cheylus and Ksar Tyr; R. Borgel. (1944), pp. 104–10 (Bir M'Cherga, Djefna).
38. Borgel (1944), p. 111; see also the report by Dr. Younès (C.D.J.C., 388-30), cited by Sabille 1954:93–103.
39. *Témoignage de A. Zitun,* (1966).
40. C.D.J.C.,-388-30: *Rapport du Doctour Younès sur sa mission au camp des travailleurs de Bizerte,* January 12, 1943; in the same vein see also Borgel 1944:114.
41. He explained "one must wash one's dirty laundry in family" (Ghez 1943: 80).
42. Ghez 1943:114: "It is most regrettable that the exemptions are generally obtained by bourgeois enjoying wealth and connections. The unfortunate poor, not having the same resources, are the only ones remaining after the sorting is done."
43. Three executions for attempted escapes were reported for Bizerte.
44. Claude Nataf, who was assigned to el-Aouina, recounts the following: "A rapport finally became established between the Germans and ourselves. A soccer club was even organized and a ball was purchased. On my birthday, work was stopped at 3:30 instead of 7:00 P.M. and we went, along with the Germans, to the Casino cafe, where a German officer presented me with a bouquet of flowers "(C.D.J.C., 388-30, December 15, 1945)." See in the same vein Maurice Taïeb, *Report on the Germans of Saf-Saf,* ibid., January 24, 1945.
45. Eyewitness accounts by J. Krief and J. Cacoub; C.D.J.C., 388-31, January 30, 1945, as well as that of Trenner n.d.:61.
46. *Rapport G. Bihnas,* C.D.J.C., 388-23.
47. C.D.J.C., 388-19: *Restitution des amendes imposées aux collectivités juives—* Communauté de Djerba.
48. C.D.J.C., 388-18.
49. Trenner gives an account of the arrest and the subsequent execution by the S.S. of a German soldier who had literally collected a warehouse full of merchandise in the Cap Bon area (Trenner n.d.: 72).
50. *Rapport I. Sperber,* C.D.J.C., 387-20.
51. *Rapport G. Binhas,* C.D.J.C., 388-23.
52. In compliance with Ribbentrop's note discussed earlier, Tunisian Jews of Italian nationality were also to be spared from forced labor till March 31.
53. C.D.J.C., 398-26: *Le Maître des Requêtes au Conseil d'Etat, Conseiller Juridique ét de Législation au Gouvernement Tunisien à Monsieur l'Amiral Estéva, Résident-Général de France à Tunis,* March 20, 1943.
54. Ibid.
55. Ibid.
56. Eugène Boretz offers an alternative explanation for the Germans forgetting to impose the wearing of the yellow star on the Jews of Tunis although they rigorously enforced the rule in Sousse, Kairouan, Nabeul, and Hammamet. According to Boretz, this omission was due to the S.S. wishing to avoid shocking the many foreigners living in Tunis, "a very cosmopolitan city" (Boretz 1944:37).

Notes

57. C.D.J.C., 387-29: *Le Préfet, Secrétaire général du Gouvernement Tunisien à Monsieur le Président du Conseil d'Administration de la Commununauté Israélite de Tunis*, Tunis, December 11, 1942. "Go into hiding!" was to be Admiral Estéva's advice to a group of Jewish war veterans who came to him to ask to be exempted from forced labor (C.D.J.C., 388-30, December 15, 1945).

58. C.D.J.C., 388-29: *Le Directeur de l'Assistance et de la Santé Publique à Monsieur le Préfet, Secrétaire-Général du Gouvernement Tunisien*, Tunis, December 11, 1942.

59. C.D.J.C., 388-33: letter from Moïse Borgel to Admiral Estéva, February 26, 1943.

60. C.D.J.C., 388-66: *Etat des Israélites déportés ou fusillés par les Allemands durant l'occupation de la Tunisie.*

61. For more on this individual, see the end of chap. 4.

62. [Pejorative terms for supporters of Giraud and de Gaulle.—*Trans.*]

63. Borgel 1944:167; Ghez 1943:60; 131 IJC, eyewitness accounts of Y. Douïeb, Y. Uzan, P. Ghez, S. Barad.

64. In his book *L'Afrique du Nord: Terre d'Histoire* (1943), el-Maadi relates the "impressions" he has gathered during one of his tours of Tunisia:

> I have wandered everywhere; I have spoken with men, women, and children; they were unanimous in their praise of the German troops' fairness and kindness. I will always remember this old worker telling me: "You see, my son, I have been working twelve to fourteen hours a day for over fifty years. Until November eighth, my highest daily pay was twenty-five francs. . . . Now I work on the German army's work sites. I have neither lessened nor increased my work input and for a less demanding job they are paying me 110 francs per day." The good old man, tears in his eyes, went on to say: "My son, happy are the justs! They are protected by God and are always victorious because their hearts are pure." I could cite hundreds of similar conversations. Fairness and kindness accomplish much more than promises, threats, persecutions, insults, boasting, and talk. (pp. 112-13)

Chapter 8. The Jews of North Africa from Darlan to Giraud

1. Both these texts pertained to enforcement procedure of the law of February 18, 1942, which defined "the status of the native Jews of Algeria."

2. C.D.J.C., 371-49: letter from R. Franceschini to G. Albou, Algiers, November 9, 1942.

3. Note no. 582/MGP/CAB of December 30, 1942, sent to the units by General Proux; ordinance of January 13, 1943, by General Giraud (*Journal Officiel du Haut Commissariat de France en Afrique*, January 21, 1943); note no. 40/C/MGI/CAB of January 1943 by General Prioux.

4. In Bedeau the volunteers were made to believe that they were leaving for the Tunisian front while they were in fact being transferred to the neighboring camp of Magenta (C.D.J.C., 385-5: le camp de Bedeau).

5. *Le Docteur Henri Aboulker, Chevalier de la Légion d'Honneur, Croix de guerre, Mutilé, à l'Amiral Darlan*, in Ansky 1950:231-32.

6. It does not appear that General Giraud was informed of the arrests before

NOTES

their execution. They were officially tied to Darlan's murder but in fact they only aimed at eliminating Gaullist and republican leaders from the Algerian Resistance.

7. See Darlan 1963:161-63 on the various events occurring during these arrests.

8. C.D.J.C., 80-11-12: *L'application du Statut des Juifs à la population Juive du Maroc*.

9. C.D.J.C., 82-12; *Time*, February 8, 1943.

10. Here are some examples of these slogans: "Roosevelt is a Jew," "The Americans have come to avenge the Jews," "American cars are decorated with the yellow star the Jews wear on the chest."

11. C.D.J.C., 80-11-12.

12. Ibid.

13. C.D.J.C., 386-23: *Rapport sur les mauvais traitements infligés a la la population juive de Beni-Mellal*.

14. Ibid., *Exposé au sujet de l'expropriation des palmeraies de Tafilalet*.

15. Ibid., *Pétition à l'adresse du Directeur des Affaires politiques à Rabat*, August 4, 1943.

16. Ibid., *Lettre au Résident-Général de France au Maroc*, September 9, 1943.

17. C.D.J.C., 386-23: *Au sujet des évènements survenu à Sefrou le dimanche 20 Juillet 1944*. These incidents led Prof. René Cassin to demand an official investigation. In his request to De Gaulle's commissioner for foreign affairs he pointed out that the rioters were encouraged by the local Pasha and militants of the S.O.L. as well as by the unlawful attitude of their French officers (ibid., August 28, 1944); on these events see also: A.E.P., *Guerre, 1939-1945* (C.F.L.N., vol. 955:32-43; 46-85).

18. *F.R.U.S.*, 1942, 2, Casablanca, December 21, 1942, pp. 485-86.

19. C.D.J.C., 385-13: *Lettre de Gérard Guttman à E. Gozlan*, Boghar, February 21, 1943.

20. C.D.J.C., 385-12: *Note à communiquer aux internés*, Berrouaghia, March 9, 1943.

21. C.D.J.C., 385-9: *Quelques renseignements sur le camp d'internés politiques étrangers de Djelfa* (end of April 1943).

22. C.D.J.C., 385-9.

23. C.Z.A., S/26/1546: letter from R. Brunschvig and B. Heller to E. L. Taylor, Psychological Warfare Division, Algiers, January 21, 1943.

24. Bentwich 1950:89-93. On November 2, 1943, Elie Gozlan praised Colonel Brister: "No one will ever forget the calm, the nerve of steel, as well as the firmness with which you have broached this most difficult task and faced up to the chiefs who commanded internment camps so often with great inhumanity. Not only did you have our unfortunate brethren liberated but you have taken them in the glorious British army and have made of them auxiliaries devoted to the cause for which all the Allied armies are fighting alongside the British soldiers."

25. C.D.J.C., 386-15: *Engagés volontaires concentrés dans les camps de travailleurs étrangers au Maroc*, August 30, 1943.

26. C.D.J.C., 380-16: cable from Elie Gozlan to the HICEM (Lisbon).

27. According to a report issued by the C.D.J. on the general situation in North Africa established in November 1943 by Donald B. Hurwitz.

Notes

28. See Avni 1975:119-36, on the situation of the refugees in Spain after November 8, 1942.
29. Avni 1975:141-42; A.E.P., *Guerre, 1939-1945*; C.F.L.N., vol. 980.

Chapter 9. Toward the Abolition of Racial Laws

1. *Congress Weekly*, November 20, 1942. In its next issue, the weekly published a message from Dr. Stephen Wise addressed to President Roosevelt in which he expressed pride of the American Jewry to see its government and armed forces deal the first blow against "the antidemocratic aggression in North Africa." See also in the same vein the stand taken by *Jewish Frontier* 11, no. 11, December 1942, p. 5, as well as Hadassah's declaration published in the *New York Times* on November 26, 1942.
2. Darlan's statement is published at length in Leahy 1950:488-89.
3. "The North African Mess," *New Republic*, January 25, 1943; "Recall Robert Murphy," *New Republic*, February 1, 1943; see Kaspi 1971:48-63.
4. See Kaspi 1971 on the circumstances surrounding this appointment.
5. Lieutenant Colonel de Linarés was Giraud's cabinet chief.
6. [Allusion to the words French king Henry IV is alleged to have spoken upon his conversion to Catholicism to ascend to the French throne.—*Trans*.]
7. "Texte du discours du Général Giraud," *Oran Republicain*, March 15, 1943.
8. Ibid.
9. Ibid.
10. C.D.J.C., 385-3: *Note portant mise point sur la situation faite aux Juifs en Algérie*.
11. Even while taking pains to emphasize they did not wish to maintain this institution that had functioned as administrative seat of the community, its leaders did however express their worries that some "hostile" individuals might consider this dissolution as a "disavowal of our actions" (C.D.J.C., 388-34: *Lettre du Conseil de la Communauté de Tunis à Monsieur le Résident-Général de France en Tunisie*, May 15, 1943).
12. F.R.U.S., 1943, vol. 2: June 29, 1943, p. 283.
13. Ibid., 284-301. President Roosevelt continued, up to November, to follow the development of these negotiations.
14. C.D.J.C., 338-7: *La situation des Juifs italiens en Tunisie* (September 1943; JOINT, Rapport D. B. Hurwitz, (November 1943).
15. C.D.J.C., 380-5-3m: *Commissariat National de la Justice et de l'Instruction Publique: Note pour Monsieur le Professeur Cassin*, March 15, 1943. See also Ansky 1950:289-92, who mentions other critical memos from the National Commissariat of Justice.
16. See, for instance, the editorial in the *New Republic* of March 22, 1943.
17. Sumner Welles's answer is cited in the *B'nai Brith Messenger* of April 2, 1943, and by V. Fry, "Giraud and the Jews" *New Republic* (May 10, 1943).
18. C.D.J.C., 385-1: *Statement Regarding the Abrogation of the Crémieux Decree Submitted to Under Secretary of State Mr. Sumner Welles*, May 17, 1943. On May 20 Henry Torrès and Pierred Dreyfus sent another report to Sumner Welles. Its key passages were developed in an article titled "The Abrogation of the Crémieux Decree" pub-

NOTES

lished in *Free World* 5 (May 1943), pp. 405-9. On this report, see Ansky 1950:301-2; see also A.E.P., *Guerre 1939-1945*, C.F.L.N., vol. 1036, pp. 60-66.

19. Jacques Maritain's entire statement was published by the B.S.J.A. in its June-July 1943 issue.

20. A.A.N. This document, which was widely diffused in Jewish milieus, is partly published in Ansky 1950:296-97.

21. Letter from Sumner Welles to Judge Joseph Proskauer dated May 20, 1943, cited in Ansky 1950:303.

22. C.Z.A., S24/15162: from Albert Cohen to Political Committee of the Jewish Agency, London, July 16, 1943.

Conclusion

1. We note as well that a *Megilat Hitler* (Book of Hitler) paraphrasing the style and content of *The Book of Esther* was written in Morocco on the day after the Allies' arrival.

Bibliography

I. Archival Sources

1. Archives de France d'Outre-Mer (Aix-en-Provence)
Series:
New call number: 16 H 115 (91) :
16 C Question Juive
16 G Question Juive
9 H Surveillance politique des Indigènes
10 H Etudes, Renseignements Scientifiques, etc.
11 H Situation politique
12 H Réformes
26 H Presse et rapports périodiques
32 H Rapports périodiques

2. Centre de Documentation Juive Contemporaine (Paris)
Note: Archival materials from this repository that were used come mainly from the large documentation of the *Commissariat Général aux Questions Juives* as well as from collections of various origins. Among general reports, the main ones are:
Algeria
28A: 28, 34, 47	Création de l'U.G.I.A.
35: 11, 31, 42, 54	Lettres d'Algérie à Xavier Vallat et Darquier de Pellepoix
81-29a	Numerus clausus dans l'Enseignement
239: 14, 16, 20, 66	Application du Statut des Juifs
371: 26	L'abrogation du Décret Crémieux
385-1	Le Général Giraud et les Juifs d'Algérie
385-18	La situation des Juifs d'Algérie (début 1943)
385-18:	Résistance juive

BIBLIOGRAPHY

Morocco
82, 5 : Rapport Bonan sur les Juifs de Casablanca (1936)
82, 12: L'application du Statut des Juifs (1943)
85-6: Rapport de l'A.I.U. sur le Judaïsme marocain (1945)
414-50: Camps de travail et transit de réfugiés

Tunisia
388: Dossier général

3. Archives du Ministère des Affaires Etrangères (Paris)
Correspondance Politique: Tunisie, volumes 130 and 131
Guerre 1939-1945: C.F.L.N., volumes 955, 980, and 1036

4. Yad Vachem Central Archives (Jerusalem)
Note: The archival material used is made up of microfilms of German documents located in Alexandria (Virginia) and of various documents gathered in preparation for the Nuremberg trials as well as documents from private collections.

Series JM (microfilms)
JM 2216   JM 3168   JM 4257
JM 2337   JM 3171   JM 4435
JM 2534   JM 3238   JM 4455
JM 3114   JM 4230   JM 4582
JM 3121

Series NG (Nuremberg)
NG 057   NG 2346   NG 3150
NG 0133   NG 2360   NG 4882
NG 2099   NG 2676   NG 4961
NG 2971

Series M2: Collection I. Shwartzbart

5. Central Zionist Archives (Jerusalem)
Series:
S 5 (492, 784, 795)
S 25 (5217, 5221)
S 26 (1396, 1397, 1400, 1546)
Z 4 (15162)

6. Central Archives for the History of the Jewish People (Jerusalem)
Fonds Hélène Cazès-Benathar sur les camps de travail et les réfugiés juifs au Maroc; temporary call number: P/229

7. Institute of Contemporary Jewry – Oral Division (Jerusalem)
Eyewitness accounts of forced labor in Tunisia

II. Newspapers

1. The Jewish Press
L'Avenir Illustré, Casablanca (1926–1940)
L' Union Marocaine, Casablanca (1932–1938)
Bulletin de la Fédération des Sociétés Juives d'Algérie (1941–1944)
Le Réveil Juif, Tunis (1930–1934)
Petit Matin, Tunis (1941–1942)
La Voix Juive, Tunis (1944)
Aufbau, New York (1941–1942)
The B'nai Brith Messenger (1942–1943)
Congress Weekly (American Jewish Congress) (1942–1943)
Contemporary Jewish Record (American Jewish Committee) (1940–1943)
Jewish Chronicle, London (1942–1943)
Jewish Comment (World Jewish Congress) (1943–1944)
Jewish Frontier (1942–1943)
J.D.C. Annual Reports (1941–1943)
The J.D.C. Digest (1942–1943)

2. The General Press
El-Rachid, Bulletin Intérieur du Comité Musulman de l'Afrique du Nord, Paris (1943)
La Dèpêche Tunisienne (1941)
La Tunisie Française (1941–1942; 1944)
Tunis-journal (1942–1943)
Tunis-Soir (1941–1942)
L'Unione Tunis (1943)
Alger Républicain (1938; 1943–1944)
Dépêche de Constantine (1940–1944)
Echo d'Alger (1940–1944)
Echo d'Oran (1941–1944)
La Dépêche Algérienne (1942–1944)
Oran Républicain (1938; 1942–1944)
L'Echo du Maroc (1942–1944)
La Dépêche Marocaine (1942–1944)
La Presse Marocaine (1942–1944)
La Vigie Marocaine (1942–1944)
Le Petit Marocain (1941–1944)
Jeunesse, hebdomadaire de la Jeunesse du Maroc (1942)
Times (London), 1940–1944
The New York Times, 1940–1944
The Nation (New York), 1942–1943
New Republic (New York), 1942–1943

3. Official Newspapers
Journal Officiel de l'Algérie (1940–1942)
Journal officiel de Tunisie (1940–1942)
Bulletin officiel du Maroc (1940–1942)

BIBLIOGRAPHY

III. Books, articles, and manuscripts

Abitbol, Michel (ed.). *Judaïsme d'Afrique du Nord aux XIXe-XXe siècles.* Jerusalem: Ben-Zvi Institute, 1980(a).

———. "Zionism in Islamic Lands—North Africa." In Moshe Davis (ed.), *Zionism in Transition.* New York: Ayer Co., 1980(b). Pp. 197-210.

Aboulker, M. *Alger et ses complots* Paris: Les Documents Nuit et Jour, 1952.

Ades, L. *L'aventure algérienne 1940-1944.* Paris: Belfond, 1979.

Ageron, Ch. R. "Une émeute anti-juive à Constantine (août 1934)." *Revue de l'Occident Musulman et de la Méditerranée* (1973). Pp. 23-40.

———. "Ferhat Abbas et l'évolution de l'Algérie musulmane pendant la Deuxième Guerre Mondiale." *Revue d'Histoire Maghrébine.* July 1976. Pp. 125-144.

———. "Contribution à l'étude de la propagande allemande pendant la Deuxieme Guerre Mondiale." *Revue d'Histoire Maghrébine.* January 1977. Pp. 16-32.

———. "Les populations du Maghreb face à la propagnade allemande." *Revue d'Histoire de la Deuxième Guerre Mondiale* 39, no. 114 (1939). Pp. 1-39.

Amouroux, H. *La Vie des Français sous l'Occupation.* Paris: Fayard, 1961.

Ansky, M. *Les Juifs d'Algérie du Décret Crémieux à la libération.* Paris: C.D.J.C., 1950.

Arendt, H. "Why the Crémieux Decree was Abrogated." *Contemporary Jewish Record* 6, 2 (1943). Pp. 115-20.

Aron, R. *Histoire de Vichy, 1940-1944.* Paris: Fayard, 1956.

Avni, H. *Contemporary Spain and the Jewish People* Jerusalem: Hakkibutz Hameuchad, 1975 (Hebrew).

Bauer, Y. *American Jewry and the Holocaust.* Detroit: Wayne State University Press, 1981.

Bennabi, M. *Mémoires d'un Témoin du Siècle.* Algiers: Editions Nationales Algériennes, 1965.

Bensimon-Donath, D. *Evolution du Judaïsme Marocain sous le Protectorat Français.* Paris: La Haye; Mouton, 1968.

———. *Immigrants d'Afrique du Nord en Israel.* Paris, 1970.

Bentwich, N. *I Understand the Risks: The Story of the Refugees from Nazi Oppression Who Fought in the British Forces in the World War.* London: Victor Gollancz Ltd., 1950.

Bergman-Sydney, G.F.J. *Im schatten der Tricolore: Erlbnisse Eines Refugies von 1939-1943.* Manuscript. Jerusalem, at the Yad Vashem Archives E/693 (n.d.).

Bernardini, G. "The Origins and Development of Racial Anti-Semitism in Fascist Italy." *The Journal of Modern History* 49, 3 (1977). Pp. 431-53.

Bessis, J. *La Méditerranée fasciste: L'Italie mussolinienne et la Tunisie.* Paris: Karthala, 1981.

Billig, J. *Le Commissariat Général aux Questions Juives (1941-1944).* 3 vols. Paris: C.D.J.C., 1955-60.

Blair, L.B. *Western Window in the Arab World.* Austin: University of Texas Press, 1970.

Bibliography

Boretz, E. *Tunis sous la Croix Gammée*. Algiers, 1944.
Borgel, R. *Etoile Jaune et Croix Gammée: Récit d'une Servitude*. Tunis, 1944.
Brunschvig, R. "Les mesures antijuives dans l'Enseignement en Algérie sous le régime de Vichy." *Revue l'Alger* 1, 2 (1944). Pp. 57–79.
Chamine, A. *Suite Française: La Conjuration d'Alger*. Paris: Albin Michel, 1956.
Cohen. N. W. *Not Free to Desist: The American Jewish Committee, 1906–1966*. Philadelphia: J.P.S., 1972.
Cohen-Hadria, E. *Du Protectorat Français à l'Indépendance tunisienne*. Nice: Cahiers de la Méditerranée, 1976.
———. "Les Juifs francophones dans la vie intellectuelle et politique de la Tunisie entre les deux guerres." In M. Abitbol (ed.), *Judaïsme d'Afrique du Nord aux XIXᵉ-XXᵉ siecles*. Jerusalem: Ben-Zvi Institute, 1980.
Coidan, E. *Le Sionisme au Maroc*. Manuscript. Rabat, 1946.
Crawford, K. G. *Report on North Africa*. New York: Farrar and Rinehart, 1943.
Danan. Y. M. *La vie politique à Alger de 1940 à 1944*. Paris: I.G.D.J., 1963.
Dawdowicz, L.S. *The War against the Jews, 1933–1945*. Philadelphia: J.P.S., 1975.
Documents on German Foreign Policy, Series D (1937–1945). *The War Years*. Washington and London, 1960–62.
Driss, R. "La Tunisie au début de la Seconde Guerre Mondiale (1939–1940)." *Cahiers de Tunisie* 27, no. 107–8 (1979). Pp. 213–75.
Eisenbeth, M. *Pages Vécues 1940–1943*. Algiers: Charras, 1945.
El-Maadi, M. *L'Afrique du Nord: Terre d'Histoire*. Paris: Edition France-Empire, 1943.
Esquer, G. *8 novembre 1942: Jour premier de la Libération*. Algiers: Charlot, 1946.
Felice, R. de. *Ebrei in un paese arabo gli ebrei nella libia contemporana tra colonialismo, nazionalismo arabo e sionismo (1835–1970)*. Bologna, 1978.
Foreign Relation of the United States — Diplomatic Papers. Washington: U.S. Government Printing Office, 1957.
Friedman, S. *No Haven for the Oppressed*. Detroit: Wayne State University Press, 1973.
Ghez, Paul. *Six mois sous la botte*. Tunis, 1943.
Giraud, H. (General). *Un seul but: La Victoire*. Paris: Julliard, 1949.
Gosset, R. *Le Coup d'Alger*. Montreal: La Revue Moderne, 1944.
Goutard, (Colonel). "La realité de la menace allemande sur l'Afrique du Nord en 1940." *Revue d'Histoire de la Deuxième Guerre Mondiale* 10, no. 44 (1961). Pp. 1–20.
Green, W. "The Fate of Oriental Jews in Vichy France." *The Wiener Library Bulletin* 32, nos. 49–50. Pp. 40–50.
Hilberg, R. *The Destruction of the European Jews*. New York: New Viewpoints, 1973.
Hirszowics, L. *The Third Reich and the Arab East*. London: Routledge & Kegan Paul, 1966.
Howe, G. F. *Northwest Africa in World War II*. Washington: U.S. Government Printing Office, 1957.
Jackel, E. *La France dans l'Europe de Hitler*. Paris: Fayard, 1968.
Jars. R. *Les Campagnes d'Afrique 1940–1943*. Paris: Payot, 1957.

BIBLIOGRAPHY

Jousse (Colonel). "La libération de l'Afrique du Nord et la Résistance Nord-Africaine." *Esprit* 1.1 (1945).

Judenverfolgung in Italien, den italienisch besetzen Gebieten im in Nordafrika. Franfurt am Main, 1962.

Julien. Ch. A. *L'Afrique du Nord en Marche.* Paris: Julliard, 1972.

Kadache, M. "L'opinion politique musulmane en Algérie et l'Administration française." *Revue d'Histoire de la Deuxième Guerre Mondiale* 39, no. 114 (1979). P. 115.

Kammerer, A. *Du Débarquement africain au Meurtre de Darlan.* Paris: Flammarion, 1948.

Karsenty, B. "Les compagnons du 8-11-1942." *Les Nouveaux Cahiers,* no. 31. Pp. 2–10.

Kaspi, A. *La Mission de Jean Monnet à Alger.* Paris: P.U.F., 1971.

Knout, D. *La Résistance juive en France, 1940–1944.* Paris: C.D.J.C., 1948.

Kraiem, M. "C.G.T. et Syndicalisme tunisien après la prise de Tunis par les Alliés 1943–1944." *Revue Tunisienne de Sciences Sociales.* April 1975. Pp. 273–308.

Kubowitzki, A.L. *Unity in Dispersion: A History of the World Jewish Congress.* New York, 1948.

Kum'a N'Dumbe III, A. *Hitler voulait l'Afrique.* Paris: L'Harmattan, 1980.

Langer, W. L. *Le Jeu Américain à Vichy* (French translation). Paris: Plon, 1948.

Leahy, W. D. *I Was There.* New York: McGraw, 1950.

Le Clay, M. "Musulmans et Juifs marocains: Etude de moeurs et de l'état des esprits à l'occasion du mouvement antisémite d'Allemagne." *Bulletin du Comité de l'Afrique Française.* November 1933. Pp. 621–25.

Les Relations entre Juifs et Musulmans en Afrique du Nord, XIXe–XXe siècles. Paris: C.N.R.S., 1980.

Lubetzki, J. *La Condition des Juifs en France sous l'occupation allemande.* Paris: C.D.J.C., 1945.

Marrus, M. R. "Vichy before Vichy: Antisemitic Currents in France during the 1930's." *The Wiener Library Bulletin* 33, nos. 51–52 (1980). Pp. 13–20.

Marrus, M. R., and R. O. Paxton. *Vichy et les Juifs.* Paris: Calmann-Levy, 1981.

Michel, H. "Le Giraudisme." *Revue d'Histoire de la Deuxieme Guerre Mondiale* 9, no. 35 (1959).

―――. *Pétain, Laval, Darlan: Trois politiques.* Paris: Flammarion, 1972.

Moine, A. *Déportation et Résistance: Afrique du Nord 1939–1944.* Paris: Editions Sociales, 1972.

Murphy, R. *Diplomat among Warriors.* New York: Doubleday and Co., 1964.

Noguères, L. *Le Véritable Procès du Maréchal Pétain.* Paris: Fayard, 1955.

Ordioni, P. *Tout commence à Alger, 40–44.* Paris: Stock 1972.

Paillat, C. *L'échiquier d'Alger.* Paris: Laffont, 1966–67.

"La part de la Résistance française dans les événements d'Afrique du Nord." *Les Cahiers Français.* Special issue (August 1943).

Paxton, R. O. *Parades and Politics at Vichy.* Princeton, 1966.

―――. *La France de Vichy 1940–1944.* Paris: Seuil, 1973.

Peyrouton, M. *Du Service public à prison commune.* Paris: Plon, 1960.

Bibliography

Rainero, R. "La politique fasciste à l'egard de l'Afrique du Nord: L'épée de l'Islam et la revendication sur la Tunisie." *Revue Française d'Histoire d'Outre-Mer* 64, no. 237 (1977). Pp. 498-515.
Rémond, R. *Le Gouvernement de Vichy 1940-1942.* Paris: A. Collin, 1972.
Richard, R., and A. de Serigny. *La bissectrice de la guerre: Alger, 8 novembre 1942.* Algiers: La Maison des Livres, 1948.
Sabille, J. *Les Juifs de Tunisie sous Vichy et l'occupation.* Paris: C.D.J.C., 1954.
Schmitt (General). "Le Général Juin et le Débarquement en Afrique du Nord." *Revue d'Histoire de la Deuxième Guerre Mondiale* 11, no. 44 (1961). Pp. 47-64.
Serigny, A. de. *Echos d'Alger, 1940-1945.* Paris: Presse de la Cité, 1972.
Sivan, E. "Stéréotypes antijuifs dans la mentalité pied-noir." In *Les Relations entre Juifs et Musulmans en Afrique du Nord—XIXe-XXe siècles.* Paris: Editions du C.N.R.S., 1980. Pp. 160-72.
Soustelle, J. *Envers et contre tout.* Vol. 1: *De Londres à Alger (1940-1942).* Paris: Laffont, 1947.
Szajkowski, Z. *Jews and the French Foreign Legion.* New York: Ktav Publishing House, 1975.
Tartakower, A., and K. R. Grossman. *The Jewish Refugees.* New York, 1944.
Torrès, H. "The Abrogation of the Crémieux Decree." *Free World* 5 (1943). Pp. 405-9.
Trenner, M. *La Croix Gammée s'aventure en Tunisie.* Manuscript. C.D.J.C.: 380-8-1, n.d.
Truchet, A. *L'Armistice de 1940 et l'Afrique du Nord.* Paris: P.U.F., 1955.
Vallat, X. *Le nez de Cléopâtre: Souvenirs d'un homme de droite, 1919-1944.* Paris, 1957.
Vanino (Vanikoff), M. *Le Temps de la Honte, de Rhetondes à l'Ile d'Yeu.* Paris: Creator, 1952.
Well, J. *Contribution à l'histoire des camps d'internement dans l'Anti-France.* Paris: C.D.J.C., 1946.
Weygand, M. *Mémoires.* Vol. 3: *Rappelé au Service.* Paris: Flammarion, 1950.
Wischnitzer, M. *Visas to Freedom: The History of H.I.A.S.* Cleveland: The World Publishing Company, 1956.
Woodward, L. *British Foreign Policy in the Second World War*, vol. 2. London: H.M.'s Stationary Office, 1971.
World Jewish Congress. *Collection of Reports and Documents Pertaining to the Jewish Situation in French North Africa.* June 1943.
Zenati, R. "Le problème algérien vu par un indigène." *Renseignements coloniaux* (May-June 1938). Pp. 49-81, 117-35.

Index

Abbas, Ferhat, 162
Aboulker, José, 107, 108, 110, 111, 144
Aboulker, Raphaël, 110, 111, 144
Aboulker, Stéphane, 110
Abrial, Admiral, 50, 52, 62, 69
Achiary, André, 112, 144
Ahmed, Taleb, 30
Ahmed Pasha Bey, 75, 76
Aïn al-Ouraq work camp, 100
Alexandre, Armand, 110, 144
Alexandre, Pierre, 110, 144
Alfieri (Italian ambassador), 77, 121
Algerian Jews: after Allied landing, 141–45; and anti-Jewish laws, 59–63, 66, 67, 68–69, 72–73; and anti-Semitism, 8, 19–34, 43, 44; community organizations of, 89–90; education for, 8, 86–88; emancipation of, 8, 24; enforcement of Jewish Statute, 76, 80–83; intellectual elite of, 10; in pioneer corps, 142–43; political attitudes of, 25, 26, 27, 33; repeal of Jewish Statute, 153–57; in Resistance, 110, 169; response to Jewish Statute, 85–90. *See also* Crémieux decree; North African Jews
Algerian Resistance, 107–10, 143, 153, 169
Alibert (justice minister), 57
Alibert law, 58, 62, 63–65
Alliance Israélite Universelle, 8, 85

Alliance raciste Universelle, 35
Allies: landing in North Africa, 105–10, 145, 153, 169. *See also* Britain; United States
American Friends Service Committee, 91, 150
American Jewish Committee, 14, 159, 161, 163
American Jewish Congress (A.J.C.), 152, 153, 155, 160
American Jewish Joint Distribution Committee (J.D.C.), 91, 92, 153, 155, 159
American Jews: and refugee aid, 13–14; and reinstatement of Crémieux decree, 160, 161, 163–64; relations with Free France, 163–65; and repeal of racial laws, 13, 152–54, 155
Amitiés Françaises, 23–24, 26
Amitiés Latines, 22–23, 30, 31, 36
Ansky, Michel, 14, 157
Anti-Semitism: in Algeria, 8, 19–34, 43, 44, 143; Algerian administration and, 26–28, 44; Arab, 20–22, 29–31, 36–39, 42–43, 146–47; campaign by Bellat, 24; charge of avoidance of military service, 28–29, 143; and Crémieux decree, 8–9, 19, 30, 44; economic boycott of Jews in, 26; explanations for, 19–20; German propaganda and, 37–38, 54, 119, 139;

206

Index

as Germanophilia, 42; Jewish soldiers as butt of, 28, 143; Jewish support for Britain and, 43–44; leadership of Father Lambert, 22–23, 29, 36; leadership of Morinaud, 23–24, 29, 30; leadership of right-wing groups, 25–26, 29, 35–36; in Morocco, 35–40, 42, 145, 146–47; police harassment in, 74, 83; political attitudes and, 27; response of Algerian Jews to, 31–34; response of Moroccan/Tunisian Jews to, 39–40; in Tunisia, 35–40, 42, 121–22, 138; Vichy, 57–59, 83, 167 (*See also* Jewish Statute); Vichy *vs* German, 167
Arabs. *See* Moslem population
Armistice Convention, 48–49, 91
Arnim, General von, 117
Arrighi, Victor, 25
Arslan, Shakib, 36, 37
Athias, Arthur, 129
Avenir Illustre, 11
Axis forces: loss of morale, 117, 118; and Moslem population, 118–19; in Tunisia, 117–19. *See also* Germany; Italy

Bainville, Jacques, 25
Bakouche, André, 90
Baranès, S., 133
Barré, General, 116
Barthelemy, J., 59
Barthélemy, René, 25
Baudouin, P., 56
Bedeau work camp, 99
Belkaïm, K., 30
Bellaïche, H., 122
Bellat, Lucien, 22, 24, 53
Bellier, Marcel, 81
Ben-Badis, Shaykh, 33
Benichou, P., 33
Benjelloul, Dr., 33, 61
Bennabi, Malek, 20
Berguent work camp, 97–98, 100
Berstein, Philip S., 153
Best, Obersharführer, 125
Bethouart, General, 155
Bidaine, Paul, 20

Bismut, Victor, 126, 129
Bizerte work camp, 131–32, 133, 134
Blair, Leon B., 106
Blum, Léon, 19, 27, 36, 49
B'nai B'rith, 153, 159
Boccara, Guy, 126, 128
Bonan, A., 133
Bonan, Paul, 126, 129
Bonnafous, Max, 51
Bonzon, L., 81
Borgel, Moïse, 76, 120, 122, 124, 125, 126, 129, 136, 140
Borgel, Robert, 15, 138
Bou-Arfa work camp, 98, 100
Bouffet, R., 27
Boujard, Louis, 27, 51, 114
Boukort, Ben Ali, 30
Boumendjel (lawyer), 162–63
Bourguiba, Habib, 36, 119
Brister, F.M., 150
Britain: internees in armed forces of, 150; Jewish support for, 43–44; Mersel-Kebir affair, 43, 48; planning for Operation Torch, 105
Brunschvig, R., 86, 87, 89, 144
Bulletin de la Fédération des Sociétés Juives d'Algérie, 13
Buré, Emile, 162

Calvet, Guy, 110
Capitant, René, 112
Carcassonne, Pierre, 110
Carcassonne, Roger, 110, 111
Carcopino, Jerôme, 82
Cassin, René, 160
Catroux, General, 164
Cazès-Benathar, Hélène, 14, 92, 93
Central Zionist Archives, 14
Centre Culturel Espagnol, 25
Centre de Documentation Juive Contemporaine, 14
Chagall, Marc, 156
Chantiers de la Jeunesse, 118
Châtel, Yves, 49, 51, 69, 85, 87, 89, 113, 141, 142, 144, 145
Chemla, Gilbert, 138
Chemla, Joseph, 138
Chemla, R., 133

207

INDEX

Cherchell agreement, 106-8
Churchill, Winston, 105, 151
Cittanuova, Jacques, 120
Clark, General, 106, 107, 109, 113
Cohen, Albert, 164
Cohen-Hadria, Victor, 128, 138
Comité d'Action Révolutionnaire
  (C.A.R.N.A.), 37
Comité de Recruitment de la Main-
  d'oeuvre juive, 125
Comité de Secours Immediat (C.O.S.I),
  122, 139
Comité d'Etude d'Aide et d'Assistance,
  85
Comité de Vigilance, 32-33
Comité d'Unité d'Action Révolutionnaire
  (C.U.A.R.), 118
Comité Juif Algérian d'Etudes Sociales,
  10, 31-32, 33, 143
Comité Musulman de l'Afrique du Nord
  (C.M.A.N.), 139
Commissariat Général aux Questions
  juives, 57, 65, 70, 80, 81
"Committee of Five," 110-12, 113
Confédération Générale du Travail
  (C.G.T.), 35
Constantine Arab riots of 1934, 20-22,
  33
Cordier, Father, 111
Costa, Lucien, 81-82
Council of Twelve, 90
Crémieux decree, 24, 26; anti-Semitism
  and, 8-9, 19, 30, 44; emancipation
  under, 8; reinstatement of, 113, 157,
  159-65; repeal of, 12, 33-34, 56,
  59-60, 157; response to repeal of,
  60-62
Croix de Feu, Les, 35

Dames Royalistes, 25
Dana, Edouard, 138
Darlan, Jean, 49, 50, 55, 109, 113, 114,
  115, 116, 142, 144, 153
D'Astier de la Vigerie, Henri, 110, 111,
  113
de Gaulle, Charles, 50, 106, 154, 159,
  163, 164, 170
Delpeyron, Alex, 53
Dépêche Tunisienne, 36

de Pellepoix, Darquier, 70, 81, 141
Derrien, Admiral, 76, 116
Deutscharabische, Lehrabteilung
  (D.A.L.), 119
Devaud, Stanislaus, 25, 26
Djelfa work camp, 99-100
Djenien Bou-Rezq work camp, 99
Doctors, exclusion from profession, 67
Doriot, Jacques, 25
Dreyfus, Pierre, 156
Drumont, Edouard, 9, 19, 62
Dubois, Marius, 22
Duniâ' al-Jadîda al-, 55

Eclair, L', 25
Education: Aryanization of, 68-70,
  71, 82, 85, 86; participation by Jews
  in, 8; private Jewish instruction,
  86-88
Egalité, L', 10
Eisenbeth, Maurice, 15, 85, 87, 89, 141,
  154, 165
Eisenhower, Dwight D., 105, 109, 113,
  148, 152
El-Rachid, 139
Entriade Israélite, 170
Estéva, Admiral, 48, 50, 73, 76, 77, 116,
  118, 120, 123
Ettori, Charles, 49, 51

Faisceau, Français, 25, 35
Fédération des Anciens Combattants
  Républicains, 39
Filori, César, 53
Flamme, La, 25
France: Armistice Convention, 48-49,
  91; colonial policy of, 8-10; decline
  of colonial power, 42-43; Free
  France, 163-65; internment camps
  in, 90-91; opposition to armistice in,
  47-48; right-wing groups in, 25. *See
  also* Vichy regime; Vichy regime in
  North Africa
Franceschini, R., 141
Franco, Francisco, 47, 48
François, General, 52
French Committee for National Libera-
  tion, 160, 164, 165
Front de la Jeunesse, 25

208

Index

Ganne, Pierre-Louis, 53
Gazagne, René, 82
Gelice, General, 77
German internees, 149, 150
Germany: armistice with France, 48; influence on Moslem population, 37–38, 54–55, 119, 139, 146, 153, 162; occupation of Tunisia, 116–19; policy in North Africa, 48–49, 55; treatment of Tunisian Jews (*See* Tunisian Jews under German occupation); and Vichy regime, 56–57, 77–78. *See also* Axis forces
Ghez, Henry, 128
Ghez, Paul, 15, 123, 124, 126, 129–30, 132, 133, 136
Gillot, F., 82
Giraud, Henri, 109, 110, 112, 113, 115, 141, 142, 145, 156–57, 159, 160–61, 164
Gozlan, Henri, 33, 85, 92
Great Britain. *See* Britain
Guilbaud, Jacques, 118

Hadamard, Jacques, 156
Hadjerat M'Guil work camp, 98–99
Hardy, G., 68, 69, 82
Harlinghausen, Colonel, 116
Hasan b. al-Mahdi, Mawlay al-, 48
H.I.C.E.M., 91, 92, 94, 95
Hitler, Adolf, 37, 47, 48, 55, 116
Husayni, al-Amin al-, 37

Internees. *See* Refugees and internees
Italian internees, 148
Italy: ambitions in Tunisia, 117; influence on Moslem population, 38–39; intervention on behalf of Italian nationals, 77–78, 120–21, 168; labor camps under control of, 131, 133. *See also* Axis forces

Jacob, Paul, 156, 161
James, Ewin L., 160
Jensen, Sturnscharführer, 125
Jewish Affairs Office, 141
Jewish Statute: administrative agency for, 57; definition of Jew under, 63–64, 65–66; enforcement of, 75–77, 78–82, 142; exceptions under, 64–65; exclusion from economic life, 66, 71, 72–74; exclusion from professions, 67–68, 71–72, 82; exclusion from public education, 68–70, 71, 82; exclusion from public functions, 64, 66; exclusion from Youth Corps, 70; Italian intervention over, 77–78, 168; limitations on property ownership, 72, 73; public response to, 74–75, 167–68; repeal of, 152–65; response of Jewish community to, 83–90, 169; Spanish intervention over, 79–80
Jousse, Colonel, 106–7
Joxe, Louis, 112
Judenrät, 88–89
Juin, General, 109, 116
Justice, La, 10

Kabyle revolt of 1871, 8, 19, 161
Karsenty, Bernard, 107, 110, 144, 170
Krief, Georges, 129

Lambert, Father Gabriel, 20, 22, 29, 36, 80, 81
Lambrech law of 1871, 24
Lanzanne, Stephanle, 53
La Rocque, Colonel, 25, 26, 58
Lautier, Henri, 25
Laval, Pierre, 50, 51, 53
Lawyers, exclusion from profession, 67, 82
Le Beau, Governor-General, 47–48
Légion Francaise des Combattants, 52–53, 78, 83, 145, 149–50
Legrand, J.-C., 25
Lemaigre-Dubreuil, 110–11, 112, 113
Levi-Valensi, A., 31
Libre Parole, 25
Libre Pensée, 39
Libyan Jews, 38
L.I.C.A. (International League against Racism and Anti-Semitism), 31, 32, 39
Ligue des Droits de l'Homme, 39
Livre d'Or du Judaïsme Algérien, 32
Lutte Sociale, La, 30

INDEX

Maadi, Mohammad el-, 139
Madrid Convention, 9
Mandel, Arnold, 85
Maritain, Jacques, 162
Martin, Claude, 25, 118
Marty, P., 118
Massieu (socialist party candidate), 27
Massigli, René, 164
Mast, General, 158
Maurras, 58, 60
Mayer, René, 113
Maynard, R.P., 161–62
Mein Kampf, 48
Mers-el-Kebir affair, 43, 48, 95
Moatti, Emile, 144
Moatti, René, 112, 144
Molle, Dr., 20, 22, 23, 62, 80
Moncef Bey, 75, 76–77, 119, 136
Monnet, Jean, 156
Monnick, 49
Morali, Fernand, 144
Morali-Daninos, Dr., 110
Morgenthau, Henry, 153
Morinaud, Emile, 9, 20, 22, 23–24, 29, 30, 62
Moroccan Jews: after Allied landing, 145–47; and anti-Jewish laws, 63–64, 66, 67, 73–74, 85; and anti-Semitism, 35–40, 42, 145, 146–47; community organizations of, 10, 90; denial of French citizenship to, 9–10; education of, 8; enforcement of Jewish Statute, 78–80; support for French war effort, 40, 41. *See also* North African Jews
Moslem population: and anti-Semitism, 20, 29–31, 36–39, 42–43, 139, 146–47; and Axis forces, 118–19; Constantine riots of 1934, 20–22, 33; influence of German propaganda, 37–38, 54–55, 139, 146, 162; influence of Italian propaganda, 38–39; rapprochement with Jewish community, 33, 61–62; response to repeal of Crémieux decree, 60–62; under Vichy regime, 53–54
Mouvement Franciste, 35
Muhammad V., Sultan, 79

Murphy, Robert, 106, 109, 111, 113, 144, 152, 153, 155
Mussolini, Benito, 38, 48

Narboni, Armand, 85
Nataf, Albert, 128, 129
Nataf, Edouard, 138
Nataf, Elie, 125
Nehring, General, 117, 121, 122
Nicolai, André, 53
Noguès, General, 47, 50, 53, 79, 109, 113, 145
North Africa: Allied landing in, 105–10, 145, 153; under Armistice Convention, 48–49; decline of French power, 42–43; Resistance in, 107–10, 143, 153, 169. *See also* Anti-Semitism; Moslem population; Vichy regime in North Africa
North African Jews: attachment to France, 11, 33–34, 40, 41, 83–84, 87, 170; and colonial policy, 8–10; community organizations of, 85–90; comparisons to fate of European Jewry, 119–20, 166–67, 168; disaffection of intellectual elite, 10–11; documentation on, 12–15; exclusion from legion, 52; exclusion from military service, 40, 41; Italian nationals, 77–78, 120–21, 159, 168; -Moslem relations, 20–22, 29–31, 33, 36, 37, 60–62, 139, 146–47, 162; participation in public education, 8; population on eve of World War II, 7; press of, 10, 13; renewal of Jewish consciousness, 85, 170; socioeconomic makeup of, 7–8; in World Jewish Congress, 170; and Zionism, 85, 170. *See also* Algerian Jews; Anti-Semitism; Jewish Statute; Moroccan Jews; Tunisian Jews; Tunisian Jews under German occupation
Nortych (interpreter), 125, 135

Oettinger, J., 95
Operation Torch, 105–10

Palestine, 30, 36, 37, 85
Parti de Peuple Algérien (P.P.A.), 37, 55
Parti du Manifeste Algérien, 162

210

Index

Parti Populaire Français (P.P.F.), 25, 35, 44, 53, 83, 118, 139, 145
Parti Social Français (P.S.F.), 25, 26, 35
Perrin, Francis, 162
Pétain, Henri, 43, 47, 48, 49, 56, 57, 62
Petit Matin, 13
Petit Oranais, 22, 30
Peyrouton, Marcel, 48, 50, 145, 153, 154
Phalange, 53, 119
Pharmacists: exclusion from profession, 67; excused from forced labor, 138
Philip, André, 164
Pioneer corps, 142-43
Pohl, Sergeant-Major, 125, 134, 135
Popular Front, 19, 22, 32, 36, 51
Presse Marocaine, 36
Pucheu (minister of interior), 53

Qol Aviv, 84, 85

Racial laws. *See* Jewish Statute
Rahn, Rudolph, 117, 118, 120
Rassemblement anti-juif de France, 35-36
Rauff, Walter, 120, 122, 123, 124, 125, 136, 137
Red Crescent, 119
Refugees and internees: emigration assistance for, 93-94; enlistment in armed forces, 91, 149-50; evacuation of, 93-94, 150-51; in France, 90-91; German/Austrian, 149, 150; Italian, 148; liberation of, 147-51; and relief committees, 13-14, 92-93, 94-96, 150; Soviet, 149; in trans-Saharan rail construction, 96-97; in work camps, 97-101, 150
Regis, Max, 20, 62, 80
Renaud, Jean, 25, 35
Républican, Le, 30
Resistance, 107-10, 143, 153, 169
Réveil Juif, 10
Reynaud, Paul, 47
Ribbentrop, Joachim von, 121
Rigault, Jean, 110, 111, 112, 113, 144

Roosevelt, Franklin Delano, 114, 115, 142, 145, 147, 152-53, 158, 166
Rothschild, Edouard de, 156, 160, 161
Ryder, General, 105, 109

Sabille, J., 14
Samama, Felix, 120
Sarrault, Albert, 24
Scherb, Jean, 118
Schlichting, Karl, 37
Schwartz, Joseph, 155
Section Française de l'Internationale Ouvrière (S.F.I.O.), 22, 39
Service d'Ordre Légionnaire (S.O.L.), 53, 83, 118, 138, 145
Sfez, H., 133, 134
Shapiro, I., 84
Smadja, A., 32
Smadja, Edmond, 129
Smadja, Isaac, 128
Smati, Dr., 61
Soir Marocain, 36
Soleil du Maroc, 36
Soustelle, Jacques, 112
Soviet internees, 149
Spain: claim to French Morocco, 47, 48; intervention over Jewish Statute, 79-80
Spanien, R., 95
Spire, André, 156
Stalin, Josef, 105
Statut des juifs. *See* Jewish Statute
Stora, Paul, 89

Taïb, J., 133
Temime, André, 144
Temman, Roger, 125, 126
Torrès, Henry, 156, 161
Trenner, Maximillian, 125, 126, 135-36
Tunisia, Axis forces in, 117-19
Tunisian Jews: after Allied landing, 158-59; and anti-Jewish laws, 63-65, 66, 67, 73, 85; and anti-Semitism, 35-40, 42, 121-22, 138; community organizations of, 90; denial of French citizenship to, 9; education of, 8; enforcement of Jewish Statute, 75-77, 78; intellectual elite of, 10; repeal of Jewish Statute, 158; sup-

211

INDEX

Tunisian Jews (cont.)
port for French war effort, 40, 41.
See also North African Jews
Tunisian Jews under German occupation: attitude of Tunisian population, 136–40; class division among, 129–30, 132; comparison with Holocaust, 119–20, 168; debt contracted during, 158–59; exceptions to forced labor, 138; in forced labor camps, 130–36; incarceraton of notables, 120; indemnities imposed upon, 121–22, 134–35, 136–37, 158; Italian intervention on behalf of nationals, 120–21, 168; propaganda campaign against, 121–22; recruitment of labor, 122–30, 138, 158, 169; wearing of yellow star, 137–38
Tunis-Journal, 118

Union des Croyants Monothéistes, 33
Union Générale des Israélites de France (U.G.I.A.), 88–90
Union Latine d'Action Française, 35
Union Marocaine des Juifs et des Musulmans, 40
Unions Latines, 22
United Nations, 158
United States: intervention over Tunisian Jewish debt, 158–59; planning for Operation Torch, 105–6; on reinstatement of Crémieux decree, 161, 163; response to racial laws, 145, 152–53, 163, 168–69; and Vichy regime, 113–15. See also American Jews
'Uqbi, Shaykh al-, 33

Valensi, Alfred, 10, 33
Vallat, Xavier, 57, 59, 65, 69, 70, 73, 74, 80
Vallat law, 62, 65–66, 67
Van Heycke, 110, 111
Vichy regime: and Germany, 56–57, 77–78; neutrality toward Axis forces, 116; refugee policy of, 91, 92, 93

Vichy regime in North Africa: administrators of, 49–52, 144–45; after Allied landing, 141–47, 153–54, 168–69; anti-Semitism of, 57–59, 83, 167 (See also Jewish Statute); collaborationist elements in, 55; control of Jewish community organizations, 88–90; Jewish census by, 66–67; legion and, 52–53; Moslem population and, 53–54; police harassment of Jews, 74, 83; press and, 53; public support for, 12, 49, 53, 167–68; refugees and internees in (See Refugees and internees); repeal of Crémieux decree, 59–62; right-wing groups and, 53; trans-Saharan rail project of, 96–97; and United States, 113–15
Vogh, General, 55
Voix Française, 36

Warburg, Paul, 153
Wazzani, Ibrahim al-, 55
Weizsacker, E. von, 77
Welles, Sumner, 161, 163
Weygand, Maxime, 47, 50, 51, 52, 68, 69
Wise, Stephen, 164
Woermann, E., 121
Work camps: refugees/internees in, 97–101, 150; Tunisian Jews in, 130–36
World Jewish Congress, 14, 155, 159, 160, 161, 163–64, 170

Yad Vashem Museum, 14
Youth Corps, 70, 111

Zaewecke, Captain, 125, 134, 138
Zahiri, Sheikh, 31
Zaoui, H., 29
Zenati, R., 20, 21
Zionism, 10, 11, 85, 170

Professor Michel Abitbol is Chairman of the Ben-Zvi Institute in Jerusalem. He has published studies in both French and English on North African history and contemporary Jewry, including *The Corcos Family and the Contemporary History of Moroccan Jewry* (1978) and *French Colonialism, Traditional Rule and Modern Nationalism in North Africa* (1981).

The manuscript was edited by Thomas B. Seller. The book was designed by Joanne Kinney. The type for the text and the display is Palatino. The book is printed on 55-lb. Glatfelter text paper and bound in Holliston Mills' Roxite Linen.

Manufactured in the United States of America.